Praise for *AntoloGaia*

"Porpora Marcasciano says of this electrifying memoir that, if she could, she would have written it in verse to better capture the wild anarchic energy of the world that fueled her activism. No need. Her life story is poetry enough. What a gift to English speakers for her story to find us now, when we need the inspiration of as much wild anarchic energy as possible."

—Susan Stryker, author of *Transgender History: The Roots of Today's Revolution*

"A fascinating look into Italy's radical queer and trans cultures and their fraught relationship with wider left-wing politics, Marcasciano's *AntoloGaia* is just as much a guide to how to live one's life with courage, conviction, and creativity."

—Juliet Jacques, author of *Trans: A Memoir*

"Marcasciano's life is a valuable part of trans history, and her account of the queer movement in Italy during the chaotic 1970s is eye-opening."

—Diana Goetsch, author of *This Body I Wore: A Memoir*

"This is a book of exploration—of gender, of one's life, of things one has dared to dream. Like the people we meet, the stories Porpora Marcasciano tells are cradled in a radical trans love, and isn't that one of the best kinds of love? As you read, you too will be cradled and never abandoned."

—Marquis Bey, author of *Black Trans Feminism*

T0355744

AntoloGaia

Titles in the **Other Voices of Italy** series:

**Other Voices of Italy: Italian and Transnational
Texts in Translation**

Series Editors: Alessandro Vettori, Sandra Waters,
and Eilis Kierans

This series presents texts in a variety of genres originally
written in Italian. Much like the symbiotic relationship
between the wolf and the raven, its principal aim is to
introduce new or past authors—who have until now been
marginalized—to an English-speaking readership. This
series also highlights contemporary transnational authors,
as well as writers who have never been translated or who
are in need of a fresh/contemporary translation. The series
further aims to increase the appreciation of translation
as an art form that enhances the importance of cultural
diversity.

Porpora Marcasciano's memoir, *AntoloGaia*, sheds light on
her experience in left-wing opposition movements in Italy
during the 1970s and early 1980s, at the outset of which
"coming out" was not yet a phenomenon in Italy and many
were forced to repress their nonnormative sexualities for
fear of social repercussions. She details her trajectory
toward an increased awareness of her sexuality and gender
identity as she moves from her remote town in the mountains of southern Italy to the bustling streets of cosmopoli-
tan Naples, Rome, and Bologna, as well as several European
countries, where she is more free to pursue her intellectual
passions and to explore her queer desires. During her
meanderings, reminiscent of the Beat Generation, she

engages in consciousness raising and eventually succeeds in uniting the personal and the political, a practice that was common to women and people in the queer community. Marcasciano's memoir is one of few Italian texts to meticulously map out the main movements and political struggles of the time from a queer perspective. Furthermore, her writing technique is far ahead of its time: *AntoloGaia* is the first work of Italian literature to use gender-inclusive language, a practice that is only starting to be taken seriously in Italy.

AntoloGaia

Queering the Seventies, A Radical Trans Memoir

PORPORA MARCASCIANO

Translated by
Francesco Pascuzzi and Sandra Waters

Foreword by
Sara Galli and Mohammad Jamali

Rutgers University Press
New Brunswick, Camden, and Newark, New Jersey
London and Oxford

Rutgers University Press is a department of Rutgers, The State University of
New Jersey, one of the leading public research universities in the nation. By
publishing worldwide, it furthers the University's mission of dedication to
excellence in teaching, scholarship, research, and clinical care.

Library of Congress Cataloging-in-Publication Data
Names: Marcasciano, Porpora, author. | Pascuzzi, Francesco, translator. |
Waters, Sandra, translator. | Galli, Sara, 1972- writer of foreword. |
Jamali, Mohammad, writer of foreword.
Title: Antologaia : queering the seventies, a radical trans memoir / Porpora
Marcasciano ; translated by Francesco Pascuzzi and Sandra Waters;
foreword by Sara Galli and Mohammad Jamali.
Other titles: Antologaia. English
Description: New Brunswick : Rutgers University Press, [2023] | "Translation
of Marcasciano, Porpora. AntoloGaia. Vivere Sognando e non Sognare di
Vivere: I miei anni Settanta. Rome: Edizioni Alegre, 2015"—Title page verso.
Identifiers: LCCN 2023007668 | ISBN 9781978835788 (paperback) |
ISBN 9781978835795 (hardcover) | ISBN 9781978835801 (epub) |
ISBN 9781978835818 (pdf)
Subjects: LCSH: Marcasciano, Porpora. | Transgender women—Italy—
Biography. | Italy—Politics and government—20th century. |
Radicalism—Italy—History—20th century.
Classification: LCC HQ77.8.M36 A3 2023 |
DDC 306.76/8092 [B]—dc23/eng/20230307
LC record available at https://lccn.loc.gov/2023007668

A British Cataloging-in-Publication record for this book is available
from the British Library.

References to internet websites (URLs) were accurate at the time of writing.
Neither the author nor Rutgers University Press is responsible for URLs that
may have expired or changed since the manuscript was prepared.

rutgersuniversitypress.org

For Marcella Di Folco...Marcellona

Contents

Foreword

Giving Voice to the Italian Trans Community

The history of Italian trans people has been examined much less than other aspects of the literary and cultural panorama both in North America and even in Italy itself. Furthermore, the narrative of this collective's experiences has often been told by those who have not lived them. Porpora Marcasciano's *AntoloGaia* is a pioneering work in documenting and reporting the life events of the Italian trans community. It is, therefore, an invaluable resource for those interested in studying queer writing.

There are examples of people who have transcended society's gender boundaries. Individuals sometimes push the limits in their jobs—e.g., Elizabethan theatrical actors—other times, they frequent clubs where they can freely express themselves—e.g., encounters in the Molly Houses.[1] As Laura Schettini explains in her preface to the original Italian version of *AntoloGaia*, many artists, actors, and actresses have utilized gender promiscuity during their careers (2015, 13). However, transcending the binary of traditional definitions of gender through experimentation with one's sexuality is not exclusive to the entertainment world.

On April 14, 1982, the government of Italy passed a bill that gave courts the power to approve the request for individuals to obtain a change in sex designation. Those who underwent sexual reassignment surgery could request a modification in their civil registration.[2] Law 164[3] marked the beginning of a new path toward inclusivity and the end of a legislative system that considered surgical and medical treatments illegal. But how was life for trans people before laws were passed in their favor? What path led members of the trans community toward achieving full recognition of their rights?

In the late 1960s, political and civil unrest due to the activism of students in France led to a chain reaction at the international level. In Italy, revolutionary ambitions were set in motion that ushered in aspirations to achieve meaningful social change. Among these movements, neo-feminism became a forerunner in political activism due to women's emancipation. In the mission statement of the *Rivolta femminile*, Carla Lonzi details, "Women must not be defined in relation to men [. . .] men are not a model to which women should conform their process of self-discovery."[4] After waves of change in the following decade, the Italian parliament passed laws regarding the legalization of divorce (1970), new family rights (1975), the institution of family counseling (1975), equal opportunity in the workplace (1977), as well as the legalization of abortion (1978).[5]

As feminism was making progress worldwide and society was gradually changing, movements involving the rights of sexual minorities started to increase. Specifically, on June 28, 1969, riots began in New York City after a raid in Greenwich Village, during which the patrons of the Stonewall Inn—most of whom were what we would define today as LGBTQIA+ members—clashed with police forces. As Porpora Marcasciano states at the end of her book, it was the action of Sylvia Rivera, a transgender individual, that sparked the clash (282). Within a few months, activists began the publication of the citywide newspaper *Gay* and other news outlets such as *Came Out!* and *Gay Power*. In the following year, there were simultaneous gay pride marches in Los Angeles and Chicago for the first anniversary of the riot, marking the first gay pride parades in U.S. history. Stonewall is still remembered as the origin of gay liberation movements.

News of growing awareness of diversity in gender identities made its way to Italy from other parts of the world, and traditional gender binarism began to be challenged. As a result, an interest in creating new terminology that could describe old phenomena began to flourish. An in-depth examination of what was at the time known as "transgenderism," "transvestism," and any other identity that falls nowadays under the umbrella of LGBTQIA+ would produce a long list of individuals who made their mark on the pages of its history.[6] In mythology, literature, theater, and even in the domestic lives of people whose stories were never told, many decided to express themselves freely even though their lifestyle was not typical of the gender that they were assigned at birth.

Within the Italian context, gender liberation movements of the 1970s were led by individuals and groups such as FUORI!, Fronte Unitario Omosessuali Rivoluzionari Italiani (Italian Revolutionary Unified Homosexual Front), who gave voice to the LGBTQIA+ community through their activism and courage in facing oppression from society.[7] On April 5, 1972, CIS, Centro Italiano di Sessuologia (Italian Sexology Center), held their first international congress entitled *Comportamenti devianti della sessualità umana* (Deviant Human Sexual Behavior) in Sanremo. The gathering would be their third homophobic, pseudoscientific conference.[8] Members of the recently founded FUORI! gathered outside the building where the event was taking place to decry what CIS professed about human sexuality. They denounced the actions of those psychiatrists who attempted to intervene with sexual and gender expression, particularly those who proposed the use of conversion or shock therapy. For the first time, FUORI! pursued their activism publicly. The event was covered by Italian national news outlets, including RAI—Italy's national public broadcasting company.

Porpora Marcasciano was one of many people whose life was directly impacted by such movements. According to her account of the events, coming out was not a personal choice but something accidentally decided for her. The outing allowed Porpora to experiment more freely with her gender expression and to take advantage of the fortuitous opportunity to understand her newly embraced side better as she began her *trip* (21). She chooses this word to define the path toward accepting her identity with open arms, without shame, and with great awareness of the individual realities that exist in the world. This means recognizing the falsehood of the prejudices and biases instilled in her.

During a meeting with Porpora, she explained to us that *AntoloGaia* was a collection of anecdotes and facts stemming from her life story, but not in an autoreferential way; for example, she does not describe her relationship with her family. Instead, she reports fundamental shared experiences. Starting from the title, we perceive her determination to present the collective journeys of the lives of Italian trans community members in the 1970s and '80s. As one can see, the word *anthology* is incorporated into the heading. The book is an ensemble of the most significant events in Porpora's transitional experience and serves as a cornerstone in the Italian trans literature genre. Furthermore, the second word included in the title, *gaia*, is a calque or loan translation from the

English, *gay*, and is a clear reference to the author's desire to create a connection with LGBTQIA+ history. The multifaceted title, with its half-literary (anthology) and half-gendered terms (gay), opens up the book to a culturally, socially, and literarily diverse audience as well as giving it a transnational dimension.

In addition to these standard definitions, we would also like to add two more interpretations that reflect the spirit of the book as a whole. The first one is also linked to the word *gaia* and the fact that this adjective indicates something that brings or inspires happiness (Treccani, *Gaio*). Indeed, Porpora's book discusses love in all its forms with much earnestness: "The widespread feeling was that everyone was happy with it, that everyone wanted to discover new things, that sexuality was breaking the rules, opening up to pleasure, chasing/following desire" (240). Also, one could sense a connection to the fact that *gaio* was the name given to the amorous matters of so-called courtly love by fourteenth-century troubadours (Treccani, *Gaio*). The second interpretation involves a reflection on the Greek roots of the word *antologia* (ἀνϑολογία) meaning *gathering flowers*—or, more precisely, selecting the most beautiful flowers. It could allude to Porpora's choice to narrate the most treasured instances of her past or the fact that flowers are a recurring theme in her works, as they also appear in the title of one of her other books, *Tra le rose e le viole*.[9]

Porpora divides *AntoloGaia* into four chapters, each representing a different period of her life. The first is "Le Début" in which she briefly mentions her southern Italian origins in a small village where people tend to leave "because it's small, because it's in the south, because it's poor, because it's up in the mountains, because it's so closed off" (5). In this chapter, Porpora writes about discovering her sexuality and queer individuals living in secrecy due to society's prejudices: "There were quite a few fags around but you needed to be all masculine, because do it but don't tell!" (9). She also describes her coming out in front of her high school peers, the verbal harassment, and how, once her journey started, she stopped hiding her homosexuality. Porpora felt a special connection with musicians and recalls dressing up and singing "ambiguously and sensually" by herself in her room, where it was possible to bring out her personality, "that hidden identity that I wanted to live with, the exact way in which I dreamed of going out, hanging around, and acting" (42).

The second chapter—"1977: Dreaming and Utopia"—begins with an account of her relocation to Naples to attend university. New political energy disrupted Porpora's life, taking her attention away from her studies. Although it was a period when people challenged everything, it seemed that it was difficult for individuals to question themselves: "The issues and above all the desires tied to homosexuality were still unmentionable after centuries of denial" (54). Social consciousness led to gender awareness even though "most people were still dealing with two thousand years of repression" (80). Porpora's views on gender minorities became a highly regarded perspective. The riots were intense with many victims, the first of whom was Francesco Lorusso, who was shot dead by military police in March 1977 in Bologna. The event led to a clash between leftist militants and law enforcement officers in the center of Rome. According to news reports at the time (*Il manifesto*, Sunday, March 13, 1977), over 100,000 students took part in the riot in which participants attacked many governmental offices. Class and gender conflicts merged, and all those involved developed a desire to go above and beyond to raise their awareness and engage in meaningful social change.

On September 23, thousands of activists gathered in Bologna. Among those present were collectives such as EPF (*Ente Protezione Frocie*[10]), AFP (*Assistenza Frocie Povere*[11]), and MLS (*Madri Libere Socialiste*[12]). Following the assembly, which Porpora compares to Woodstock, they began to parade through the streets of central Bologna. She adds that the occasion helped the LGBTQIA+ community to achieve tangible improvements by overhauling how it was represented and paving a path toward greater visibility).

Returning to Naples, Porpora met the world of the *femminielli*[13] and their lifestyle. It is there that we encounter the origin of her name, which was given to her by Pino Simonelli, a professor and famous anthropologist who introduced her to the local queer community and showed her the hidden culture of the city. Inspired by the protagonist of Dominique Fernandez's work *Porporino ou les Mystères de Naples* (Porporino or Naples's Mysteries), she was given the name Porporino, which later became Porporina and, finally, Porpora). The world was changing. The author explains the importance of self-awareness and clarity of mind in overcoming the sense of guilt and *autocastrazione* (self-castration).[14] According to Porpora, these elements were crucial to getting one's life back).

As Porpora explains in the third chapter—"Extravagance (1978–1982)"—concepts of queer identity and revolution were closely linked. In fact, in the spring of 1979, with the help of some friends, she announced the creation of a new collective in an advertisement in *Lotta continua* (the paper of the extreme left-wing party of the same name), hoping to make yet another step in connecting the life experiences of gay people with revolutionary movements. The *Narciso* collective—later renamed the *Circolo Mario Mieli*—was created following the first meeting, in which only five people participated.

Porpora enriches her narrative with colorful and intense stories. She depicts the "campeggi gay" (gay camps) in Isola Capo Rizzuto as a place where "everything flowed peacefully without limits of time, space, and the usual rules" (163). She recalls how activism was evolving and becoming more visible. The first congress of the "Movimento gay rivoluzionario" (Revolutionary Gay Movement) was held in an old, deconsecrated convent in Rome. Various groups and delegations participated in the event, including activist Mario Mieli, the author of *Elementi di critica omosessuale* (Elements of Homosexual Critique), whose book is still fundamental to Italian gender studies. Although positive changes had been made— e.g., the weekly publication of *Pagina frocia* (Fag Page) in *Lotta continua* (The Struggle Continues)[15] every Thursday— it was still commonly expected for *frocie* (queers) to put up with being the object of ridicule. In an atmosphere characterized by anticonformity, Porpora continued to work on political revolution and, together with other comrades, she organized the first Italian gay pride event in Bologna on June 28, 1980.

While the 1980s brought a new punk artistic scene, Porpora's travels to Bologna became more frequent. She began to pursue the idea of transforming her body—a deep-seated desire—not to become a woman but a transgender person although starting the transitional process was "like taking a leap in the dark" (216) because, at the time, there was no law to support it, nor was there any health counseling service or legal assistance. The only way for trans people to earn money was through sex work, and there were frequent police roundups. In 1981, Porpora was arrested and jailed for lewd and lascivious behavior in public and spent time in a small, dirty cell. The file bearing the reason for her arrest indicated *travestito*[16]

(227). She recalls seeing the names and the tally marks left on the walls of the isolation cell by those who suffered the same punishment as her. The gay movement was reaching a global level and, at the same time, detaching itself from the idea of class struggle. Political engagement was fading away), and there was a perceived atmosphere of disenchantment). Nevertheless, those years were also filled with positive moments, such as campaigns in favor of Law 164, *occupazioni gaie* (gay occupations), public gatherings, and victories for the queer community.

This season, however, ended sadly with the outbreak of HIV and AIDS sweeping across Italy and the rest of the world. In her last chapter—"Transition, An Epic Passage (1983 . . .)"—Porpora recalls the acts of violence against the LGBTQIA+ community, the disappearance of infected people, and the inhumane conditions with which the healthcare system treated them. Darkness overshadowed the exuberant joy of prior years. Mistrust started shaping the nature of human relationships in a way that foretold that nothing would be as it once was.

Porpora's writing style appears as natural self-expression that goes beyond the binarity of the Italian language's two-gender structure—a system that she wanted to challenge. There are many examples of gender-neutral language in Italian, such as the use of double endings and the *, in some instances, to emphasize the fluidity of gender. However, the most original linguistic aspects are the addition of the suffix -*essa* to inflect nouns that are already feminine[17] and the introduction of neologisms to give sense to realities for which there were no words in the Italian lexicon. An interesting way to achieve inclusive language, in our opinion, is Porpora's switching between the masculine and the feminine forms when referring to herself. For example, in one sentence or paragraph, she switches between the two grammatical genders: *turbato* (troubled, 7) in one line but, a few lines later, *corteggiata* (courted, 8), *arrivata* vs. *sfiancato* (arrived, exhausted, 47), *rigidissima* (very rigidly) vs. *perplesso* and *atterrito* (perplexed, terrified, 82). What might appear to a native Italian speaker as a syntactic inconsistency was a conscious strategy[18] to express herself according to how she self-identified at that time. Additionally, she confirmed that the alternation of the two genders is rooted in the motivation that pushed her to find a way that would allow her to express herself neutrally since she never desired to identify as either a man or a woman.

The switching between masculine and feminine forms allows for better self-expression. It does not violate any phono-morphological rules of the Italian language, though it does challenge the rules of syntax. Therefore, Porpora's method works perfectly both in written and oral communication, as it does not change the morphology of the lexicon. This strategy could be used in Italian language courses in order to give nonbinary students a tool to express themselves.

Porpora's narrative is fundamental to understanding the collective experiences of the Italian transgender community, and her linguistic choices are an essential tool since they represent a valid approach to using Italian in a neutral way. Throughout *AntoloGaia*'s structure, we witness the lives and the struggles of those who fought and are still fighting for the trans community. With her work, Porpora has provided us with a privileged and original point of view that gives voice to one of Italy's marginalized groups. The text reminds us of what has been achieved and what still needs to be done. We are confident that *AntoloGaia*'s translation into

English marks an important step in Italian gender studies, helping the field expand broadly and internationally.

Sara Galli and Mohammad Jamali
University of Toronto

Notes

1. *Molly House* is a term used in the eighteenth and nineteenth centuries to refer to gay bathhouses; https://blog.british newspaperarchive.co.uk/2020/06/19/18th-century-molly-houses -londons-gay-subculture/.

2. The bill, however, was later updated in 2011, when it was established that the surgical procedure would no longer be required.

3. Passed in 1982, Law 164 legalized sex change in Italy; https:// www.gazzettaufficiale.it/eli/id/1982/04/19/082U0164/sg.

4. "La donna non va definita in rapporto all'uomo [. . .] l'uomo non è modello a cui adeguare il processo della scoperta di sé da parte della donna." The complete Italian text can be found at https:// www.internazionale.it/notizie/2017/03/08/manifesto-di-rivolta -femminile.

5. The law regarding abortion went into effect following a referendum in 1981.

6. While these terms are considered offensive today, this was the terminology used at the time.

7. FUORI! was a Marxist association that was dedicated to the fight for equal rights for the LGBTQIA+ community. It was one of the first gender activist groups in Italy and was established in 1961, in Turin, by Angelo Pezzana. The group officially disbanded in 1982, at the request of its founder.

8. On May 11–12, 1963, in Rome, they held a *Convegno sugli aspetti patogenetici dell'omosessualità* (Congress on Pathogenic Aspects of

Homosexuality) and, subsequently, on June 12, 1965, in Turin, *Simposio sugli aspetti medico-legali e medico-sociali dell'omosessualità* (Symposium on Medicolegal and Medicosocial Aspects of Homosexuality).

9. *Tra le rose e le viole* was first published in 2000 and revised in 2020.

10. Queer Protection Authority.

11. Poor Queers Support.

12. Free Socialist Mothers.

13. The *femminielli* are a third gender community in traditional Neapolitan culture. For those interested in learning more, we recommend Marzia Mauriello's *An Anthropology of Gender Variance and Trans Experience in Naples: Beauty in Transit* (Palgrave Macmillan, 2021).

14. Regarding self-limitation, Porpora mentions *educastrazione*—coined by Mario Mieli—in a previous passage. Mieli had used this term to refer to that societal system that confines everything in predefined patterns and, by doing so, limits people's free expression (27).

15. A far-left monthly publication founded in 1969 by a political group of the same name; https://www.lotta-continua.it/.

16. During her interview, Porpora confirmed to us that, at the time, the term *travestito* (transvestite) was the only word used to refer to transgender people, despite it being incorrect.

17. For example, *sigarett*essa, *borsett*essa, *Porpor*essa, etc. (185).

18. She confirmed this to us in an interview in February 2021.

Translators' Note

Gendered and Pejorative Language in the Italian Version of AntoloGaia

Italian, much like its sister languages French and Spanish, has gendered nouns and adjectives, as well as some verb tenses. In Italian, there are two genders: masculine (generally words ending in -o) and feminine (generally words ending in -a). Unlike German and Latin, Italian does not have a neuter form. Conversely, a system of grammatical gender no longer exists in the English language.

For example, consider:

- *Un gatto bianco* (sing. masc.): a white cat (male)
- *Una gatta bianca* (sing. fem.): a white cat (female)
- *Sono stato a Roma* (1st per. sing.): I have been to Rome (male subject)
- *Sono stata a Roma* (1st per. sing.): I have been to Rome (female subject)

In this memoir, Porpora's representation of herself in gendered terms is fluid: she uses both masculine and feminine nouns and adjectives, as well as a new form of genderless or all-encompassing modifier: the asterisk (-*, or the schwa), which is becoming more and more popular in Italian as a way to overcome gender binarism in its written form and make the language more inclusive. Porpora's approach to the rendering of gender representation is quite groundbreaking in this sense; however, this effort would be lost in a word-for-word English translation, since English does not feature gendered nouns, adjectives, or any appropriate modifiers to convey such fluidity.

As the book's translators, as well as queer-identifying individuals, we both strongly felt that this gendered representation needed to be evident in our English translation. We have decided to denote certain terms with {f}, {m}, and {*}; specifically, we do this in passages where gendered language is essential to the rendering of a deeper and more complex meaning. Porpora may freely switch among these within the same sentence, going from one to the other to the next; we maintained meaning as close to the original as possible, to the best of our ability.

Porpora similarly adopts and uses various loaded, dated, and pejorative terminology which she reclaimed for herself to refer to herself and others: *finocchio/a*, *frocio/a*, *travestito*, *transessuale*, etc. While we express no judgment on the use of such language, we recognize that some readers might find it inappropriate and/or offensive and/or triggering, and we want to acknowledge that as valid unto itself. Nevertheless, we attempted to reproduce such terms in English to maintain the author's point of view and the color of her writing. As such, the translation will feature terms such as fag, faggot, fehg, faggola, faguette, transvestite, transsexual, etc. with any appropriate modifier when needed.

Sandy would like to thank the participants of Peter Constantine's workshop at the Bread Loaf Translators' Conference in June 2022, especially Don Henderson. Additionally, without the eagle eye and wordsmithing skills of Eilis Kierans, this translation would not be quite so shiny. We would like to thank our husbands Gil and Jonathan, and our cats.

Francesco Pascuzzi and Sandra Waters
Rutgers University

Preface to the Italian Edition

*The Unbearable Lightness of Gender in
History and Biography*

Porpora is not the first to have played, experimented, dared, and in any case to have succeeded. Over the years and centuries before Porpora, other men and women have changed their gender over the course of their lives. For fun or for necessity, for desire, sometimes for fear or for passion, as a form of eroticism and political gesture, sometimes for seduction. Cross-dressing saints, pirate women, virgins in uniform, bearded women, mollies, men-women, Leopoldo Fregoli in a skirt, virile tribeswomen, bishop nuns, the femmes, the butches, the faggy . . . History is full of examples of people from all social classes, places, and cultures who manipulate their own gender for one occasion or for a lifetime. These examples have created a rich repertoire of neologisms and appellatives that give their own account of the variety and plasticity of this phenomenon.

If the production of genders—the assigning of sex to functions, tasks, attitudes, but also different and specific desires—is one of the most fertile grounds on which social organization is based and historically has been based, then the transgression of these codes has occurred and is still happening in many different ways and for the most varied reasons and circumstances. To the point that on one hand it is unsatisfactory to find a fairly comprehensive historical category that encompasses all these infractions (Transvestism? gender ambiguity? eccentric subjects? And more recently: Transgender? drag? queer?), on the other it is almost unrealistic to talk about "one" history of what has slipped out of dominant gender models in the past. Instead, it seems more appropriate to talk about many stories, many strands, and different traditions: some that confirm social hierarchies and others that, on the contrary, undermine them.

For example, there are dozens of stories of saints in disguise, written mainly between the fourth and sixth centuries within monastic communities, which tell the heroic deeds of young women who, moved by a faith that transforms into passion and then self-denial, "become" men to escape arranged marriages and thus preserve virginity and are able to dedicate themselves to the Church, but above all to participate in monastic life or to become hermits.[1] If we take a leap of centuries we arrive on the threshold of the Molly Houses, real clubs for homosexuals set up in private homes or in taverns which began to flourish in England at the end of the seventeenth century. Here men met to listen to music, dance, and seclude themselves in private rooms. The patrons adopted feminine movements and nicknames, which often referred to their profession, and spoke in falsetto. Although it was not the prerogative of all customers, dressing in women's clothes was widespread and reached its apogee in December, the month dedicated to masked parties.[2]

If we jump over a few more centuries and switch from England to Naples, we unexpectedly hear some echoes of these evenings. In 1904 the police raided an apartment where they suspected meetings between "pederasts" took place and whose owner, Giuseppe C., was known as none other than Peppe "a Signora": "In a sitting room you could see some young men dressed as women, who exchanged caresses with their lovers and adventurers. [. . .] Scattered over a few arm-chairs were women's silk dresses, wigs simulating feminine hairstyles, covered up papier-mâché breasts to simulate a woman's complexion with reddish wax. Silk busts and gold-embroidered little shoes sat on a low-lying chair."[3]

We do not know of similar female gatherings in past centuries, but this does not mean that there have not been women who disguised themselves or pretended to be men because of love or desire for another woman, nor those who played with male accessories and symbols, such as the exercise of seduction and eroticism. In this vein we could name Cornelia Gerits van Breugel and Elisabeth Boleyn, tried in Leiden in 1688 because they married each other, with one of them posing as a man,[4] and also Caterina Vizzani, an implacable Don Giovanni of the 1640s, one of the few Italian women transvestites of which news is preserved.[5] We can also think of the artists and writers who animated the festive community of Capri where, in the early twentieth century, around sumptuous villas, some of the most famous gay women of the period intertwined passions, even stormy ones, many of them with the habit of wearing men's clothes and accessories, first of all the monocle and the cigar: Romain Brooks, Natalie Barney, Renata Borgatti, Mimì Franchetti, Checcha Loyd, Baby Soldatenkov, and Faith Mackenzie.[6]

The list of examples of more or less characterized traditions of disguises that have followed one another over time can still be greatly enriched: there is the deep-rooted tradition of actresses and singers who often impersonated men on the stage and who then transferred this prerogative into daily life—like Julie d'Aubigny, who went down in history under the name of Mademoiselle de Maupin, first wanderer and swordswoman in masculine clothes, and then acclaimed singer of the Paris Opera, celebrated a century after her death by Théophile Gautier's novel *Mademoiselle Maupin* (1835). Another legendary transvestite figure, in this case a theater actress, is undoubtedly the Englishwoman Charlotte Charke, who also owes her fame more to the eccentricity of her life— narrated in the autobiography *A Narrative of the Life of Mrs. Charlotte Charke* (1755)—spent largely in men's clothing, than to her stage career, which was thwarted by her father.[7]

The personification of roles of the opposite sex is not an anomaly within the history of theater or opera; rather, as already highlighted in numerous studies, it represented a particularly appreciated variant both for the appeal it exerted on the public, seduced by the virtuosity of its actors, and because it aptly interpreted the great theme that is at the heart of the theater: the reflection on representation and identity.[8] Shakespeare's plays, to take just one of the most famous examples, are so full of games and misunderstandings about the gender identity of the protagonists that the long history of their staging includes a copious list of actresses *en travesti*. Even *Hamlet* did not escape, counting Sarah Siddons and Sarah Bernhard among the best interpretations of the prince, and was brought to the stage by at least fifty professional actresses during the nineteenth century alone.[9]

Actresses who transferred the freedom of customs they enjoyed on the stage, the ability to play with different identities and destinies, to daily life, becoming figures of indisputable charm (as wanderers, financially independent, nonconformists, and sometimes masculine in manners and in their dress), often represented a model of freedom for other women, as demonstrated by the interweaving between the emancipationist movement of the late nineteenth century and a certain artistic scene of those years, skillfully recalled in various studies by Laura Mariani.[10]

Other stories of cross-dressing could be added, with at least one reference, lastly, to female soldiers, perhaps one of the most long-lived and celebrated traditions of female cross-dressing that Europe has known. Cases of female soldiers in the modern age abounded, as well as celebrations paid to particularly valiant figures or those dear to certain national imaginations. For example, the deeds and biography of Catalina de Euraso,[11] known as the "ensign nun" who in sixteenth-century Spain transformed from novice to soldier and reached South America, have become very popular; Phoebe Hessel, who served as a private soldier in many European countries during the first half of the eighteenth century; Sara Emma Edmonds, one of the most famous female soldiers of the American Civil War; Nadezhda Durova, the Russian woman who served in the cavalry in the Napoleonic Wars, and remained in service in the army for another ten years; Doctor James Barry, née Miranda, medical inspector of the English Colonies; Dorothy Lawrence, an ambitious young reporter who enlisted in 1915 to write about her experiences on the Western Front; and many more.[12] Printed memories, ballads, dramatizations, and contemporary and subsequent oral stories have handed down the myth of these women and of the many who have carried out similar feats. Between the mid-seventeenth and mid-nineteenth centuries the deeds of at least one hundred female soldiers were sung in about a thousand variations of ballads circulated in Great Britain and America.[13] Similarly, from the analysis of about three hundred plays staged in London between 1670 and 1700, it has been calculated that at least eighty-nine represented women who became soldiers.[14]

Gender changes, therefore, have a long and varied history; they have many stories, and in many cases they have become figures of the theatrical repertoire and more generally of the cultural traditions of many European and non-European countries. I believe that from these hints it emerges what interweaving of desire, freedom, emancipation, play, and experimentation called these practices into play, but also how for centuries the ways in which authority and society have received them have also been extremely heterogeneous: celebration and condemnation gave way to each other, with many nuances, depending on variables such as social class, political conjuncture, or cultural seasons.

Faced with this polymorphism of gender change, its representations, and the reception to which it has been subjected over the centuries, the panorama tends toward a marked homogenization and seems to be characterized by a strong radicalization of tones and topics over the course of the long twentieth century, when important innovations intervened which tended to obscure this plurality and which led us up to Porpora and her work.

Historical studies particularly attentive to the history of sexuality and the history of gender models, policies, and practices agree that the last decades of the nineteenth century and the early twentieth century constitute a key passage in these narratives. Decades in which sexuality and the question of the boundary between male and female assume unprecedented public relevance and, at the same time, in industrialized societies, in the new and confused mass societies, a certain new obsession with "identity" spreads, above all a longing for useful tools to define and fix it.[15]

In the space of a few years, gender changes, gender and sexual ambiguities, transvestism, but also hermaphroditism, that is to say everything that refers to the infringement of the boundaries between male and female, whether they are considered biological sex or facts of customs, behaviors, became a question that ignited souls, which found space in journalism, in daily life, which attracted the attention of public safety and the scientific community, which, in some ways, took on the features of a real social emergency. This kind of story was then recounted in a timely and recurring manner on the pages of newspapers, studied by psychiatrists and criminal anthropologists, and counted among the expressions of a pathology that had just been identified as sexual inversion.

As some important studies have already reconstructed, the diligence with which stories of gender and sexual changes and ambiguities in medical texts and newspapers of the period were addressed and discussed has to do with various cultural and social reasons, rather than with a hypothetical multiplication of these cases compared to the past.[16] In the first place, these were the years of scientific dissemination and communication and of the pooled press, with a proliferation of places (among which magazines and newspapers stand out) where the most disparate studies and clinical notes, cases, chronicles, and adventures were noted, resulting in more cases being documented. Above all, however, there is no doubt that at the end of the nineteenth century doctors, scientists, social investigators, and journalists attributed greater importance to gender and sexual ambiguities than in the past, that they researched cases with greater diligence, and that, around them, they often contested for attribution of paternity. This greater interest in the determination of sex and gender would be linked to some great social processes of the period and to the anxieties they aroused in culture and society, especially in the ruling classes.

In particular, we should look at the emergence of new forms of female (and feminist) visibility and sociability, but also at homosexuals, and more generally at the great changes that industrialization and urbanization triggered in gender and sexual models. The new paths of female autonomy and fulfillment opened up by schooling, by new family models, by a greater presence in wage labor and in the professions, as well as the appearance of jobs and consumption that were no longer the exclusive prerogative of men but shared by men and women, to give just a few examples among the many already extensively investigated by historiography, were the ghosts that agitated a large part of the cultural establishment of the period. Much of journalism, especially the positivist kind, reflected the concern that the advent of "modern civilization" brought with it the erosion of gender hierarchies in the family and productive world—the traditional foundation of a solid social organization. It is not surprising, then, that theories about the natural and stable division between the sexes served in these circles above all to legitimize the idea that the social boundaries between men and women had a natural, biological, and inviolable foundation.

The cultural anxiety that developed during the twentieth century for changing identities, and for games with gender identities, therefore seems to be sought in the metaphor that our society has made of the transvestite, trans people, drag: a threat to the stable division between the genders. But not only this. Marjorie Garber went further and hypothesized that cross-dressing draws a field that intrinsically refers to the credulity of the spectators, to their having let themselves be duped, but also to the discovery that reality is not what one believed. The disguise, unmasked, thus refers to the mutability of the categories within which reality is organized; in this sense cross-dressers would play a fundamental role in Western culture: they not only presented a challenge to the binary and stable division between male and female, but they represented the very act of questioning, the space of the crisis of reality.[17]

But during the twentieth century, there was an increase not only in the intensity of the obsession in culture and society with those who betrayed the separation between male and female, the stability of identities, but also the regulatory tools that were used against such transgressions. In this regard, I think at least one consideration is appropriate: in Italy the sanction of gender transgressions has historically been delegated to all the administrative police measures and to the security measures, above all starting with the promulgation of the Consolidated Law on Public Security (TUPS) in 1926 and the new criminal code in 1931 (what is known as the Rocco Code, which still represents our set of reference rules in criminal matters). These sources by their very nature and in their differences had two very important common traits: these measures were applied to subjects deemed "socially dangerous," and they were characterized by the indeterminacy of the measure applied, which could be renewed from time to time in turn until the supervisory judge decreed that the condition that had given rise to the sanction had been fulfilled. How not to go, then, to the story of Salvatore M., a man who in the early 1930s was assigned to the security measures to be served in the House of Rest and Cure in Aversa because he was considered socially dangerous? The decree assigning the measure states that this man used to walk around the city "with feminine attitudes and hairstyles" and that such a "serious reversal of meaning" was nothing more than a clear sign of "psychic bewilderment" and "social danger," since the man, feeling and behaving like a woman, was inclined to seduce young men. Making Salvatore M. particularly dangerous were, above all, some of his games with gender identity and his sex life.[18] From a young

age, in fact, he was known to all by the nickname of Namminella, precisely because of his effeminate ways and because
he had always shown a marked predilection for "women's
work," such as that of a washerwoman. Over the years, then,
he continued to style his hair in a feminine way, using hair-
pins, and to show off necklaces and other costume jewelry,
as well as to "entertain" young men.[19]

It is worth emphasizing that Salvatore M. did not become
the object of attention from public safety and judges for other
reasons: for example, he did not commit thefts or fraud. It
was only these habits, therefore, that made it desirable for the
authorities to remove the man from his environment and
from the city. He remained in Aversa for a year and a half,
until the director of the institution certified that "during his
long stay in this institution he never gave rise to complaints
about his sexual behavior, which is the only origin of its social
danger."

But how can we not go to more recent memories, such as
that of Romanina, who, forty years after Namminella, in the
middle of the Republican age, was sent into internal confinement, also removed from her environment, because she
was considered socially dangerous, armed with lipstick and
a wig. Memories that Porpora has already dealt with in *Tra
le rose e le viole* (Among the roses and violets) and to which
the volume that is published here, in a new revised edition,
also looks, albeit indirectly.

At the heart of my long excursus of cross-dressing in history, in fact, is the intention of emphasizing some elements
which I hope and pray will contribute to the reading of Porpora's work on different levels.

If I have gone so far to return to Porpora and her work,
it is not only because what she tells in this book and how she
does it does not, trivially, need to be "introduced" but above

all because I intended to contribute to returning to the fresco of the seventies that Porpora Marcasciano gives us in all its historical depth.

First, *AntoloGaia* is a biographical narrative of the path that leads to the big city from the southern province, to the collectives from the groups, from joining the extraparliamentary left to the gay movement, to the first cross-dressings and adventures, from questions and personal doubts to the political and collective dimension. A tortuous but always exciting and pulsating path, where the sedimentations of centuries of the art of cross-dressing are recognized, even beyond the intentions of the protagonists{m} and protagonists{f}: where theater, performance, seduction, desire, politics, but also transcendence, mix together to definitively and finally crumble the boundaries between these traditions, up to demonstrating that playing with gender is an art that must be recognized, which requires commitment, preparation, study, courage, passion.

Secondly, the epic narrated by Porpora, her biography and that of the many unforgettable characters that she introduces to us up close are the key to reconstructing various issues, first of all the seventies from a special observation point, and many different seventies traditionally told juxtaposed to each other: that of militants of the extraparliamentary left, creative types, feminists, homosexuals, provincial kids. Biography thus becomes an instrument of social investigation—to quote Arnaldo Momigliano—and not a way to escape from it. These biographies, which do not refer to exemplary lives and stories, which are not memoirs of "illustrious men" nor of great "political" leaders of organizations—through which the history of opposition movements has so far been told of the protest and the counterculture—represent a tool for building the investigation and narration of the social, historical, and cultural reality which is no longer conditioned only by the politics of memory of mainstream subjects and narratives, which it finds in the margins and no longer (only) in the center the point of irradiation of the "truth" and of the story itself. In this sense, biographies, memoirs, and historical narratives such as those that Porpora has given us become precious tools for glimpsing the terrains where historical agent and social structure intersect and modify each other, where personal history and collective history intersect and forge each other.

Laura Schettini

Notes

1. One of the most complete texts dedicated to cross-dressing in the Middle Ages, where we find many accounts of the second wave of "saint transvestites" celebrated between the eleventh and twelfth centuries, is Valerie R. Hotchkiss, *Clothes Make the Man: Female Cross Dressing in Medieval Europe* (New York: Garland Publishing), 1996. See also Clementina Mazzucco, *"E fui fatta maschio." La donna nel Cristianesimo primitivo (secoli I–III)* (Firenze: Le lettere), 1989.

2. A rich study dedicated to the Molly Houses is Rictor Norton, *Mother Clap's Molly House: The Gay Subculture in England 1700–1830* (London: Gay Men's Press), 1992. Norton is also the editor of a website where he has published in full a vast amount of procedural sources used for his research and is, in general, dedicated to homosexuality during the nineteenth century in *England: Homosexuality in Eighteenth-Century England: A Sourcebook*, edited by Rictor Norton, https://rictornorton.co.uk/eighteen/. See also Morris B. Kaplan, *Sodom on the Thames: Sex, Love, and Scandal in Wilde Times* (Ithaca, NY: Cornell University Press), 2005.

3. Abele De Blasio, "Andropornio," in *Archivio di Psichiatria, Scienze penali ed Antropologia criminale per servire allo studio dell'uomo alienato e delinquente* (1906), 288–292. The Neapolitan press also covered the case: "L'arresto di Peppe 'a Signora,'" in *Il Mattino*, April 14–15, 1904.

4. In this regard, see the classic text on the history of cross-dressing in the modern age: Rudolf Dekker and Lotte van de Pol, *The Tradition of Female Transvestism in Early Modern Europe* (London: MacMillan Press), 1989. For the reference to the case cited, see 59–60 and passim for other cases. See also Lillian Faderman, *Surpassing the Love of Men* (New York: Morrow), 1981.

5. Her story was collected and handed down by Giovanni Bianchi, the doctor who performed her autopsy and who through various vicissitudes had known her as a man. The pamphlet that narrates the story of this young Roman trans is Giovanni Bianchi, *Breve storia della vita di Catterina Vizzani romana che per ott'anni vestì abiti da uomo in qualità di servitore, la quale dopo vari casi essendo in fine stata uccisa fu trovata Pulcella nella sezione del suo cadavero* (Venezia: Simone Occhi), 1744. See also Marzio Barbagli, *Storia di Caterina che per ott'anni vestì abiti da uomo* (Bologna: Il Mulino), 2014.

6. A recent work that reconstructs in detail the homosexual communities and acquaintances in Capri is Claudio Gargano, *Capri Pagana. Uranisti e Amazzoni tra Ottocento e Novecento* (Capri: Edizioni la Conchiglia), 2008. See also Robert Aldrich, *The Seduction of the Mediterranean: Writing, Art, and Homosexual Fantasy* (London: Routledge), 1993. We are also indebted to the Scottish writer Compton Mackenzie, Faith's husband, author of two novels that recount the passions, intrigues, and life on the island of this community of women: *Vestal Fire* (1927) and *Extraordinary Women* (1928), translated into Italian decades after their initial publication.

7. See Charlotte Charke, *Vestita da uomo. Un resoconto della vita della signora Charlotte Charke*, ed. Sylvia Greenup (Pisa: Edizioni ETS), 2012.

8. Even though it is not about cross-dressing, the great diffusion of castrated singers in Italy during the modern age also deserves mention in this discourse. If the official justification for this practice is circumventing the prohibition imposed on women from treading the scenes, one cannot ignore the fascination that the peculiar tonality achieved by children's voices exerted in the courts and on the European scenes until well into the nineteenth century, when the work was also open to women. In the same century, then, in many operas, from Verdi's *Rigoletto* to Mozart's *Marriage of Figaro*, the success of characters of indefinite gender was recorded. Mozart's Cherubino, for example, is male, but his voice must be mezzo-soprano. The plot then dictates that in the second act he disguises himself as a woman to deceive the count. Here, then, we find a woman who plays a male character who, however, at a certain point, disguises himself as a lady. For some notes on the subject, see Naomi André, *Voicing Gender: Castrati, Travesti, and the Second Woman in Early-Nineteenth-Century Italian Opera* (Bloomington: Indiana University Press), 2006, and *En Travesti: Women, Gender Subversion, Opera*, ed. Corrine Blackmer and Patricia Juliana Smith (New York: Columbia University Press), 1995.

9. See Marjorie Garber, *Intressi truccati. Giochi di travestimento e angoscia culturale* (Milano: Raffaello Cortina Editore), 1994, particularly chapter 1.

10. In this regard, see: Laura Mariani, *Sarah Bernhardt, Colette e l'arte del travestimento* (Bologna: Il Mulino), 1996, and *Il tempo delle attrici. Emancipazionismo e teatro in Italia fra Ottocento e Novecento* (Bologna: Mongolfiera), 1991.

11. For the story of Catalina de Euraso, see her autobiography: Catalina de Euraso, *Storia della monaca alfiere scritta da lei medesima* (Palermo: Sellerio), 1991.

12. For the figures just mentioned and more insights into the theme of female soldiers, see: Julie Wheelwright, *Amazons and Military Maids: Women Who Dressed as Men in the Pursuit of Life, Liberty, and Happiness* (London: Pandora Press), 1989; and Daniela Danna, *Amiche, compagne, amanti. Storia dell'amore tra donne* (Milano: Mondadori), 1994, in particular 56–61. For another famous case of a woman in uniform, that of Valerie (alias Victor) Barker, see also James Vernon, "'For Some Queer Reason': The Trials and Tribulations of Colonel Barker's Masquerade in Interwar Britain," *Signs: Journal of Women in Culture and Society* 1 (2000): 37–62. Nadezhda Durova's memoirs originally published in 1836 have been translated and published in Italy in recent years, with the title *Memorie del cavalier pulzella* (Palermo: Sellerio), 1988.

13. Dianne Dugaw, *Warrior Women and Popular Balladry, 1650–1850* (Cambridge: Cambridge University Press), 1994.

14. Simon Shepherd, *Amazons and Warrior Women: Variety of Feminism in Seventeenth-Century Drama* (Brighton: Harvester), 1981; Lisa Jardine, *Still Harping on Daughters: Drama in the Age of Shakespeare* (Brighton: Harvester), 1983.

15. The obsession with identity in Western societies in the contemporary age deserves to be discussed much more widely, but here it is necessary at least to refer to the fact that the cultural and anthropological disorientations induced by colonialism and the first forms of globalization are not extraneous to this drive related to the technical innovations in the means of transport and communication, as well as the government need of nation-states in the age of nascent mass society and which materialized in the birth of the first signaling and identification systems.

16. For example see Alice Dreger, *Hermaphrodites and the Medical Invention of Sex* (Cambridge, MA: Harvard University Press), 1998.

17. See Garber, *Intressi truccati*, particularly the introduction to the volume.

18. The custody and care home in Aversa was annexed to the local Judicial Asylum with which it shared personnel, spaces, and functioning. Salvatore M.'s medical records are kept in the Historical Archive of the OPG of Aversa. The medical records are mainly collected in folders sorted by date of discharge or death of the inmates. Salvatore M. resigned on June 6, 1933. The documents cited below are all contained in his medical records.

19. Romina Cecconi, *Io, la "Romanina": perché sono diventato donna* (Firenze: Vallecchi), 1976.

AntoloGaia

~ 1 ~

Le Début (1973–1976)

To write is to always
conceal something
So that it may be discovered.
—Italo Calvino

Somewhere in the West

There are many beginnings, like all those events in life that make us feel emotional and capture our attention. Every beginning is enclosed in a moment, in a situation, in a time!! So what better beginning than, "once upon a time"?!

Once upon a time in Italy, much like many other places across the world, there was a reality somewhat different from the one we know and imagine today, a reality in which trans, gays, lesbians, women, and others revolutionized their own life and, from there, that of the entire world. It was a scene waiting to be invented, before others could invent it for us: it was necessary to give meaning, shape, and above all substance to our liberation. If I had to stick to the rules of writing, of cultured writing, I would have never been able to relate the testimony of a moment in time so important in the history of the LGBTQIA+ movement. If I could, I would have narrated in verse, because poetry—better than anything else—may fully capture that scene animated by artists and dreamers, vagabonds and intellectuals, creators and revolutionaries, witches, wizards, Martians, and happy gypsies. An intense time, rich in events and ideas, a time embodied by the figures of those I call "pioneeresses" (I'm using the feminine form because it gives a more accurate idea). A revolving door of new, exhilarating, and shocking experiences that created and invented our reality and then, little by little, led us toward the abyss that in the '80s would swallow everything and everyone: AIDS, the so-called third millennium plague, which marked the end of an era and the beginning of a new one.

Much like I already said in *Tra le rose e le viole* (Among the roses and the violets): "pas de document pas d'histoire": if we ignore our history, and the path that led us here today, we cannot build our future. To fill the void of gay literature, a shortage that is profoundly Italian, I'm starting from me, using my narrative as a powerful means of reappropriation of that world from which we were always excluded{*}, starting from that asterisk!

In the '70s, a popular graffiti used to say, "live your dream instead of dreaming about living," words that best describe the desire that pushed me to change my life in the entire world around it. Maybe because of the sun, maybe because of the heat, maybe because of what was burning inside of me, the summer of 1973 represented a turning point in this transformation. Maybe the planets in my astral chart lined up in a configuration that induced a change, a search, a revolution, because my exodus started at that moment—what we called back then a *trip* or, as we refer to it today, a "transition" from alienation to realization. Looking up from the earth, closer to the ground that I was covering in sweat, the sky would appear thick with clouds and heavy with turbulence. I would wrack my brains to find a way to survive in a reality that I felt profoundly hostile, in a world where I felt out of place, unfit, wrong, and let's just say it: different. I felt imprisoned in a finite, discrete, closed-off environment, which was the cause of a suffocating feeling of social and cultural claustrophobia.

That was the summer Mia Martini released "Minuetto" (Minuet) and Patty Pravo took everyone by storm with her faggoty anthem "Pazza idea" (Crazy idea), two songs that had me and a thousand other faggots-to-be raving. Back then, the world seemed to explode like a meadow in bloom in the springtime and, surrounded by the colors, the scents, and the sounds of those explosions, my fantasy turned alight with wholesome fury. I kept looking in a state of fascination to a bunch of articles that I cut out of my mom's magazines: Amsterdam, thousands of happy hippies in desecrated churches and public parks; London, millions of butterflies freed by Mick Jagger while his hypersexual lips mouthed "Sympathy for the Devil"; San Francisco, music and free love across the streets of California; Paris, transvestites, artists, and rebels out and about in the streets of the Latin Quarter. From those magazine cutouts, from what I heard on TV, I felt that something was changing while I, wrapped up in my dreams, tried to break away from that rusty world in which

I felt imprisoned—the rust slowly eating away at my life but luckily not at my imagination! All across the world it appeared as though imagination was rising to power, and it served as a guiding light during my transition. Still holding out all around me, I felt what Mario Mieli called "educastration." It was steeped in a cultural system that has the capacity to enclose the universe and nature in schemes, perimeters, laws, codes, inside of which everyone sooner or later feels constricted if not altogether imprisoned. A system that today, after many years, has come back to threaten us. A *lex* meant to preserve society, or a specific society in particular, I should say. Any plurality is not taken into consideration because that society posits itself as the one and only: Western society! Its "veterosexual order," as Nicoletta Poidimani would call it, or its *"straight mind,"* according to Monique Wittig, engenders suffering. So much conflict, so much malaise, so much violence justified to maintain and protect its order! In that West that posits itself in the singular form, that considers itself unique and unrepeatable, there exist other places, other stories, which all contradict that pretense of uniqueness, which all contaminate its malodorous purity, and tell us a different story!

Once upon a time, there was a faggot! Someplace else, in one of those many Wests, my deviant, scandalous, and degenerate experiences flourished to my own delight and everyone else's disapproval, giving colors to a story that, across centuries, flowed along silent, wiping away infinite other stories or "stories of otherness," robbing them of colors, of words, of life, of "fabulousness." My life against nature, at first like a brook and then like an overflowing river, began on September 15, 1957, but I will only narrate a part of it, my *pride*, which began sixteen years later, in September 1973, to be exact.

Traces of Dreams

I never felt{m} I was a male, or a female at that. I never even felt like my name belonged to me. Among heteros I felt gay, among gays I felt trans, among trans folk I felt other or more exactly "beyond!" As our dear friend Aracne who left us in 2007 would say: onward! In motion, in travel, in transit, just passing by. In order to encourage me and boost my mood, my mom would repeat, "strength and courage, life is transitory." I never felt{f} like a man, or that I was perceived as one, but I never thought I was a woman because of that, or that I was born{f} in the wrong body, but rather in the wrong world. Never been so very masculine, maybe a little more feminine, in a world where the logic of "it's six of one and half a dozen of the other" rules—I could either be one or the other. Everything about the male universe always bothered, embarrassed, and scared me, but at the same time attracted and perturbed me, in the positive connotation of the word.

The town where I was born and lived in up until I was nineteen is one of those places that sooner or later you end up leaving. You run away because it's small, because it's in the south, because it's poor, because it's up in the mountains, because it's so closed off. A town where ultimately nobody is born because people have kids elsewhere, away from home, in city hospitals. A town along shepherd routes following the transhumance among the mountains of Abruzzi and the lowlands of Puglia or Campania, a borderline town that never offered me a clear sense of belonging, in this or that region. Whenever I was asked where I was born, I would usually hesitate before answering because, my town being so unknown, I had to answer "in Campania," a geographically correct statement that didn't really relate. To answer Molise or Puglia was only partially correct and wrong for the rest. Later on, I realized that a more accurate answer regarding my origins was "Sannita," because Sannio lies transversal in relation to those three regions and it is the one that best represents me: a land of anarchists and thieves, of peasant revolts and trade union mobilization, a land that pushed back against the Romans up until the end without ever folding. A borderland if you will, much like my borderline sex and gender identity. An attraction toward movement, toward transit and travel, toward *trip*, as we used to say back then.

Even my name never belonged to me. The first one, the one you'd find on documents, I inherited from my maternal grandfather, but because it was so bizarre and uncommon, my parents figured they would add the name of the other grandfather but forgot to officialize it with the registry office. Then they just kept on calling me by my second name, dismissing the first one, the original one if you will. In sixth grade, I figured out that my real name was the first one, not the second one that everybody knew me by. Records showed I never attended elementary school, and after a number of adjustments and bureaucratic maneuvers, I had to start signing with a new name that in reality was the old one. I solved this problem later on when I chose a different name that felt like mine. So I have different names, one for the registry office, one for parents and acquaintances, one for friends, one for lovers. The borderline, the half-breed, the uncertainty, the hybrid, years of exodus caused by uncertainty—all this represents my poetics today, a search and a construction of meaning, my personality and my outlook on the world. I feel like a nomad, transversal, hybrid, extraterritorial. My only certainty is my 5′7″ by 154-pound body, the central hub of my happiness, the starting point and the finish line of all my needs and desires.

The Source of Consciousness

As soon as I started my third year of high school, I attended a crowded assembly about the coup d'état in Chile and the violent repression that resulted from it. I listened to the older students talk about fascism and torture, repression and liberty, revolution and justice. These were new words and conversations that made an impact on me because they opened a breach inside me, which afterward became successively a chasm and a conscience, a struggle that was real and lived. My story starts there because my liberation begins there.

For some time, I was upset by a deep crisis: I was a teenager, I lived in a Southern European country at the beginning of the seventies, and I was homosexual. To whom could I entrust that tremendous reality that was so bold for the time?

So, like in most little cities, the only person predisposed to listen was the priest. He was certainly not capable of understanding what was considered a mortal sin, which could invoke the worst feelings of guilt in me. But after years of useless and repetitive confessions, I really didn't want to hear him ask: "With whom did you do it, how did you do it, how many times did you do it, and where did you put your hand?" Questions that embarrassed me, made me feel guilty, made me feel stranger than what I was, because to repeat in confession that I had committed impure acts with my friends and therefore with other boys, to explain to what point I was pushed, was tiring and above all excruciating. After confession I felt free from that sense of shame, but a caress or a simple look was enough to make me fall back into temptation.

When I was young, I was supposed to play with toy cars or pistols, but I preferred dolls instead. I was supposed to be aggressive, come to blows, piss in groups, and woo little girls, but instead I minded my own business, I didn't piss in the company of other people, and I liked to be pursued myself, but not by little girls who were my friends but by little boys with whom my personality didn't gel, and to whom my many complicated parts were unclear. To tell the truth, they were also a mystery to me.

I was a teenager and like everyone at that age I was confronted with the world, a world that I felt was deeply hostile, a world in which I didn't feel accepted or understood. That same world belonged to those who threatened to kick me out of school a few months earlier because I was homosexual. Paradoxically, those who proposed my expulsion were the same ones with whom I had pleasant exchanges of effusion.

Effusions, and lots of other stuff, I, living in solitude and isolation, believed to be part of a unique, isolated experience. Later, while confiding in my faguette friends, I understood that, as they say, it's a small world, that every fag in her own environment had her little stories, and that famous saying "do it but don't tell" represented (and still represents very well) Italian culture. A way of doing things that left me perplexed. Why are they all like that? I mean, it's they who search me out, and then they don't accept my homosexuality? Why, I asked myself, did that guy I made out with last night in a wheat field say today that if I'm really a fag it would be better if I left school? The only logic was precisely that of "do it but don't tell," because when you talk about it, its pillars collapse. Someone felt outed, someone regretted it, someone else had a guilty conscience, but regardless of all that they continued to seek me out, and therefore I was popular{f}. As often happens, and as I have been able to verify in the course of my experience, the more intolerant and violent ones are those who have a guilty conscience, like the straw-tailed fox of the fable. I think that social control with relative repression has always worked through people censoring, exorcizing, and squeezing out the part of themselves that is not accepted, and destroying it in others as well. To be clear, given the widespread homophobia, I'm convinced that there were really a lot of repressed faggolas! The famous gay poet and writer Dario Bellezza—who I had the chance of hanging out with because of a strange affair with Marco, the love of my life—claimed in an interview that women's sexual relations with men had declined since women began "giving it up" (using his words), which coincided with sexual liberation. On the other hand, I believe that men have gone downhill because they couldn't or didn't succeed in coming out, so they all seemed like a particular kind of man; what appeared to us was a world divided in two, men on one side and women on the other. There were quite a few fags but you needed to present as all male, because do it but don't tell!

When accusations and threats were made against me my world collapsed. I was scared; I felt like a fox being hunted down by a pack of dogs. Unfortunately it was a condition that concerned not only me and my town but all of Italy and the whole world, let's say. In the early seventies gay liberation had just begun but wasn't shared by everyone yet. Something had happened and was happening, but I didn't know anything about it. Sylvia Rivera had thrown a bottle at policemen three years prior. The preceding year Mario Mieli and Alfredo Cohen, along with a bunch of others in Sanremo, had staged their sit-in against sexologists who still considered homosexuality a disease. That was the first gay protest in Italy, but I didn't know anything about it. Two years earlier, Romanina had finished serving a sentence of two years of personal confinement in a small village close to mine because she was transsexual. I remember that in the sticks some people talked about a person who was half-man and half-woman, about a transvestite who had gone to live in Volturino, in the province of Foggia (ten kilometers from my town) and I couldn't understand exactly who it was and what it was all about. It was Romina Cecconi, today a dear friend of mine, who had been sent to live in a small town (otherwise known as confinement) because she was considered a socially and morally dangerous subject. She lived in Florence and didn't hide her identity, but rather flaunted it. For this display—which was very provocative for the times—Pier Luigi Vigna thought it was a good idea to confine her to a little village ten thousand miles from Florence. He needed to watch over and punish her because she was trans, or rather, a transvestite. I use the term "transvestite" because at the time "transsexual" didn't exist, or if it did, I was not aware of it. Previously I had seen some transvestites in the streets of Naples. My sister pointed them out to me; otherwise in my naivety I wouldn't have been able to imagine that they could be men dressed like women, despite the fact that doing so was my favorite pastime. I dressed up like Madonna, Saint Lightning Flash, and Saint Kneeling, as unlikely queens of imaginary countries wearing veils, turbans, feathers, lace, and costume jewelry found among my female relatives' things. After this initial religious phase I began to imitate Sandy Show, who sang barefoot, and Patty Pravo, who at the time had released the songs "Oggi qui domani là" (Today here, tomorrow there), "Ragazzo triste" (Sad guy), and "La bambola" (Doll). Both had worn their first dizzying and scandalous miniskirts. I did a kind of karaoke, wearing a towel as a miniskirt; it was a simple, innocent game all for me and my people. The first miniskirts caused a sensation, upset morals, and tickled the imagination. For boys it was one thing, for girls it was another, and for me it was that shocking fabulousness that I felt inside but still couldn't give a name to. Miniskirts, men with long hair, and so many other events and cultural phenomena of the time were strong signs of an unprecedented uprising.

Coming Out

Much of what was happening around the world remained unknown to most people. The vast majority didn't know anything about it or couldn't decode the signs of this revolution. In the big cities, the fuses had been lit and we could smell the sparks coming from Vietnam, the Prague Spring, Bolivia, Chicago, and Woodstock. I sensed it, but nothing and no one had clearly communicated these things to me. You could feel it in the air but there was no verbal confirmation. So-called counterinformation ran on particular channels that were more difficult to discover. There was no Google where you could type in "gay liberation" or "trans" and find all there was to know. Even the term "homosexual" wasn't used and, to take back a title from a pamphlet in FUORI!, it was an "unmentionable practice." The first time I'd heard about it publicly was in November of 1975 after the murder of Pier Paolo Pasolini. News programs on TV made allusions rather than actual statements about his ascertained or presumed homosexuality. It was precisely on the occasion of the school assembly that was held after his murder that I first came out, supported by my friends in the collective.

Almost all students usually participated in the assemblies, except for those few who weren't interested or the small minority of little fascists. I remember that moment well. I was so very excited because speaking in public was a big deal for me. Introducing the topic to the agenda, a friend from the collective said that someone who was living the experience of being gay would talk about Pasolini's murder. I was so agitated and emotional that I don't remember the exact words nor the reasoning the speakers who preceded me offered, nor do I remember what I said. I only remember that one of the few fascists who bothered to show up said something like "now even the fags get to talk," and was promptly invited to leave.

The ritual of coming out didn't exist yet, or at least I didn't know about it. At any rate we didn't call it that, and it wasn't an acknowledged rite of passage in a political sense. My spot on the agenda was decided within the student body, which usually met in the afternoon when the school remained open at our request in order to strengthen our studies, although more than filling educational gaps we wanted to change the world. And so we engaged in politics. At my school we were allotted four hours a month for assemblies that we normally stretched to five or six. These extra hours were requested or required for what we considered to be urgent or an emergency, and Pasolini's murder was considered just that. The student body decided to allow my participation. Since my new path had begun I no longer kept my homosexuality secret. Rather, supported by friends and comrades and strengthened by a new conscious, I{*} proudly went to the assembly.

We barely discussed homosexuality and to talk about one's own was taboo. There was a lot of talk about sexuality, or at least we tried. I think that only in feminist circles were the issues dealt with on a deeper level, perhaps stemming from oneself, being self-aware. I talked about my sexuality more easily with my friends who were girls than my friends who were boys. With the girls I felt less embarrassment, there was a kind of sharing, almost a common feeling, a deeper understanding of problematic implications, an increased sensitivity. My friends who were boys were much more curious; they posed infinite questions that were more useful for reassuring themselves and guaranteeing their integrity, rather than questioning themselves. As soon as they had determined and verified their preferences and their gender normality was recognized, we indulged in degenerate practices. I slipped{*} in and out of so many beds, so many meadows in bloom, barns, basements, attics, barracks, riverbanks, under the sun and under the moon, in the snow and rain, everywhere, but in silence and in the shadows. I couldn't say it, but I entertained affairs and affection with everyone, continuing to ask myself if my experience was an exception, isolated, or shared by others. All of this amused me, excited me, intrigued me, made me feel exactly how I wanted to feel: nonconformist, rebellious, and desecrating.

Usually, my companions had mixed feelings about me, somewhere between pity and understanding: "I understand how you feel; I'm sorry but there's nothing I can do about it," was the most common expression. During this wave of political correctness, we launched into contests of solidarity and understanding and, great gossipers that they are, the boys accused each other of incorrect behavior, false feelings, and vulgar sex. Everyone let themselves go and then they accused and shamed each other. In any case, given the times, I had begun to think—who knows how profoundly—about sexuality and homosexuality, topics that had been unapproachable until that moment.

During those years the frequent school occupations were composed of days and, above all, nights, that I will never forget: assemblies, photocopies, guard duty, sandwiches, beer, sleeping bags, and lots of fabulous sex.

One thing I can say for certain is that in all of those years of changes, of revolutions and upheavals, so many people began to look at themselves closely, questioning themselves via a radical criticism, but none of this was about masculinity in any way. This is one of the biggest political and cultural defeats of that revolution that so many got sucked into. Self-awareness, self-analysis, and deep self-reflection are concerned almost exclusively with women, gays, or other small groups. Except for very rare cases, guys weren't interested in the idea of observing their own identity and questioning it.

Their crisis, if you can call it that, was a reflection of feminism, of the changes that women, gays, lesbians, and trans people had set in motion. In the alternative culture, of the left or of the movement, if you prefer, men had been the great speakers of the past decades; they were the ones who handled discussions, debates, by speaking—or rather by yelling—about the powers that be and by pointing to all the world's problems, but never to their own. They discussed revolutions that needed to happen somewhere, sometimes in our public squares, other times in faraway countries, but always and in any case outside of and far away from themselves.

I had so much sex with sixteen-year-old straight boys, a lot with so-called comrades, alternative or revolutionary, but I never heard one of them talk about sex calmly, or they claimed it was not really a personal relationship but more like a revolutionary political act. And this wasn't my frustration but their failure. I was not aware of this during the years when I came out; I was too young, naive. Perhaps the times weren't yet ripe enough for calm and polite discussions about sexuality, homosexuality, transsexualism, and bisexuality.

It Happened

And yet somewhere something was happening. I read a flyer from FUORI! that a sensitive soul brought me from Rome. FUORI! stood for Italian Revolutionary Homosexual

Unitary Front (Fronte Unitario Omosessuali Rivoluzionari Italiani). I had already read something about it in an article in *Re Nudo* (Naked king, one of the most important sources of counterinformation), written by Mario Mieli, a name that at the time I knew absolutely nothing about. I was very curious and every time that I read or heard about this joyful group, I didn't feel alone anymore, evidently because somewhere else there were other faggots who shared the same experience with me, despite that in that moment I couldn't imagine there were so many. In the end, I reconfigured a different image of homosexuals, that of the young militant in step with the times, as opposed to that of the old pervert who went to the movies luring boys and begging for love. The presence of gay groups made me happy and at the same time upset me. I felt a mix of curiosity, fascination, and fear that gave me anxiety. I often passed in front of the FUORI! office, at the Radical Party headquarters in Naples, I hung around in the neighborhood by Port'Alba in Piazza Dante, pretending to be interested in the books displayed in the windows of the surrounding bookstores and closely observing everything that happened inside. Despite all the people who went through the entrance, not even one of them seemed homosexual to me. It was absurd, but I believed that all homosexuals were somehow visible, that they had some sign on their body or clothing or how they carried themselves that transmitted their way of being. After all, the only homosexual I knew was me; I had caught a glimpse of others in the crime section of some newspapers, but certainly not on Rai 1 or Rai 2, the only two television channels that existed at the time.

The vision that I had of them was the fruit of the widespread stereotype: half-, truly half-disguised, effeminate queers wearing tight bell-bottoms and shoes with high heels, sporting penciled-in eyebrows, and carrying a little leather bag that was popular in those years under their arm, the kind that guys held in their hand in a certain way, and the fags, less manly, held under their arms! Hair combed back with Brylcreem and a languid gaze. The image that distressed me the most was the shady guy who approached boys at the movies or who was beaten up like clockwork at the train station. The image of the bashed fag was a foregone conclusion, almost an automatic association that many made. That model distressed me, the fear of becoming that kind of guy and of inexorably ending up like that. Every so often I saw Paolo Poli on TV, and I thought that his very evident gay mannerisms were staged, something that seemed like jauntiness to me because of my mental distortions. Paolo Poli was the most obvious, but he wasn't the only one: I remember Don Lurio, Alighiero Noschese dressed up like a woman, Elio Pandolfi, all of whom were real characters who made me curious by making me think more about a strange way of being male than a particular way of being gay. Thinking about it now, I was really twisted{m} and baffled—in the worst sense of the word—by the "veterosexual" rank, from his unique and one-directional vision of the world. How many more, I asked myself, were in the same situation? Given the estimates, the percentage of real surveys, there had to be hundreds of thousands or even millions, but I couldn't see them because I thought that homosexuals were all like me, that is, not very masculine. I didn't imagine there could be homosexuals with beards or mustaches. I didn't think that among so many guys with fiancées, married with children, there were so many faggots hiding. Could I have been stupider?! The famous sixth sense that I developed in those years was at that time completely absent, to the point that when a man went to bed with me, the mere fact of him being engaged to a woman made me perceive him as hetero.

Only years later did I develop those antennae that would have let me perceive elective affinities, by making me coin the relative concept to a precise homosexual trait that made me recognize one fag among a million individuals: the "parabola glance." It's a particular way of looking, common to 99.9 percent of faguettes, which consists in scrutinizing a person who you're interested in for a great number of reasons, almost like gaydar: the unmistakable sign of sin! When I hung around outside the FUORI! offices these particularities escaped me. I was convinced that the men going inside all came for the Radical Party offices and certainly not for FUORI! Maybe out front, besides me, there were others lurking in a kind of cathartic waiting.

The news of the existence of a gay group spread through my school to the point that my circle of friends often asked me ironically or jokingly when I had opened a branch in our town. Someone started to write it on the bathroom walls, in the corridors, and even in the classrooms, together with a list of all of the alleged homosexuals in the town. First on the list in large letters: my name. It didn't bother me at all. In fact, I found it amusing. The fear of being discovered that had accompanied me for years had vanished and, in its place, a deep pride was taking root, a pride of being different: a pride nourished by my age, sustained by the environment of those years, by the air that I breathed. For that reason, I consider having been adolescent and young in the 1970s a great godsend.

Trip

At the time everything was extraordinarily interesting, enticing, fantastic, not only because of my age but because it was a time for tasting and experimenting. We didn't know what the future would hold, but we liked to fabricate it with that exuberant fantasy that set us apart. Things to do, to see, to follow, and above all to discover were so abundant that even my homosexuality took a back seat or, much more simply, was itself part of that landscape.

I lived in town until 1976, the year of my high school graduation; I was nineteen and, in spite of the want and need to escape, I was fine there because even in my little town something interesting would occasionally happen. The magic of those years spared very few places in the world and very few cultural hubs, and above all it spared very few zones in the consciousness. That entire dimension appears now ever so distant, arcane, so different from the current one. In times of stress, when time flies by or doesn't feel like it's enough, I think that back then even the passing of time and its effect on things and on people were different. In order to go to Naples I would take the bus to Benevento, then a train, and if everything went without a hitch and without delays, the trip would take about four hours. The city as seen from my town was far away, an altogether different dimension, and whenever I'd get there everything appeared new, particular, fascinating. Today, the same trip by car takes me no longer than an hour, I already know where to go and what to do, I keep in touch with those I'm leaving and those who are waiting for me over cell phone, I never get lost, and even if that were to happen I could immediately get in touch with someone. Back then, you would place phone calls from a bar or from a phone booth, and homes didn't have answering machines yet. From Rome to Milan by train would take me eight hours, hitchhiking would take up to two days. My fist with a thumb pointing straight up was the most common mode of transportation. Hitchhiking remains one of the most iconic symbols of that time: inherited from Kerouac, from the Beat Generation poets, from hobos, it was a way to travel not just physically but also culturally.

At sixteen I took my first trip to London. I left from Foggia at 4 P.M. on a Wednesday, and I arrived in London at 9 A.M. on a Friday. Nowadays I fly into London, I leave on Friday then come back on Sunday and I no longer need a sleeping bag. I still keep my diary from the trip with all sorts of detailed notes:

Bought the ticket to London, spent 46,500 liras, have 20,000 liras left, the train left at 4 P.M., I arrived in Milan at 5 A.M. in the morning. Had breakfast, wandered about the sprawling and smoky station, kids with a backpack and a sleeping bag headed in all directions across the world, one asked me for some money and a cigarette, he was headed to Amsterdam. How wonderful, what an emotional dimension, I feel great, I feel free. Took another train for Dunkirk which I'm not exactly sure where it is, left at 7. Traveled all day across Switzerland and France, at customs we were asked for our documents and our bags got searched, emotions running wild, it's the first time that I'm outside of Italy, felt hungry and really, really cold. I arrived in Dunkirk at 11 P.M. Got off the train and got in line to get on the ship. The cold is biting and I left with only a T-shirt and a denim jacket on, everything is so exciting that I don't even feel cold. Many kids waiting for the ship, almost all of them with long hair tied back with a scarf like Native Americans or with wide-brim hats on. I had only ever seen this many hippies all together in a magazine. Got on board and headed straight inside, it's too cold outside but so many are out there with their sleeping bags and their guitars. I fell asleep and was awakened by euphoric screams, I looked outside from the bridge and there I saw the white cliffs of Dover. Got off the boat at 6, made it through customs, took a train full of backpacks and sleeping bags. Someone was smoking a joint. So thrilling to cross the English Channel my dream of seeing London is coming true, and at 9 A.M. there's London! I could not have imagined that it would be so cold here or that the food would be so different from Italy. Found out today that this world is completely different, far away, unthinkable compared to my little town. After the currency exchange, I realized that I don't have a lot of money.

This was an excerpt from a diary for my great trip dated June 1974, I had just finished my third year of high school, had failed math, off to my first exciting journey, my first *trip*. I couldn't possibly know that the British climate, food, and so many other things would be so different compared to Italy. The first sandwich I bit into, and almost spat out, was filled with sweet mustard and herring. I began to understand the value of money when, at Victoria Station, I exchanged 20,000 Italian liras for four British pounds that could only buy me a few disgusting finger sandwiches for a couple of days; on the third day, I just had to make do. London was the destination and the symbol of an entire generation, the archetypal free city, the capital of rock music, the harbor for rebels from across the world, much like Paris had been years back for artists and bohemians. I would gather information about London on *Ciao 2001*, a weekly publication for music, art, and entertainment which was incredibly popular among younger kids because it had a permanent feature dedicated to London with all the concerts, festivals, music news, groups and bands, places to sleep and eat for cheap, among them the Portobello Market which lent its name to that magazine featurette.

Other Dimensions

Thinking back to that dimension seems like making a jump backward thousands of years, when time and space seemed bigger. Now they are concentrated, abstract, relativized with cell phones, computers, satellites, faxes, planes, high velocity, and super engines. A journey like that was truly a trip because you could go through different dimensions. Now it's a much more expensive simple trip, where adventure gives way to comfort.

The term "trip" was used a lot and had different meanings—all, however, traceable to the concept of pursuit. "Trip" wasn't only displacement, movement, adventures in pursuit or discovering other places, but through other dimensions, other words, or . . . worlds beyond! "Trip" meant, above all, an LSD trip or those other hallucinogenic drugs useful for broadening consciousness, dilating it, or according to widespread opinion, making it. Hallucinogens weren't simply rocking drugs, but powerful ways of gaining knowledge. They came back in full force in the experience of the times, confirming themselves as an integral part of the counterculture, whose best-known people were Jerry Rubin, Timothy Leary, Allen Ginsberg, and Abbie Hoffman, whose texts were like bibles for me.

"Trip" meant the journey that comprises my whole path that I had started in September of 1973, when a new world opened wide to me, when I began to understand many things, becoming aware, when I stopped being ashamed and I understood that all that had been said to me until that moment was false. Indians weren't the bad guys, communists weren't cannibals, anarchists weren't assassins, and homosexuals weren't monsters, and the assholes who wanted to make you believe it were the real assholes, assholes through and through. Awareness was a path, an established practice of those years; before then the vast majority of people still blindly believed in what the assholes said and wrote, in a world that had rendered crooked all that had been straight.

The political environment within my school was crucial for me, above all the encounter with a group of hippies who afterward became my best friends. Not only my school, but schools in general were fermenting. More than a row of desks facing the teacher's desk, they were a big political and cultural laboratory. Everything was discussed, especially knowledge, which we had always been forced to learn passively, a constructed knowledge, set up and assembled for the use and consumption of bourgeois power. A vertical, one-sided knowledge that needed to be passively absorbed and then transposed without the necessity of engagement. Challenging and questioning this type of learning concerned not only its subject matter but also the ways in which knowledge is organized and transmitted. Even if I wasn't perfectly aware of it, I felt the need common to so many others to regain possession of that knowledge, to develop some knowledge from the ground up, which would make us active subjects and producers and not just sterile receivers. A need to be the protagonist and not a spectator, to be the subject and not the object of history in the making. Today all of this might seem like a foregone conclusion or irrelevant but at the time it had become so urgent that it drove us to study, to deepen our knowledge, to elaborate. For this reason, it's not surprising that reading books, newspapers, and so on was widespread and cut across all categories: students, workers, and intellectuals.

At my school we had many professors who supported us, sustained us, and stood by our side. Among them all, the Maoist stood out the most. That's how everyone in town called the philosophy professor who was a true teacher for me and many others. Today he'd be called a bad teacher. It was he who inspired us to study, offering us a different reading of history, another vision of the world. It was he who taught us to better understand how the world turned, opposite from what had been conveyed to us by tradition. The Maoist had a beard, round glasses with metal frames, and he wore corduroy jeans—all signs that communicated a very specific identity and belonging. Don't judge a book by its cover, they say today, and the signifiers are no longer tied to the signified, aesthetics don't necessarily correspond to a cultural belonging, and in this I rediscover that confusion that characterizes our times, or what I would call the "hermeneutics of postmodernity." In town, the professor wasn't well respected; there were many people who considered him a dangerous subversive, especially when he gained disciples by gathering a large group of young people around him. The Maoist was part of the Manifesto-PSIUP (Socialist Party of Proletariat Unity); he was like the glue that kept together our school, student collectives, Neapolitan factories and neighborhoods, and the base of the PCI (Communist Italian Party), which in those years was very strong in the country, as it was in the whole region. The base of the Communist Party was formed by old Marxist-Leninist comrades who were still waiting for the big revolution that sooner or later would have burst out and for which we needed to prepare ourselves. Activities between school, the political party, collectives, and committees were intense and highly productive, not only politically but also socially and culturally, assuming these three things can be separated.

Early on, my school became one of those famous "communist lairs" that were practically everywhere. In those years we were able to carry out a theatrical spectacle denouncing some aspects of the life of our town and investigating the economic and social conditions of the local working class. Then we rented a little house in the working-class quarter of the town for after-school services for the kids who lived there. It was a successful experiment of great socialization.

My town bordered the provinces of Benevento and Foggia, places with a strong communist and anarchist tradition: from the first anarchic republic of Benevento at the end of the nineteenth century and the first anarchic cells of the province of Foggia (Nicola Sacco was born in a little town about thirty kilometers away from mine), to the labor riots and the land occupations of the farmers in the fifties. A land of bandits and rebels, set between mountains and green valleys crossed by transhumant flocks, where it seems the famous walnut tree was. Witches danced in a circle around this tree on nights of the black moon or winter and summer solstices. The women spun around with their backs to the tree, looking at the infinite universe represented by all points of the circle that they crossed over while dancing. A land from which you needed to escape, sooner or later, because of hunger or prejudice. A land destroyed by a logic of power that we opposed in every way in those years, and that now, with no more obstacles and objections, openly manifests itself.

Now here's a libertarian tradition in the seventies that we profoundly felt was ours, trying as much as possible to protect and respect: we got together with students at the high school, with companions at the party headquarters, with the hippies at Studio Uno Underground, with the local community at the cafe by the jukebox listening to music, in our homes to eat and drink with other people or in the fields to smoke a joint. We walked around for hours until the dead of night to discuss the revolution and other dimensions including mine that, however different, was always a topic of discussion and luckily also an object of another kind of reckoning.

These discussions often concluded in someone's bedroom, in a car, in a dark alley, and in all of the places where you take your foot off the brakes. Despite being an unmentionable practice, homosexual relations were widespread and widely exercised—as far as I'm concerned—relationships and practices that I was trying to include in my fabulous revolutionary kit.

Changing the World

When we talked about politics and the powers that be, positions overlapped with the ends but rarely with the means and much less on the way to get there. Among us young people there were some divergences, more or less emphasized with respect to the way of doing politics. The main line of demarcation and contrast was between hard and pure companions, militant communists—or army asshats—on one side; and the freaks, the stoners, the dreamers, the mavericks, and the anarchists on the other. Differences and divergences that sometimes excluded the other and at other times attracted one another; sometimes grew apart, other times wove together; that in time produced and gave life to interesting and particular experiences. Wanting to synthesize and simplify: on one hand there were some who theorized the revolution and on the other those who put it into practice because they didn't want to wait anymore . . .

As usual, I was stuck{*}, poised between two realities. Among the army asshat companions, there were the PCI guys, the *Manifesto* people (who were the strongest component at my school), the Lotta Continua guys, and various Marxist, Leninist groups; the autonomists hadn't yet appeared.

The communists accused the anarchists of lack of commitment, of childishness and utopianism, and especially of using and abusing drugs. There wasn't a real distinction between light and heavy drugs; the use–rather the abuse–of them wasn't as widespread as it is today. The knowledge of different substances was scarce and heroin's power was still a long way off. The anarchists thought that the communists were boring and far away from real needs, not yet well defined and coinciding with a somewhat nebulous idea of freedom to live everyday life by not giving up anything. Rather, taking everything!

I wasn't able to settle down in a serious and definitive way—let's just say it—in a masculine way! I followed my heart that always beat right in the middle, more or less on the edge! The deep perception of injustice, the conscience of a "dirty" society made me angry, an anger that became political commitment, class struggle, need and desire of changing the world. At the same time I wanted everything right away. I didn't want to wait for a revolution day that had been dreamed up by companions that I knew, that inspired nothing good in me. To imagine a society like the Soviet or Chinese ones in which everyone was equal and above all where everyone had to work, as leaders there would be other bureaucrats but certainly not libertarians. I didn't like that at all.

However, in order to be coherent, we had to take countries where none of us would have wanted to live as a model and that was our biggest contradiction. Every time we talked, discussed, or argued, there was always someone who said: "Why don't you go to Russia or to China?" And all of us explained that those countries had a different history than ours, that conditions were different, that perhaps it wasn't so bad living there and that the problem rather, was information, that in the West it wasn't correct and it was subject to censorship. Certainly, today I would have more arguments to support those analyses, but that confrontation was a cursed trap that you got stuck in every time you talked about politics, especially with someone who disagreed, which was often the case.

On the other hand, I perceived a wonderful but not very real situation. I couldn't yet put into focus a clear idea of liberty, to say nothing of freedom, which remained the most feasible path. I reasoned in maximalist and categorical terms, dreaming about the famous utopia. I think that my indecision was due to my age, to a lack of deepening and information. The alternative world, the dispute, political conscience in the first half of the seventies traveled on channels that were gradually discovered. Reality was under construction, yet to be discovered, it wasn't super packed like it would be a few years later. Let's say that our world, that which we try to imagine, was built without precise concerns, because they were models, these concerns. Goals were all being defined and studied. We dared because we didn't know the future, but we liked to imagine it. Fantasy built unimaginable reality, worlds, universes until that one moment.

The Underground

As I said, my *trip* began in the fall of 1973, in that assembly about the Chilean coup d'état, but my entire experience cannot be separated from the Studio Uno Underground which for me was a place of dreams, a place of fairy tales, the other dimension, the cradle of my conscience and its expansion. Every time I think about the Studio I get emotional and I relive the sensation of my first time walking in there, which for me was like discovering a new world: a mind-blowing cross of a hippie commune, a community center, a tea room, a political hub, and an art gallery. It was a big, old basement in the old part of my town. It was *the underground*. A group of guys, rather unusual looking especially given their country roots, had rented and transformed it, bringing it back to life. By the entrance you would see a quote from a song by the Doors, the band that, together with Jefferson Airplane, was the soundtrack to that place. For a few years already, that group of weirdos had caught my attention and especially my curiosity. They were known around town as the Sowbreads, a moniker derived from "flowers' sons," the Italian term used to describe hippies. That group was initially made up of six so-called big-haired ones, because they all had long and unusually shaped hair, patched-up jeans, colorful shirts, bracelets, pearl necklaces, amulets, earrings, sheepskin jackets, and canvas tote bags. This kind of description nowadays wouldn't make much sense, given the popularity of different styles and fashions that have no real purpose other than profit, but back then, on top of representing a true novelty, those kids represented a clear and tangible sign of rebellion, of opposition to the bourgeoisie.

The Sowbreads would never go unnoticed and in spite of people pointing and laughing at them, they seemed to live in a different dimension and couldn't care less about people's negativity. A few years earlier they had spent a few months camped out in a colorful truck just a few steps from my place. I would stare at them every day as they busied themselves fixing up that truck—they painted it black and orange like a tiger's skin, they flipped the back into a spacious truck camper (at a point in time when those didn't exist yet), they even installed a small chimney on the roof; after months of preparation, one fine day they began to load trunks, food, and blankets, and among the jubilant screams of the kids that would hang around them, they took off. Only after they came back, about a year later, did I learn that they had gone to

Morocco by way of Tunisia and Algeria and, upon their return in the summer of 1973, they rented out that big basement which, just around the time of the Chilean assembly in October, opened to the public as Studio Uno Underground. My *trip* began the first time I walked in there, feeling at once embarrassed and fascinated by Pink Floyd's *Meddle* playing on full blast, among scented incense and cinnamon tea served in original barberry tea sets. A bluish fog set among the smoke of an enormous chimney and the smoke coming out of all sorts of different cigarettes, giving a surreal touch to the overall atmosphere. I spotted my philosophy professor in a corner talking to a bunch of kids and, in order to hide my embarrassment, I sat down on a pillow and grabbed a book, the first one I could put my hands on: *Paradise Now* by Julian Beck. What a trickster that book was! I kept reading and turning those pages, and reality began to acquire a different shape. I was so struck by a few quotes in that book that I began writing them everywhere, on desks at school, on notebooks, on walls. These same quotes would later be included in *Seven Meditations on Sadomasochism*, a smash hit show that the Living Theater, the anarchist theater par excellence, would take around Italy on tour. Everything, literally everything felt intoxicating and jolted me further and further away from that old road, which appeared ever narrower, monotone, oppressive, and above all banal because it had been traced by others and not by me. Those quotes would play like a jingle or a poem that said, "I want to love whomever I want, I want to make love to whomever I want, I want to travel around the world without a passport, I want to walk naked, kiss and caress everyone to convey peace, revolution, and many other sidereal dreams." The perfect distillation of the sexual revolution manifesto that, according to a certain left-wing intelligentsia, was taking place during those years. Studio Uno was also a legitimate art gallery because some of its patrons, who came from the Academy of Fine Arts, had turned it into a lab where they experimented with new artistic trends. There I learned a new and original drawing technique that allowed the transfer of images and colors from newspapers on a white sheet with trichloroethylene, creating a psychedelic, intensely colorful base on which I would draw with ink and watercolors. I had always loved drawing, and that technique represented for me a powerful means to express my dreams. Critics called it Pop Art. I brought my drawings with me on my travels and I would sell them on the street, or more often just gift them to people.

When it came to traveling around the world, all of us had turned it into a commitment first and a pleasure second. It was the primary way to pass the time; we felt like nomads, wanderers, insatiable Ulysseses always ready to board rafts or transatlantic liners, kites or spaceships. Some of us left with full sails and a tailwind, leaving our birthplace, others would alternate between times of rest and times of faraway journeying. New landmarks were created elsewhere, chiefly in those places where hosting opportunities were to be found. One of those places was definitely Florence, where some friends had moved including Vagaiolo, with whom I had come to share something deeper than a friendship. Vagaiolo was a dreamer, restless and unpredictable; all of a sudden, bored of the same old landscapes, he would run away and disappear only to appear somewhere else across the world, soon to disappear from there, as well. While everybody's mind was set on ten, his own would run at two hundred, and nothing was ever enough to satisfy his frantic search for new emotions. As someone born in a proletarian family, his biggest aspiration was a well-off life with all sorts of comforts and amenities. His problem was that he wanted it all at once, so he would often be plotting get-rich-quick schemes that weren't always legit and legal. He was incredibly beautiful and fascinating, with dreamy green eyes that would stab right through one's heart, leaving victims in his path. My love for him was no mystery, and he had promised himself and me that one day we would go off and have an incredible time together in a beautiful locale, the same locale I would dream of and paint with the bright colors of falling in love; a place that had so far remained undiscovered, a place we'd try to reach with different magic potions. He lived in a house somewhere in the whereabouts of Santo Spirito square in Florence, a hub for first-generation drug addicts.

It was there that, one evening, he introduced me to Carlina, the first trans woman I had the honor of talking to—about nothing really, considering her absolute, dissociative obsession with drugs. Vagaiolo had already mentioned her, telling me that she was engaged in sex work, but I didn't quite understand what any of that meant. I would ask myself what exactly she was doing, who her clients were, what kind of rapport she had with them. Knowing her mainly as a heroin addict, I immediately linked her addiction to the transsexual experience. All of this was particularly disturbing to me because I associated everything that would deviate from normalcy to illness, craziness, drug addiction, and suicide. At that time, no one knew about transsexualism, and my own mental image reflected it back as that of transvestism—as in someone who would dress as a woman to feel more like herself or rather, someone who would disguise themselves as a woman. I would ask myself plenty of questions that would often remain unanswered. Before then, I had had the opportunity to observe a few transvestites in Naples, from a distance, as part of those nighttime tours that were organized in order to look at the local attractions that remained otherwise mostly unknown. I was deeply taken with those people even though I wouldn't profess that publicly, and when, in the company of a few acquaintances, we would decide to take a nightly tour of the city, I would always suggest a pit stop by Corso Vittorio, their habitual gathering spot. To me, they looked gorgeous, sensual, fascinating, and above all incredibly feminine, but I wasn't aware of the different steps, their trajectory wasn't very clear to me, I couldn't tell where the natural stopped and the artificial began. I didn't know anything about hormones, surgery, or even makeup, wigs, padded bras; I just took everything at face value, and that was that.

That night, in Santo Spirito square, Vagaiolo insisted that I become friends with Carlina in order to pick up a couple of johns and make some money; he told her, as well, even though she immediately changed the subject. I read her indifference as a basic lack of consideration for me, perhaps because she didn't see me as capable or good enough. Years later, with a much clearer mind, I realized that her indifference was instead a form of protection and of control of the square from any new arrivals, jointly with the fact that her attention was completely absorbed by heroin. Back then it wasn't easy to pick up johns as a transvestite, in either Lungarni or Cascine, and the various procedures to get there were dangerous and time-consuming. I would eventually understand that on my own only a few years later.

One night we stopped by to meet her in Lungarni, in the whereabouts of Ponte alla Vittoria, where she worked with other trans women. A close encounter, all the more shocking for me because it made me feel excited, anxious, confused, but also fascinated and captivated, in particular because of all the cars that would drive around from which you could make out both the type of the demand and that of the financial means, as I understood in the following years.

Eventually, the search for the island that doesn't exist made Vagaiolo set sail on the wrong boat. Instead of a sailing ship, he boarded the Titanic and slammed against an iceberg. They found him with a needle in his arm and his gaze toward the sea in July of 1986.

Technical Rehearsals of Resistance

In the meantime, my small-town life passed by; school's out, quick pit stop at the local cafe, then lunch, then off to the community center where, already in the early afternoon, reunions and debates were beginning and usually led to the preparation of a dazibao that would be published in front of the institute and around town. Back then, we would print out fliers with an old mimeograph, which required the manual insertion of a stencil typed on an old Olivetti, so that it would line up exactly with the roller, and then lots of elbow grease on the crank to churn out bulletins that would always come out either too dark or too light. Our hands, faces, and clothes would get soiled with the powdered or liquid ink that fed into that old coffeemaker, leaving behind indelible traces of guilt. Nowadays, you'd simply put together a bulletin on a computer, select print, input the number of copies in the printer and, in thirty minutes, you'd have hundreds of copies of the flier or, if you wanted to be even faster than that, you could just send it out in an email and have thousands of people read it in a matter of minutes. And yet, in spite of all that effort, we'd print out hundreds of documents, and they meant something different from the fliers that people publish now—perhaps they meant something because they had been written and produced that way. I remember one that I typed up by my own accord about the Brescia massacre, in which I proceeded to lash out against fascists, bosses, cops, directly incriminating the Italian Socialist Movement (MSI). That flier angered the overzealous Carabinieri marshal, who summoned me to the local station threatening lawsuits and arrests.

I made a habit of keeping copies of all those fliers alongside interesting articles and various issues of some newspapers. I piled everything up into a few big boxes that I kept at my country house. A few years later, while my aunt was cleaning around, she mistook those boxes for scrap paper and threw everything out: three full years of *Lotta Continua*, a few special issues of *Manifesto* and of the newly issued *Repubblica*, *Paese Sera*, *Avanguardia Operaia*, a few issues of *Re Nudo*, *Il Pane e le Rose*, *Rosso*, *Metropoli* . . . all garbage. It was like the burning of the Library of Alexandria.

I would stop at nothing to keep myself in the loop about what was going on in the world; I would ask my sister or those friends who lived in the city to buy me specific newspapers or magazines and to gather bulletins or other materials that could be of interest. In all of this, the turning point was receiving a mail subscription to the catalog of Arcana Editrice, whose address I had found in *Ciao 2001*, which enabled me to order and receive all the books that I wanted directly at home in a sealed envelope. Arcana would publish all sorts of Italian and international counterculture books, which were otherwise rather hard to track down as they were either too revolutionary or too extreme for a regular bookstore. I relied on Arcana from 1974 to 1976, the year I left my town, and I still fiercely guard the books that I acquired that way as the crown jewels of my library: *Ma l'amor mio non muore*, *Do It* by Jerry Rubin, *Jail Notes* by Timothy Leary, and many others, among which was *Homosexual: Oppression and Liberation* by Dennis Altman, the one I guarded most fiercely and secretly and would only show to a select few, as it moved and inspired me so deeply. To own it was for me a clear sign of belonging, like a card that proved the politicization of my sexuality, and the acknowledgment of the revolutionary potential of my experience. Alfredo Cohen had written in the introduction, the part that I understood most clearly. In it, there were a number of different nods to the Black Panthers and to the Gay Liberation Front as well as other liberation movements that, back then, would converge and collaborate.

Once my work at the community center was done, I would run to Studio Uno which would always be open, night and day. There I began to know and appreciate good music, like the early Pink Floyd (*Meddle*, *Atom Heart Mother*, *Ummagumma*), Grateful Dead, Van der Graaf Generator, King Crimson, Cream, the Who: that music motivated me and made me dream. The booming voice of Grace Slick, the singer of Jefferson Airplane, kidnapped, electrified, moved me most of all, perhaps because it was the voice of a woman. Jefferson Airplane quickly became my favorite band as well as the soundtrack of all those years.

Eventually many youngsters became interested in Studio Uno, and a growing number of people slowly added itself to the founding group so that, in a few months, the Sowbread tribe shot up to about thirty members. As the number of hippies grew, people around town started murmuring about a conspiracy of some kind. Priests, moralists, even the police, everybody started to conjure up obscure or otherworldly plots, as though the USSR, China, or Martians were about to invade town: hippies, communist professors, rebel students, restless sons, *magic buses* from Morocco and India, funny-smelling cigarettes, eccentric figures landed more and more often on the boring town soil. Apart from the Russians, the Chinese, and the Martians, others worried it was really about drugs or free love. According to some, those were the three plagues that were destroying the world. After a few years, a particular agreement between the Vatican and the United States took care of the first one, heroin took out the second, and AIDS erased the third one. That Soviet experiment, the so-called communism that none of us were able to justify to ourselves and to others because it failed right after its inception; the relentless search for psychedelics which placed us in front of our own belabored insanity and kept on terrorizing us; and love, free yet not liberated, of which we got but a little taste until AIDS, the so-called divine judgment, descended like manna from heaven for our enemies to put a stop to all that relentless depravation. Everything that I had been ashamed of as a child and as an adolescent had turned into pleasure, happiness, pride, and later on, after the arrival of AIDS, suddenly engendered a sense of terror and loss. Morality, with its pangs of guilt and its load of pain, peeked out its head stealthily, without anyone noticing, and systemically destroyed everything we were enjoying. Yet, all this would take place years after the events I'm discussing.

The Best of Youth

Within the Ciclamini tribe, some planned an escape from their homes, others from the town altogether, and all of us from what we called a "shit society." Problems with my father began very early at home. He neither accepted nor tolerated my choices. Tensions transformed into real tragedies, when he began to see me hanging out with the longhairs, or walking together with the philosophy professor, that communist, for whom my father nevertheless had a lot of respect. For him, a fervent supporter of the Duce (Mussolini), having a son with those acquaintances was a tremendous humiliation. My father was the classic hard-ass with sound principles who would never have imagined that his son could question his ideas, his values, his rules, or his world. Actually, it had never happened before that children rebelled against their parents, that a large number of young people questioned that ancient system, including all of its representatives. A contrast between children and parents has always been endemic, but in those years, it was not a simple contrast in place but the birth of a new culture that rejected and destroyed the world that was protected and represented by its fathers. I certainly wasn't the first—another generation before mine had begun the demolition work and we, staying in tune, were pursuing it. We sought to understand by studying and debating; we knew what needed to be thrown out, destroyed, or questioned. The incredible thing was that despite the hard work, our work was still at the beginning; there was still so much to discover, to do, to understand. We had the feeling or were under the illusion of having all the time in the world at our disposal, that this would never be finished, there was still time to plan, to think, to build, and we certainly didn't lack the imagination necessary to do it.

The moment of greatest tension between me and my father was precisely the 29th of May 1975, the day after the massacre in Brescia. Having learned about the attack, the collective met immediately to discuss it and decide what to do about it. We prepared flyers and manifestos in which we denounced the fascist hand of the massacre, openly accusing the Movimento Sociale Italiano (MSI, a neofascist political party). After having followed the newsletters that reported that some violent clashes had erupted all over Italy, we organized a demonstration for the following day that, however, wasn't authorized. At the end of that feverish day, when I got back home, I found myself in front of my father in the grip of anger, who was cursing while waving a piece of paper that he had in his hand. I didn't understand what had happened, but I understood when I read the piece of paper: it was a summons to the police station for an unauthorized demonstration and slander against a political party, referencing the posters accusing the MSI. I confess that I was scared. In effect it was exactly what the marshal of the Carabinieri wanted: to scare us! He was a fervent and cocky supporter of the Fascist period who hounded us, spied on us, and attacked us. I remember that during an occupation of the high school he came in the middle of the night, ramming the door open with his shoulder so he could enter and liberate the school from communists, but one of the occupiers—who today is a serious party leader—who had drunk one too many beers welcomed him with a "golden shower" from the window.

On the news they were giving updates about clashes in the piazzas that led to wounded people and arrests all over Italy. There was really a lot of anger and indignation. After Piazza Fontana, the attack in Piazza della Loggia was the second fascist massacre, and once again the finger was pointed at the usual anarchists. I had heard a lot of talk about Piazza Fontana, but when it happened, I was only twelve. But that time, for sure, I understood it better and also got a sense of how much had really happened. I also understood what would be needed in the years to come, including the Bologna massacre and the hundreds of fascist attacks with no one found guilty. I think about it and I think back and I can't stand it. I find it incredible that in Italy there were hundreds of deaths due to the fascist massacres of which the guilty parties were never found and sentenced, while really all of the members of the extreme left ended up in prison, those women and men who had believed in a violent overthrow of that system.

What happened in Brescia made my anger and conscience grow in tandem. In my town nothing particularly striking happened, but looking out over the world through the television porthole, there were protests, clashes, and uprisings every day. Living in town I had never attended or participated in protests that flowed into clashes in the streets. The only ones I had attended were those that punctually broke out at pop music concerts between the police and the gearheads.

Rebel Music

In February of 1974 I went to a Genesis concert at the Naples arena, the first concert of my life, and since it was the first, it was a mind-blowing experience. The concert was supposed to start at 9 P.M., but I was at the gates at 6 P.M. because I liked to enjoy and live the event in all its glory. And like me, all the other eccentric people, dressed in even stranger ways, were united by an unstoppable desire for freedom. That concert had a particular significance for me because Peter Gabriel was a representative of rock music who made dressing up a very important component of his performance, a style whose principal icon was David Bowie. The excitement grew gradually until the lights went out and a beam of blue spotlights illuminated Peter Gabriel dressed as a bat, singing "Knife." I was very excited, it was my first time at a concert so huge, one that had a famous artist on the stage and—what's more—in costume.

Music was a fundamental element of those years, a powerful instrument of communication and youthful association. Tickets cost 5,000 liras but there were many people who didn't have money, and there were so many people who thought that music should be free. So, it often happened that fights broke out with the police at concerts, and they were sometimes very violent. That night with Genesis, the mess was limited to some broken windows, but two months later at the Traffic concert, at the same arena in Naples, the clashes took on a much more violent disposition. The concert began one hour late and ended early without an encore, because clashes had continued inside the arena as well, rendering the air unbreathable due to the tear gas filtering through the broken windows. I was angry and at the same time fascinated. I wanted to listen to the music, follow the concert, even if emotionally I felt very involved in the rebellion in progress.

If on one hand music represented the desire for freedom and liberty—especially in the words and messages that various groups or artists sent out—on the other it signaled the failure of those values because it was completely enslaved by the industry, and its representatives always appeared so distant from our lives. I think that political violence signaled the point of no return at the Lou Reed concert in Rome, if I'm not mistaken, in 1975—the last hurrah of foreign bands in Italy. The next one would be five years later with Patti Smith. In between those two concerts, only Italian bands performed at festivals and concerts, where there was a strict rule in place of "Italian things only." I remember that at an Area concert at the Tenda theater in Naples I paid only fifty liras. So many concerts were organized around Italy, almost always associated with political events of the extraparliamentary far left. All those groups and solo artists who performed made up a rainbow of Italian pop music: Banco del Mutuo Soccorso, Premiata Forneria Marconi, Area, Napoli Centrale, Eugenio Finardi.

Another event that I remember fondly is the festival at Licola, held in June of 1975. Three days of music and counterculture by the sea, close to Naples. We read the announcement in *Lotta Continua* and immediately organized our departure—rather, our escape—because I left in a car with friends as soon as class had ended at school, and with perfect timing we met other friends at the beginning of the concerts only to leave again at the end, in the middle of the night, arriving the next morning just in time for the school bell. Maybe it's because of the big joints we smoked, but the only thing I remember was the FUORI! kiosk, a shack decorated with veils, colored paper, and posters. It was run by three gay daredevils who raved about, making a public display of themselves among their distraught and bewildered respondents. The three gays gave out kisses and caresses to bystanders but, paranoid as never before, I was careful not to get close. That too was a missed opportunity. I would have liked to talk to them, to communicate, but I didn't have the courage. I was scared that the meeting would involve all the ritual effusions that I couldn't manage or maybe didn't even want to.

Rock music represented an important point of reference on my journey; it was not only the soundtrack of my *trip*; it was, more generally, communication, formation, and transgression. Several years prior, my sister had bought *Ziggy Stardust* right after it came out, the mythical David Bowie record. And then *Aladdin Sane*, where Bowie appeared on the cover in close-up with makeup, transformed into a transvestite, even though he was nude. Even before arriving at Studio Uno, I listened to it and listened again; I scrutinized the cover with that character who teased and fascinated me beyond belief. I spent entire afternoons holed up in my room listening to David Bowie, imitating the way he dressed, his makeup, and his gestures. And the Rolling Stones too, dreaming about Mick Jagger, his mouth, his made-up eyes, and the huge swelling of his pants, the Stones who were not yet shamed, who managed to thrill an entire generation with their transgressive pieces and their shocking concerts. I clearly remember the pair of boots with very high heels that I secretly took from my sister. I wore a tight velvet shirt, I put makeup on, I straightened my hair back, and I allowed myself to sing ambiguously and sensually in my room by myself. I emphasized my nature, that hidden identity that I wanted to live with, the exact way in which I dreamed of going out, hanging around, and acting. I still didn't know anything about dressing like a woman, about transsexualism or transgenderism; it was all still far away from my little town, from Italy, and from the life of its people. Let's say that it was all confined to the world of spectacle, the only place where it was allowed to be.

To tell the truth, in my daily life I adorned myself with bracelets, necklaces, and various frills, making those ornaments fall more in the hippie style than in a clear sign of transvestism. For a while I{m} took to making bracelets with those little colored beads that I then sold to my school friends, those typical bracelets that for many young people were a clear sign of belonging. I was able to overcome the fear and I even got my ear pierced. It was so exciting for me to wear a tiny gold hoop that seemed to me a fantastic jewel in the crown! But I had to hide it from my father by putting a Band-Aid on my earlobe every time I sat at the table, claiming that I had an infection. One day I managed to get him to accept the earring, after which I did the second, the third, and the fourth hole until my ear was full, but at that point the earring began to lose its original meaning. Like the earring, all the other signs that characterized "counterculture"—tattoos, amulets, clothes—were slowly absorbed and transformed into fashion and, later, into a market: definitively debased and denuded of their subversive potential.

Only when I left for my trips around the world did I bring all those accessories in my backpack that I had failed to put on before: scarves, veils, jewels, shiny things, patchouli, eye kohl—and at that point Cinderella turned into a princess!

Exodus, Displacement, Transition

In 1976, I had taken my high school graduation exams, scoring a mediocre forty-two. Immediately after that, I left with two of my friends for a much-anticipated trip, destination Copenhagen, where we were supposed to visit Giorgio, a dear artist friend and wanderer who lived in Christiania, a liberated and liberating place, a true myth back then. We made a pit stop in Ravenna, where a big pop festival was taking place. The three of us had set off in an old Seicento which had been fixed, rearranged, and restored. It was blue with purple hues and innumerable tiny silver stars spread all over the body—they used to call her Blue Hotel. Unfortunately, the traffic policemen in Rimini sequestered it upon arrival because we didn't have I don't know what paperwork. Blue Hotel was abandoned, remaining parked in the whereabouts of the Rimini station for a long time, and it was still there when I stopped by again after a year, hosting vagabonds and pilgrims. After losing the car, our original group split up; I stayed back in Rimini with a Swiss guy, who was also headed to the Ravenna Festival, whom I hosted very willingly in my welcoming Blue Hotel.

That was a time of interesting encounters, undefined or undefinable adventures, midway between the sexual and the sentimental. After the Swiss guy, whose name I no longer recall, I moved along with Francesco. When I met him, I thought he was experiencing a bad *trip* and I tried to help him. He vacillated between moments of tranquility, when he would hold me tight, hand in hand, and delirious outbursts where he would go on about utter nonsense, repeating over and over that he didn't want to go back home, begging me not to abandon him. I stayed with him three days, long enough to fall in love but also to understand that this was not a *trip* gone wrong, but something much more complex. I took him to the festival ER, and while he kept staring at me holding my hand, an ambulance took him away.

Among the diverse fauna populating Ravenna back in that time, I also recall Maga, a rather extravagant character who became an integral cog of the alt landscape. She was a thin, borderline scrawny faguette, with a huge black hat. Like a spider spinning its web around its victims, he was always surrounded by pretty boys, charging at them with spirited eyes and catching them by surprise, perhaps scaring or perhaps fascinating them, but always binding them to himself. In the following years, you could see her every night in Piazza Navona reading tarots at her small desk, the first of a now infinite series of annoying card readers populating public squares, until one day I read on *Messaggero* that she had gotten murdered, yet another gay killing in the capital.

Meanwhile the festival went on; it was meant to last an entire week, but there was a certain tension and unrest in the air that only subsided when the music started. All the big names of Italian rock were in attendance, as well as a few acts from the British scene. I remember that one day, while I wandered around the city, I witnessed a so-called proletarian expropriation. A group of people would walk into a grocery store, filling up their carts to the cry of "proletarian expropriation," and leave quickly without paying. The practice of expropriations had always existed but it became a constant reality of that time. While I looked around, amidst a great fracas of screams and slogans, some woman I had met the night before put a whole salami in my hand and told me to run at the same time that I heard police sirens getting closer. I ran in a crowd that became bigger and bigger, and together with the sirens I could also make out the dry blast of tear gas. The air quickly became unbreathable amidst upside-down cars and flaming dumpsters. In spite of the danger I didn't let go of the salami, holding it tight like an important war trophy. As the clash intensified, I heard arrests and people getting wounded. Many reported that a so-called Crazy Horse had been hurt or killed. We later became accustomed to the performances of Crazy Horse, a fixture of all the meetings in our movement and different happenings in the Radical Party; he was completely bonkers, and his sensational behavior walked a thin line between heartfelt protest and egocentrism.

Many similar messes like the one that blew up in Ravenna had already happened a month earlier at the Youth Proletariat Festival in Parco Lambro in Milan; however the violence there was not directed toward the outside, but rather to the inside of the alt scene, also at the expense of some gays whose stand was destroyed while the protesters took over the stage. On that occasion Mario Mieli, after occupying the stage together with a group of homosexuals in order to denounce male aggressiveness, declared: "From now on we won't just work the streets, we will work the good fight together. Proletarians around the world, let's fuck each other." Parco Lambro represented the beginning of a new phase, giving visibility and body to a certain wing of the youth proletarian movement that joined Autonomia en masse; I gladly followed in their footsteps.

Following those revolts, I left Ravenna together with a hundred other degenerates heading to France and continuing to the Isle of Wight, where rumor had it that another festival was going to take place, like the really famous one from 1969. We were a kind of wandering tribe of about two hundred vagabonds, Indians, gypsies, and Martians.

The destination had changed again from England to Copenhagen, but it wasn't over yet. The train car we had hopped on without a ticket was disconnected in Bologna and, before the cops could get to us, we ran away across the rails. I hopped on the following train with a small group of survivors headed to Turin. We talked, we told stories, we dreamed, and we were tripping. I had my sleeping bag, and sleeping together in close ranks facilitated an intimate communion, enhancing points of contact and touch; no matter what, we were part of a revolt, against everyone and everything, "nature" included. Waking up the following morning you'd act like strangers with some; with others the flirting would go on and it all felt so dreamy.

Around that time you'd take off with nothing on you and you would eventually find everything; nowadays you take off fully equipped, condoms included, and you come back with all of them not because you had unprotected sex but because you had no sex, period. Compared to those times, I believe that nowadays it's a lot harder to have sex because there's less closeness, reduced communication, a culture of estrangement, a general lack of trust, and it's all so widespread and poorly acknowledged, so you never really know who's in front of you, let alone behind you. Sex and sexuality back then were categories without distinction that roared loudly within each one of us like something uncontainable pushing to break free. We'd talk about sex, we'd joke about it, we tried to understand it because there was a potential ready to burst, compared to today where there is an inability to expand. You would try it with everybody and among everybody, everything was meant to be discovered and lived. Starting the following year, in 1977, sexuality became much more central in relationships, in flings, in reflections, in manifestations, and in large swaths of our movement. From then on, attention and tension were no longer centered only on sex but also on sexuality. Desire was placed squarely at the center and the games began!

Escape

So I left. My studies were the official reason, but it wasn't just about that. I left because I no longer fit in my town, because I felt the need to get to know that world that appeared so distant from up there, so unknown and fascinating. From that outside world would arrive news, messages, impulses, stimuli that made my feeling of nonbelonging to the reality of my town grow ever more. The city was far away, its lights and chaos at once so fascinating and terrifying, so attractive and repellent, and I felt deeply that the metropolis was the only place where I could survive.

After resolving the fear to leave my home alongside the certainties and the feeling of safety with which I had grown, I started my journey. The road that opened in front of me wasn't straight, nor paved, nor plain. An old lady from my town would often say, "The devil you know is better than the devil you don't." As soon as I arrived in the city, I was welcomed by utter madness: protests, screams, blasts, the bitter smoke of tear gas, fires, Molotov cocktails, and war dances. It was the fall of 1976, the big prologue to the madness that would soon ensue.

I enrolled as a sociology major in Naples for the 1976–1977 academic year. I got there quite exhausted already due to a profound crisis that hit me right at the time I was adapting to this new dimension with all the insecurities, the doubts, and the fears that it brought out from within me. Up until that moment the dream had been to escape, but when I actually found myself on the train out of my hometown, I became enveloped by a feeling of dread. I would no longer be able to rely on my parents or operate within the narrow yet comfortable landscape of my little town. Luckily, I didn't have much time to think and worry about it; I was ejected into a bewildering yet fascinating new world. Everything happened at a rate and speed that felt breathtaking. First Parco Lambro, then Ravenna, almost setting the stage for the fires that climaxed into the violent protests the evening of December 8th in front of the Scala in Milan. The Milan haute bourgeoisie had set a date to celebrate the Prima, but the party was ruined by protesters that the newspapers kept calling "a small group of unrepentant provocateurs," who threw everything under the sun on the fur coats of the ladies in attendance and on the oversized jeeps of the riot police. The lyrics from Paolo Pietrangeli's "Contessa" echoed over the proceedings.

∼ 2 ∼

1977

Dreaming and Utopia

My house will continue to travel on two legs
And my dreams will have no frontiers.
—Ernesto Che Guevara

And 1977 Exploded!

We knew it was a dream but we liked believing in it. The sensation was something new, something powerful was happening; ashes had caught fire. More and more often we talked about Autonomia Operaia (Workers' Collective), which, until that moment, had been a minority of the antagonistic movement, while the most consistent part was represented by

Lotta Continua. It wasn't only Autonomia Operaia that occupied the scene but a series of groups, little groups, theme songs, and singles that made up the great, diversified galaxy of '77. Everyone's will and ability to lose themselves in that healthy and saintly delirium that had always been denied us made all the difference. Those happenings filled me with joy, a thrill that went up and down my spine and that of the best of youth.

The first months, those autumns were useful to me for settling in. I hung around the department, I went to almost all of my classes, some interesting, others less so. Above all I preferred anthropology and sociology, especially the two seminars organized by the respective department heads, one on "magic and popular traditions" taught by Pino Simonelli—with whom later on I would become friends, accomplices, and other things; the second on "communicative forms of movement," taught by De Masi, a very prominent professor, especially within the movement of which he seemed to be an integral part because he was present at all the initiatives. One day, during one of his classes, a group of about ten people with their faces covered with balaclavas or bandanas barged in. They interrupted the class, read a statement, and after having accused De Masi of manipulating the movement, they smeared the chalkboard, desk, the record books, and the professor himself with red spray paint, identifying themselves as Masok Collective.

Even if they weren't so invasive, I remember so many more blitzes like that one. They were a part of the normal rhythms and rites of the university. Every once in a while, someone came in, read a document, shouted out a slogan or sang a song. University corridors were filled with manifestos and writings; a simple, rhythmic slogan with some handclaps was enough to transform everything into a party or into one of those processions that started with ten people and ended with three hundred. I remember that it was precisely one of these occasions that turned into the first occupation of the year, at the Departments of Sociology and Law at the University of Naples. I'm able to remember events and the time period because I wrote everything down in my Savelli Red Notebook of '77, which I still have saved and hidden away. It was a late January afternoon. There were still classes being held in classrooms, and in the department hallways there was a big to-do: little groups that were talking, someone putting up flyers, and another little group that was banging out a beat on the benches. Then other people with painted faces showed up and the banging got louder and grew to the point that everyone there was banging out that rhythmic slogan differently in the two versions of "Hey, Hey, Hey, Oh!"—with their hands, jars, bottles, and all kinds of tools—that would mark the rhythm and succession of the year's events.

After a little while an enormous conga line formed that unwound first in the hallways, then in classrooms, interrupting classes (to the great dismay of the professors who were teaching), and ending along the entrance stairways to the university and off into the streets. A happy and creative dance line, improvised without any evident political motivation except for that of enjoying spaces, taking them back, cheering them up and painting them, the university, life, the world, and everything else. This improvisation was not tolerated at all by those little hard and pure groups that stayed to watch with deplorable and contemptuous expressions. They were all those military types who had confused the revolution with political order, communism with China or Russia, rebellious joy with militant severity. They were all those guys who populated the galaxy with Marxism and

Leninism, with Maoism, with Stalinism, and with that myriad of slogans that abounded in that time period. The dance line went around the entire university, blocking traffic during rush hour, and when the express mail showed up after the dance line's daze, it went back into the department, having decided to occupy it. I don't know how long I stayed there because I lost my concentration. I realized it only a few days later, when I came across my roommate in the curious crowd that was observing the occupation. He told me about a phone call from my mom. I recall a sort of dissociation between reality and fantasy, between what was necessary to do or be and what we wanted. I was supposed to be studying and going to classes, but I increasingly convinced myself that in the moment it was more important, maybe also more fun, to do what I wanted. Rebelling made me feel truly myself and above all in the right place, in the beating heart of the protest. I waited for that moment for years. I had heard so much talk about the events of 1968 that not having lived through it made me feel as though something was lacking. It was time for a new '68, said one of the famous slogans directed at the enemy on duty: "Pack your bags, a new '68 is here!"

In the following days, news of occupations in other cities came, and all of this electrified matters, and shivers of joy crossed the universe. At the occupation, everything was happening: assemblies, seminars, megaphones, rallies, parties, music, theater. But the new and extraordinarily exciting element was the joy and happiness with which everything developed. Every time that the old-school militurds took the floor trying to bring everything back to the banks they were buried in imaginative screams, shouts, and slogans. There was a profound need to be protagonists, to directly live through the revolution that was taking place, but all that it involved did not coincide at all with the orders and rules that the militurds wanted to impose. That "fucking" Soviet Union or China which we'd been banging our snouts on for years, every time that we talked about liberty and someone retorted "go live in Russia." Even if we didn't like capitalism at all, I believe that there were few who saw communist countries as a possible alternative. We sincerely dreamed about something better. Often when a militurd took the floor there was someone—almost always a woman or a gay guy, or a creative type—who made fun of him by turning him around, touching him, laughing, making an ironic comment, or mimicking improbable conditions.

It was in one of these situations where I met Pina and Antonello, who later became Valerie and Antonia, the two faguettes of the movement. During one of those mega-assemblies at the university, together with other companions, they were making fun of a super macho guy, a militurd, or, as we used to say, a stubby. I had already seen Valerie before. I'd met her one morning in front of the Orientale, the languages department, as she spoke on the megaphone about gathering signatures in favor of abortion. Maria Teresa Di Lascia was with her, a well-known historic, militant radical who died in 1994. Valerie was a very young faguette: tall and thin with thick hair like Angela Davis. Stiff and proud, exactly as she is today, she invited passersby to sign her petition for abortion rights, arguing against machismo in a feminist key. Her courage and above all her pride astonished me, yet at the same time she intimidated me. Rather, that air of confidence and her stern and contemptuous gaze vexed me. I felt like it was a reproach to my political commitment to the movement and its disengagement in the gay liberation struggle which was much closer to us.

I still couldn't comprehend a gay struggle inside the movement. I didn't really understand that my being homosexual could be revolutionary. I was still encrusted with that rigidity typical of Marxist-Leninists—the fruit of an old, cultural heritage. I was still experiencing a major split between the personal and political. I lacked the connections between homosexuality and revolution. Let's say that my conscience was in the process of formation. I felt the need to channel my experience into a more general struggle of liberation. I was able to insert the revolutionary process into my personal experience, into my being homosexual, but I couldn't do the opposite and pose or propose my homosexuality as revolutionary praxis. As the situation evolved, becoming red-hot, we talked more and more about the relationship between the personal and the political, about how much these two levels overlapped, but although my homosexuality was obvious, I still couldn't find the courage to start from it and make it central to the struggle and in the barricades.

Thinking about it now, it seems absurd that, in such a revolutionary phase as '77 where everything, really everything was questioned, it wasn't simple and not even a given to start from one's own homosexuality. It was all too easy to question the world, society, and others, but it was truly difficult to question yourself. The issues and above all the desires tied to homosexuality were still unmentionable after centuries of denial. Sooner or later, however, the questioning of everything would have irreparably led to questioning one's own person. And so it was! Confrontation with oneself was tiring and—regardless of reading Fromm, Bakunin, Nietzsche, or Baudelaire—it exhausted us a lot more than police raids. The need and more than anything the desire to scream out to the world your own homosexuality was pressing, but there were very few who were able, and those few were considered foolish: they were crazy! I was very naive to the point that I considered someone gay only if they showed it off or flaunted it. The others were all hetero, as if to say that the only fehgs were Valerie, Antonello, and the few others that I had met at that juncture. In the following years as liberation gradually materialized, I began to see old companions of the barricades come out more and more. First five, then ten, a hundred, a thousand, and the scene was reversed.

Occupations grew more numerous, together with a red-hot situation in schools among the young people generally. For that reason, Luciano Lama, at that time secretary of CGIL (Italian Workers Confederation), decided to hold a meeting at the University of Rome that turned into a battle after which the unions were left battered. I was in Rome in the days leading up to that date as a guest of my old high school companions who were enrolled in the Political Science Department, another department that was hot and lively in those days. All the departments had a collective that was characterized by political trends or affiliations, and almost all of the collectives had a large component of Lotta Continua, which until that year remained the most consistent group and also the most characteristic of the years preceding '77. The Political Science collective made references predominantly to Lotta Continua, with a consistent presence of a so-called creative wing or those who didn't identify with any specific group. In those days the collective was pretty much buzzing because the fascists had shot and killed a companion right in their department.

The First Lesbian

I remember that my friend introduced me to Maria Grazia, a lesbian member of the collective who was there during the fascist raids. She was the first lesbian that I knew personally. She had long blonde hair, a wide-brimmed black hat, a blue velvet shirt, black clogs, and a round Tolfa bag: more of a feminist model than a lesbian one. Lesbians weren't very present or visible yet because they were weak or inserted into the women's movement; let's say that I couldn't yet read and decodify the signs, so I couldn't yet see the reality that was slowly emerging. I wasn't familiar with the galaxy of feminism at all, much less the separatist kind in which the majority of lesbians operated. After all, it wasn't easy to know that experience well because feminist places and situations were off-limits to me anyway since I was a guy. I must have passed{f} by the occupied building in via del Governo Vecchio a hundred times, peeking inside with a deep desire to go in, but it was impossible. In those years I used to go with my girlfriends a lot to Governo Vecchio for gynecological appointments or various assemblies, but I had to stay at the front door. I didn't even really ask why; it was just like that. There were few gays and lesbians who were visible or *outed*, like we say today. As soon as we figured out or heard about a gay or lesbian acquaintance or friend, our ears pricked up, we got emotional, and we went into palpitations in order to get in contact with whomever was having the same experience. We sought to correspond with them, their way of life, of being and remaining in that phantasmagoric space represented by the anti-movement.

Maria Grazia welcomed me radiantly, taking me around the university (Sapienza) on a guided tour of the hottest university in Italy. The tour was mostly about the Chemistry, Political Science, and Humanities Departments, those that were situated around Piazza Minerva, the main hub of the university. We wandered around groups who were debating, others who were writing manifestos, people who were putting up flyers, and others who were selling revolutionary newspapers and magazines: *Voce del Popolo* (Voice of the people), *Pane e le Rose* (Bread and roses), *Foglio di Interfacoltà*, and so many others, among which was *Lotta Continua* (The struggle continues), the most read and widespread that was sticking out of every backpack or purse, every jeans or parka pocket. There were people announcing assemblies, processions, teaching blocks, alternative classes, group games, hide-and-seek, cops and robbers. There were people writing on the walls and chalkboards. "Love, love make me come with the revolution" was written on the stairs leading up to the humanities building, which was a mythical meeting place mostly during the day that competed with the more famous Piazza Navona, Campo de' Fiori, and Santa Maria in the Trastevere neighborhood. Maria Grazia strolled around—and I with her—to stop and say hi, chat, and joke around.

We would stop to listen to an improvised assembly on the subject of teaching, or an aesthetics lesson about the movement's communication, and from there we would head to the interdepartmental feminist group, and from there to the sixth occupied classroom, where the intergalactics prepared the revolution on Jupiter, planning on turning Pluto yellow and putting dots on the Colosseum. And so on throughout the day with a lunch break at the cafeteria in via De Lollis, coffee at the university center, and then heading to the stairs leading up to the Humanities Department.

It was right there—among the circulating joints, guitars and tambourines, ring-around-the-rosy circles, and daisies—where I saw the faggola who was crazier than the entire galaxy. I heard a scream coming from Piazza della Minerva, and Maria Grazia poked me with her elbow, inviting me to look. I saw this fehg dressed like a feminist who was screaming at the top of her lungs: "We are women!" She wore the classic black clogs, a jean skirt of shitty quality that was probably homemade given its poor fit, a scarf tied at the back of her head like the companions used to do, the inevitable parka, and a scratched-up luxury purse that I later found out was acquired with a five-finger discount, or, as she called it, a fag-gotorium. Her makeup was conspicuous and in very bad taste: fire-red lipstick, smeared because of the many kisses that Madame gave out, light blue eye shadow from the '50s, black eyeliner a centimeter high, and two round balls of brick-red rouge on her cheekbones. Copies of *Lotta Conti-nua*, *Manifesto*, *Voce del Popolo*, and *Corriere della Sera* were peeking out from her bag. She pushed forward, proud and fearless, screaming with her raspy, grating voice, "I'm serving fish," after having stopped again and again to kiss everyone who came up to her for one, and started singing "Beware, battalion; the fags have arrived!" again, banging out a rhythm and imitating the popular Neapolitan character "pazzariello" (jester). Having arrived at the bottom of the stairs, she paused, tossing her luxury bag—which she clearly couldn't stand anymore—on the ground and, turning toward the hundreds of people sitting around what seemed like an arena, began her meeting. She took the *Corriere della Sera* out of her bag, opening with, "Dirty communists, terrorists, lazybones." I was shocked! I don't know if it was because of how she looked, her personality, or what she was doing or saying. I could hardly understand, I could not understand who she was and what she wanted, and when she began with "dirty communists," my confusion was absolute. Maria Grazia reassured me: "She's crazy," even if I didn't exactly understand that *matta* in the feminine form. Even the reaction of those present, who seemed to know her well, helped to reassure me. After the opening statement she continued to introduce herself as "the Countess Mancinelli Sforza," and opening the *Corriere della Sera*, began to read an article about what was happening at the university: "You want to destroy the university after you've destroyed Italy, ugly communists, but I won't let you, whatever it takes, over my dead body, my ass, my skirt, my lipstick. It's true that my name is Sforza Mancinelli," and while saying these last few words she simulated cunnilingus by moving her head and masturbating with her left hand, exactly like Mancinelli. She stopped talking, was silent for ten seconds, and then burst out into a thunderous laugh. With her arms raised in a sign of triumph: "Dears, little girls, darlings, looooooooves, I'm taking you all to bed with me. Rather, to she-bed (*lettessa*)." She made all the words grammatically feminine, and the words that were already feminine she emphasized with an *-essa* (-ette) at the end. I{m} was shocked, fascinated, and terrified at the same time. It was the first time I had heard such a strategy. I continued reading my copy of *Lotta Continua*, or at least I faked reading it, and I followed the crazy lady's whole delirium, saying hi to everyone, giving kisses, touching genitals, bursting out into thunderous laughter. Then suddenly, having arrived at the top of the stairs, she paused, and with her closed fist began to yell: "Pasolini is alive and you'll see him in every man who falls." She suddenly became serious, walked down the stairs, and just like she arrived, she left. Afterward, I saw her other times, at assemblies, at rallies, at parties, and every time I saw her, her delirium disturbed me. Later we would become friends, or, as she said, friendettes or dickfriends (*amicazze*).

We Want Everything!

And while history always drains the now dried-up well of invention, a frantic and weak prayer tries to postpone the continuation: "The rest for the next time." "This is the time!" yelled the happy voices. Thus the wonderland was born and slowly, one by one, bizarre events were explained.

The atmosphere of those days, their taste, their color, and all of their noise, stayed within me like that children's book, *Alice's Adventures in Wonderland*, mostly written on the walls, on flyers, and on our hearts. I was staying with my former high school classmates at Civis, a dorm that was far from the university but not far enough to avoid hearing the ruckus coming from it. What was happening in the university classrooms and corridors was also happening there in the dorm. In the evenings there was a constant coming and going between the various rooms in a collective excitement by which it was difficult not to become infected. Trysts and adventures materialized in those Civis beds that lasted a few nights but were enough to give birth to new loves, those many new loves that dotted my twenties—I had one in every city, in every place, and one for every situation—to the point that my friends called me "Cotta Continua" (continuous crush). Each fling had its own uniqueness, path, and importance, and although they were exclusively affairs regarding sex, they also aroused fantasies and feelings. Periodically, like clock-work, there was a most engaging tryst that made me dream and write poems, many of which I still have. A fling that turned my life upside down, and although I used to turn upside down with everything that came within reach, love remained the ingredient, the magic potion that made me have visions or ecstasies like Saint Teresa.

The people who most disrupted my peace in that period I remember well: Ziggy and Osaio, with whom I went to live for some time in the classrooms that they had occupied in the Faculty of Medicine together with others, the same one that today has given way to the gloomy and cold Second Polyclinic. The collective they belonged to was intriguing and quite interesting, and even if they called themselves "mavericks," they referred to that creative wing of the movement which had its center in Bologna, between the occupied Department of Fine Arts and the defunct Radio Alice. Situationists, Dadaists, Transversalists, and more. It must be said that the whole university abounded in political collectives. In fact, each faculty had several. The one that Osaio and Ziggy belonged to was not the only collective of medicine but certainly the most attractive. Their leader was Teo, often accompanied by Angela Putino, a great feminist philosopher who died a few years ago, and there were also Lorita (a crazy Calabrian creative type), Marilena, Tina, and many others.

That rich and consistent area had its most visible part in the Metropolitan Indians and in the Bolognese Transversalists. Collectives, microcells, and creative groups existed in all the cities, sharing public squares and places—not always peacefully—with the so-called tough guys of the opposition movement. In addition to physical spaces, the two experiences shared the idea that reality as it was had to be changed, indeed reversed, but there were divergent visions on its means and objectives. The difference in position and means of expression was particularly highlighted by the media, which in their articles separated the movement into good and bad using that monotonous refrain still very common among the few bad apples who ruin everything. On the other hand, the creative types used irony as a means of communication, and it often happened that their tight grip on the ass of the system was so subtle that it was not always understood by everyone. And in fact, many fell into their linguistic or semiotic traps. Like when they printed up a flyer that claimed their innocence and naivety with respect to some street clashes that they distributed and sent to press agencies. In the leaflet they distanced themselves from violent sects, declaring that they had received a few boxes of flowers and fruit as a gift from the bad fringes, in which they had found strange bottles with unknown contents which, to their amazement, caught fire when thrown.

It was Zanza himself, the crazy faguette I had met on the steps of Letters and Arts, who was handing out the flyer and gave me a copy during a demonstration. He placed a hand right "there," and with protruding lips overloaded with lipstick he said to me: "Star of the firmament! Where do you come from?" Then, squeezing his hand on the fly of my pants, he continued: "May God bless it and you." I was shocked; it was a blow to the stomach, and I had no ability to react. I didn't know whether to laugh or be serious. She had the same clothes on as the previous time, but instead of the feminist scarf, she was wearing a purple hat, eyeglasses as thick as Coke bottle bottoms, the usual exaggerated and kitschy makeup caked over greasy and pimply skin. I can't say that she was a little flower, but I think she used that ugliness of hers to be ironic and to make fun of the whole world. I still had to recover from the shock, as he had already told me about the COM and the COP, occupied houses in via Morigi, Alfredo Cohen and all the fehg patrols in Europe; it was the first time that a queer himself gave me news of experiences that I had only read and dreamt about without even knowing if they were legend or reality. I was speechless and stunned while meanwhile he had put his arm under his other arm, continuing to say: "Do you know that Mario Mieli eats shit? Do you know that the Queen of Sheba is at court in drag and that the UFO (Unidentified Faggy Object) was fucked in the ass by Mario Capanna? You know that Valerie, the Neapolitan, has slept with the entire architecture collective . . ." She spoke while continuing to greet everyone. Every now and then she told me to wait for her for a moment because, after aiming for someone particularly cute or more virile than the others, she put her hand on his fly and began: "Honey, are you a boy? And aren't you ashamed? In your place I would get buggered, but then if you're really a guy why don't you bugger me?" She continued in her delirium, improvising speeches, jokes, and slogans. When the victims recovered from the shock, she laughed out loud and said: "L . . . L . . . Love, I'm going back to my friendette (*amicazza*) now." I wasn't yet used to anyone referring to me in the feminine, I couldn't process everything that was going on, I couldn't make sense of that character. Zanza was truly nuts, beyond the boundaries of reality. After all, she placed herself exactly where most of those who populated the scene tended to end up.

All that had been buzzing for months and perhaps for years exploded when Luciano Lama, secretary of CGIL at the time, held a rally at the university. On the morning of February 17, we woke up early to be there in time for what was the movement's great debut. As soon as we got to campus we immediately sensed that something was going to happen; it was in the air. The trade union security service was near the entrance gates—which wasn't particularly reassuring—while the sound of a loudspeaker broadcasting songs and slogans came from Piazza della Minerva. Our more politicized comrades were inside the buildings, discussing what to do, but an increasingly large crowd formed by the so-called mavericks was gathering in the square on either side of a truck being used as a stage. It was clear that a mess would soon break out, but no one would have guessed its extent. Before Lama took the stage, a small group had written a huge inscription on the facade of the rectory overlooking the square: "The llamas are in Tibet."

When Lama began to speak there arose a tide of boos, the square thundered, and the slogans became increasingly threatening. A conga line of creative types wound up among those present. That day they had painted their faces like Native Americans, and they were in fact called "Metropolitan Indians." The three little pigs sang in rhythm: "We are three little pigs, CGIL, CISL, and UIL, no one will ever divide us . . . tra la la la," or "Tanassi and Rumor are innocent, we are the real criminals," and then on their knees, "Lama, whip us. Lama, whip us."

The energy of the creative types infected the more agitated ones, but it was a masculine force that took over.

Security began to start pushing, and from the shoving they soon passed to aggression, and the situation degenerated from there. Everything began to fly through the air: sticks, bottles, stones, and bolts. At first Lama invited the violent provocateurs to isolate, but when he realized that besides his security service the rest of those present were all so-called provocateurs and that there were thousands of them, he left the square. The clashes lasted a couple of hours, during which I took refuge together with many others in the College of Arts and Sciences which had been occupied for a few days.

In the sixth classroom, which became famous for having been occupied for about three years, the Indians had set up a veritable laboratory where people painted their faces, arranged feathers and frills in their hair, and prepared slogans to chant and write on the walls. In all this frenzy, while the war continued outside, a small group with painted faces and plastic axes in their hands came out of the sixth room to read a statement on the megaphone: "Today the people of men have unearthed their hatchets to respond to the attack of the pale-faced Lama and declare the state of permanent happiness open." There was a roar and everyone began to beat out rhythms with their hands, feet, and voices. A huge line formed, which began to turn in the corridors, in the classrooms, and then out of the building.

Signs of the battle—which in the meantime had moved toward the exits—were visible in the square. The big snake that came out of the Humanities building chanting "Hey, hey, hey, oh" grew bigger and became a procession of thousands of people on campus heading toward the gates, where the hard-liners were putting up with the police who had by then replaced security forces. We were literally surrounded. And that's how we occupied the University of Rome, Sapienza. We remained locked inside until 9 P.M., when the police allowed whoever wanted to leave through De Lollis Street. The air was unbreathable. The police fired hundreds of tear gas canisters which a team of comrades threw back out. The wind and rain were also favorable that day, as they pushed all the smoke back toward the police. Among the flash-bangs, the smoke, and the slogans there was also Garibaldi, an old bearded anarchist comrade who played "Internationale"—the workers' hymn—on his trumpet. Garibaldi was a well-known character among our companions. He made his living playing the trumpet in the taverns of San Lorenzo, the popular neighborhood bordering the university that was considered its antagonistic stronghold.

While the battle continued at the gates, "the state of permanent happiness" was organized inside, and between bongos, flutes, and dances I had a vision. Seated on the ground in a circle with other Indians was Mauro, with very black hair down to his ass, bright eyes, and two lips that looked like cherries. Our eyes met and a few sparks flew because he began to smile at me while passing me the joint. I was very clumsy trying to speak but he put his hand over my mouth to ask me to be silent, he took me by the hand and we went out, but as we went down the stairs of the Humanities building I heard a scream that I never wanted to hear at that moment: "L . . . L . . . Love! Shitty friend." It was Zanza, who was making the magic of the moment disappear. He stood in front of us, putting his hands on both of our cocks and with that absurd and disarming expression of his: "Where were you running away to, cowards, scabs? Fine, abandon the battlefield, but I'm coming with you." I felt a mixture of embarrassment, anger, and excitement. Mauro, who in the meantime had seen a friend of his, took the opportunity to slip away and leave. I would see him again a few years later in a restaurant in Trastevere where he worked, still as beautiful as the first time, but already clearly marked by heroin. That time we managed to escape together, despite the white powder that blocked energies and pleasures. After a few years he ended up in a ward of the infectious disease department of Spallanzani: AIDS.

Meanwhile, there was excitement in the classrooms and corridors of the occupied university, also due to the news broadcasts by Radio Città Futura, the movement's radio station. The main stories were Lama's expulsion and the occupied university in Rome, but news of clashes and occupations came from all over Italy. The other occupied universities were the Statale in Milan, the Normale of Pisa, the Polytechnic of Turin, the Federico II of Naples, and then those of Bologna, Padua, and Palermo. All universities and many middle schools were occupied or in turmoil. An electrifying situation; we felt good!

I returned to Naples, where my things were waiting for me, my commitments, not least of which was my studies. In that season, however, the thing that was most difficult for me was precisely that of studying: there were simply too many stimuli and events to be able to concentrate on books.

And when it happened that I found the concentration and disposition to immerse myself in my studies in front of a book, and full of good intentions, my roommate with whom I entertained a pleasant and controversial political-sexual relationship had other thoughts and intentions. We were already friends in high school and we moved to Naples together in order to go to the university there. We both came from the same high school and from his political collective but he, unlike me, was one of those serious comrades, determined and decisive, one of those according to whom extremism is infantilism and communism is a serious matter not to be confused with bullshit freaks, university occupations, and feminists, let alone fags. He did not participate in the events of those days, keeping his distance from them; he was the true representative of "male communism": in addition to declaring himself strictly heterosexual, his founding myths were Joseph Stalin and Mao Tse Tung. He had always accused me of childishness and lack of political seriousness, and every time he talked about it, after having railed about my way of doing and being, he also tried to make me feel guilty. Then he slowly relaxed, softened, the tension eased, and he began to get excited. He would touch himself, he got closer to me, first touching and then clinging to me. That was the awaited moment, the one I knew was coming and that I was waiting for with joy. In fact I had a strong sexual attraction to him. The ceremony was always the same: he began to court me like a peacock, touching himself, self-satisfied by marking his absolute masculinity; I naturally played the part of the excited and flattered faguette, while he was the male who doesn't give in. But that is precisely the key to hidden things, indeed to the "hidden thing." The more they insist upon their heterosexuality the more they want; they need it in order to quell the sense of guilt but at the same time to bring out the hidden narcissist. He knew I liked him and that I couldn't resist. I thought the same thing about him, but I made him believe what he wanted to. Sometimes the game went on for hours; he pushed forward and withdrew while I played the part of the seductress or perhaps the seducer. The recitation of that role, including all the preliminaries, excited me perhaps more than the final act when, paradoxically, the parts were reversed, so that I had to play the role of the active player who makes moves while he did what he wanted, bursting with desire but withdrawing because he wants to be taken. He's super macho and I'm super queer. I was intrigued by his being brutally male, even if at the end of the preliminary ceremony when we inevitably ended up in bed, I sensed that all his masculinity would be gone in an instant if I only wanted it to. At that point I was in charge of the situation and the peacock magically became docile and tame. His erogenous and sensitive zones weren't exactly the most properly masculine ones: when in fact I decided to make him come, it was enough to kiss his nipples and tease his little ass with my finger. And yet, despite the type of relationship, the ceremonial aspect, the erogenous zones, I continued to be gay and he was macho.

I continued to have relationships of this kind and I still wonder today if it was repressed homosexuality, the nonexistence of the real male, self-defense, or hypocrisy. Gender purity is profound conceit; it only rarely exists and is a pure cultural construct. At the time I didn't ask myself questions; it was just like that. I was the disgraced and deplorable faggola while the others were the boys. I was a fag because I was visible as such and I had ambiguous, unmasculine features, while the other, apparently impeccable, muscular ones were the so-called normal ones. Today I laugh uproariously and I am convinced more and more because appearances do not always correspond to the truth; what they want us to believe is often the exact opposite of reality.

The house in the university area of the historic center that I shared with my sexy tenant represented a place of return, a link with normality, with my studies, with my family, a sort of decompression chamber to which I returned every time I needed physical rest or to take stock of the situation. My heartbeat was elsewhere, and Naples never felt completely mine, because Rome remained the city I dreamed of.

The house was behind the church of Santa Chiara, in the square where the comrades of the movement met. The evening and nocturnal rendezvous in Piazza del Gesù became a ritual recognized by the whole movement. I didn't have much confidence yet; in fact I was quite shy, so when I arrived in the square I observed and stood quietly on the sidelines. One evening I saw Valerie arrive with Antonello, haughty and proud as always. Seen from the outside, her way of being, in some ways fascinating and for others irritating, instilled fear, so communication with her was practically impossible. As usual she walked past me with the attitude of someone deliberately ignoring you, even though I perceived that I didn't go unnoticed. After saying hello to half the piazza and doing her fashion show, she took a can of red spray paint out of her bag, shook it before using it, and wrote on the wall: "Free Gloria Swanson." I didn't know exactly who Swanson was but I understood that the writing and her gesture should be read in the key of gay militancy. Antonello, charming as always, joined her in the fun. in Naples he was famous in the movement for his particular beauty.

Both Valerie and Antonello were blatantly and openly gay, or as they say in Naples, *femminielli*: Dressed and dolled up in keeping with the style of the time, with that extra touch typical of queer creativity. They moved quietly and at ease, clucking and frolicking as if at a party with friends. I still felt quite removed from them, from that blatant visibility. After all I came from a small town where, in my own way, I was super visible. Nevertheless, there were still many milestones to reach that were all linked to self-acceptance upon coming out, and at that moment some practices appeared difficult to me, and distant from my perception of the world. Still, I would soon begin to follow these practices.

I remember one evening when *Mistero Buffo* by Dario Fo was shown on television, an important show of denunciation that was repeatedly censored, which is why many of the visitors to the square decided to watch it together at the home of some of our comrades: Alfredo, Annalisa, and Edoardo. There must have been about thirty people in the house among bottles of wine, spliffs, flyers, and constant potshots from Valerie, who kept running around between one group and another, completely ignoring me. There were at least five particularly cute guys who attracted the attention of many of those present, both women and queers. Apparently very determined guys of which every other possible dimension escaped me, all their hidden nuances did not reach me, so I strictly adhered to appearances. Years later I used to find several of them with variations in sex and gender not exactly like those of that evening, decidedly more gay and relaxed.

The evening ended very late and I was given a ride home in an old FIAT 600. There were five of us in the car and in the back seat there was one of the guys sitting in the center between me and Valerie, who stubbornly continued to ignore me. We passed by Corso Vittorio, a place that was famous because at night the most beautiful transvestites in Naples were always there. I saw them as fabulous and so distant that I would never ever have imagined sharing their experiences and paths and above all I didn't think that the haughty and unfriendly disguise I was wearing in the car would have paved the way for me. One of those present paid a compliment, nice and not unpleasant, about the ass of one of the trans men on the Corso. God forbid! Valerie snapped with screams and hysterics: "Asshole! Sexist, reactionary, conservative." She said so many insults that I found it disproportionate as a reaction; I honestly couldn't grasp its meaning, I couldn't get a word in edgewise. She made the driver stop the car and got out, all indignant: "Enough! I'm getting out here." It was four in the morning and I didn't understand how she wanted to be left in that area at that hour. This increased my fascination with her. Geez, what courage, I thought. I found out later that she lived right there and so she was already home. The nerve of some girls! Before getting out she turned toward me, pissed off and hard, the first time she'd deigned to say one word to me: "And don't you say anything!" Despite her bitterness, I was happy because I had finally received recognition as a queer from her.

Alice in the City, Transversalism, Situationism, Fantasy

The situation was effervescent, gradually increasing in pace, power, and imagination. After Lama's expulsion from the university, a national assembly of the entire movement was called in Rome at the Faculty of Economics and Business. I went there with a mixed group partly from Lotta Continua and partly from Autonomia. I remember that a heated discussion broke out in the house where we were guests, which bordered on a brawl between the two factions, and in the end Lotta Continua left the house. From that evening I too began to move around, not exactly with Autonomia but in the area of the so-called mavericks or wild dogs. The Roman assembly was very crowded, and in addition to the plenary there were many other meetings in the various halls: faculty and factory collectives, feminists, precarious unemployed people, Indians, and creatives.

And that's where I saw Zanza again, who was nothing short of spectacular that day. There was the general staff of Autonomia Operaia, with its very male militants all arrayed in a muscular manner around the table and the microphones. The Volsci stood out, the Roman collective that took its name from the street in the San Lorenzo district, all gathered around Daniele Pifano, their undisputed leader. Zanza was dressed like a feminist and yelling out "goddamn comrades and damn god comrades." She made her way through the crowd and, having arrived under the table, turned to Pifano and began to shout: "Shut up, idiot. Instead of standing here and wasting our time, go home to wash the dishes." A thunderous laughter arose from the audience while an intransigent guy from Autonomia Operaia pushed Zanza, causing her to fall. Would that he had never done it! An angry Zanza got up shouting and cursing, giving chase to the pusher, who ran away among those present. She, who couldn't keep up with him because the "femme" was faster than she was, stopped under the stadium cheer that had infected everyone present and, taking off one of her feminist clogs, took aim and . . . got him! The guy got a kick on the back which was greeted by thunderous applause from the audience. Zanza turned toward that warm audience and with open arms thanked them: "Thank you! Dears, friends, companions, it's time to hit all the macho men. We'll cut it off with the scythe and we'll paint it over with lipstick." Then she took the microphone and, addressing Pifano, dedicated a poem to him that became famous because the next day it was reported by various newspapers. I remember the big article in *Espresso* on the 1977 movement in which Zanza's poem was reported in its entirety under the big headline "Zanza Takes Care of the Tough Guys."

Immediately after Zanza's exploit, yet another spontaneous procession of Metropolitan Indians formed who, punctuating their "Hey, hey, hey, oh," took the microphone and read the press release of the newborn people of men. I was very excited, and everything boded well. The rhythms and roundabouts of the Indians were occasionally covered by the hard-and-fast slogan, "Workers' Autonomy organization, armed struggle, revolution," to which others responded with "Workers' astronomy fourth dimension, we choose the stars for the revolution." And then it continued with "Gastronomy worker cannibalization, knife and fork, let's eat the boss." All in a holy atmosphere of celebration and revolution, as it should have been. The slogans, the graffiti, and the posters were varied and colorful, the fantasy was overwhelming, underlined by the huge writing that stood out on the main facade of the university: "Fantasy will destroy power and laughter will bury you."

Strawberries and Blood

Unfortunately, the first victim arrived with the month of March. In the university quarter of Bologna during a few confrontations that broke out between companions and provocateurs from Communion and Liberation, the cops rushed into via Mascarella, killing Francesco Lorusso, a companion of Lotta Continua, the group that paid the highest price that year. Besides Francesco, in fact, Giorgiana Masi was killed on the 12th of May and Walter Rossi was killed on the 30th of September. They were both in Rome and with Lotta Continua, even if the radicals were claiming Giorgiana's membership in their party of late.

The energy became white-hot, more than it already was. The battle ignited and increased in power, then spread like wildfire. The movement was preparing for a national demonstration announced in Rome for March 12, but Lorusso's killing the day before changed the scenario. The news coming from Bologna was anything but calm because not only the university quarter but the whole city center was interested in guerrilla warfare, at times a real battle that increased with the passing of the hours. We were all angry, confused, and at the same time excited. There was trepidation for what was happening, and the belief that something without precedence would happen. The night passed sleeplessly. We were all stuck to the various pirate radio stations that spread press releases and news from all over Italy, each in their own area. The appointment was for seven 7 P.M. at the Naples train station, where there were already thousands of people headed to Rome. Four trains left, all full of red eyes, dark faces, attentive ears, clenched fists, and "Red bandanas in the wind, one companion dies and another ten are born." Silence prevailed, however. A silence full of tension that didn't foreshadow anything good. Once we arrived in Rome we met up with our companions from all over Italy. The silence grew and grew until it became deafening. Outside Termini station a thick and persistent rain made the atmosphere even more gloomy. Everyone flowed toward Piazza Esedra and the silence was broken only by the slogan that resonated more than any other: "Today our flags are at half-mast. You will pay dearly; you will pay for everything."

Effectively, the price to pay that day was high. I continued to look around me and, seeing thousands of angry people, I asked myself how the situation would unfold. Near the fountain in Piazza Esedra was the subway's construction site that was literally dismantled, just like how the cobblestone paving was dismantled; it all ended up in backpacks and parka pockets. Unlike previous times, that day was about attacking, and no longer about defending. Via Nazionale—deserted as never seen before—opened up in front of it, with hundreds of cops barring entrance from start to finish. In front there was a barrage of companions with helmets and bandanas covering their faces, challenging them. They observed each other in silence, basically betting on who would be the conquerors that day.

Wandering around the crowd I caught a glimpse of Zanza wearing makeup and dressed like a woman with a small group of gays who were also rather eccentric. They were handing out flyers and selling *Zut A/Traverso*; I still have a copy of this creative newspaper titled "Wow." Under the title, "After Marx April, after April Mao, and after Mao . . . June!" was written. I had just met up with them; it was time to process the emotional impact and buy *Zut* that echoed the slogan throughout the piazza, but this time it was more powerful and profound. Hundreds of companions who had just arrived from Bologna were scanning the scene. They were walking across the piazza with their fists closed, staid, their eyes puffy from exhaustion, rage, tears, and tear gas. They held an enormous banner that said: "Francesco is alive and fighting with us." The crowd opened up to let them in and chanted the slogan with them.

After having walked around Piazza Esedra promising revenge, the leader of the procession went down via Cavour like a river in a flood that nothing and no one could stop. I had lost sight of the little group of gays as well as the companions with whom I had left Naples, and in the crowd I met the last person I would have liked to meet: my sister, who had also arrived on one of the many trains from Naples. This cheered me up, but at the same time worried me since, given the scenario that lay ahead, the piazza was suitable for those who were practical, and my sister was not practical at all. But the fact that there were about 100,000 people in the piazza reassured me. Soon the silence was broken by the unmistakable blast of tear gas and other shots, the nature of which became clear to me shortly after. We went down all of via Cavour pretty calmly; in all the cross streets that led towards via Nazionale there were thousands of cops in riot gear but, despite their disturbing presence, everything ran smoothly, or at least that was my impression. When we arrived at via dei Fori, all of that tranquility disappeared, giving way to restlessness. A few hundred meters away, Piazza Venezia was literally shrouded in smoke that rose high with tear gas and burning cars. At that point the procession divided into two: the calmer part passed by via Sacra—at that time still open—rejoining the rest at Teatro di Marcello; the other branch, the tougher one that I followed, passed by Piazza Venezia under the Vittoriale and the Campidoglio. The scene that presented itself in front of me was incredible. I will never forget it. On the opposite side, the one toward via del Corso, there was a double police barrier made up of buses and armored cars, behind which the policemen protected the buildings of power from the movement's attack. The clashes had begun when the head of the procession, held by our feminist companions, found itself in the middle of the attack on the headquarters of the Christian Democrats in Piazza del Gesù and of the attempt to widen the attack on via delle Bottegghe Oscure, then the seat of the PCI. The police split the procession in two, which, however, rejoined the Lungotevere, crossing the maze of alleys of the historic center. Where I was crossing the square between us and the police there were about fifty comrades of an impromptu bodyguard service, lined up to defend the passage of the procession. Someone among them flaunted a gun and then I understood the origin of those shots I had heard before. Others continued to throw Molotov cocktails, and the flames, fueled by burning cars, rose for tens of meters. Bursts of tear gas continued to arrive from the police side which, fortunately that day, did not obtain the desired effect due to the rain. I felt a rush of adrenaline, fear, and excitement mixed together.

Suddenly Zanza appeared out of the smoke with her mascara all smeared from the tears due to the unbreathable air: "But don't you realize? These idiots are serious, instead of staying at home doing the dishes!" The situation escalated and gradually got out of control because after a while there were very violent clashes throughout the center of Rome, literally under siege by anti-riot troops, while news of war continued to arrive from Bologna. I think on that day many of us thought that the revolution had broken out, at least in the forms in which we had most easily imagined it: the taking of Palazzo d'Inverno. I continued to wander among barricades, fire, tear gas, and a persistent rain of water and objects of all kinds. Once in Piazza del Popolo it seemed like we were in Stalingrad because it was really difficult to understand how to continue, where to go, what to do. After various vicissitudes and a violent police arrest we managed to reach the station and leave for Naples, just in time to avoid the violent charge launched by the police inside Termini station.

Meanwhile, final exam time was approaching, and even though I spent most of my days at the university I had hit the books very little. I began to assiduously attend courses in medicine, the department actually furthest away from my interests, but in fact the one I felt closest to because of the members of its collective: interesting, cute, tender, and colorful. In the spring I decided to go and live with them in the occupied classroom where I stayed with my sleeping bag for a few weeks. With the arrival of spring, activity in the movement increased.

On April 25 I left for Bologna, which would become my adopted hometown. The national assembly of the movement was there, the first after the events of March which in Bologna had taken on a particular character, both with regard to the level of conflict as well as the political and cultural development of the movement. In that period radio stations played an important role, and Radio Alice in Bologna represented something more. It had become a symbol, an idea, a way of being for us. I remember perfectly the live broadcast during its removal, when we heard the police enter live with the microphones still on, who, after breaking down the door, destroyed whatever was destructible. We listened as anger and excitement formed an explosive mixture. Not only in Bologna but on the walls of many other cities there were pieces of the Alice in Wonderland fable along with other slogans signed by "Alice in the City."

I left by hitchhiking, the most popular and beloved means of transportation, because it allows you to meet people and have adventures while offering the possibility of traveling for free. There were about thirty people in our group. We got organized for our departure, dividing up into groups of two. I left with Clara, a fellow sociology student. We arrived in Bologna in the late afternoon, right in the middle of a hot and crowded sports hall assembly where Franco "Bifo" Berardi—who was at the time a fugitive—spoke. I remember that he arrived surrounded by a large group in which everyone had their faces covered. I remember the assembly as serious but with bright tones, and on the stands of the sports hall that day lots of trousers, mustaches, and muscles.

After the assembly we ate in a cafe on via del Pratello, the street where a few years later I would live—not even meaning to do so—in the building right next to Radio Alice. After dinner, as usual, we all went to Piazza Maggiore, the main square; I would need a special pen and notebook in order to describe it. The square was a spectacle of sounds and colors, of cheerful comings and goings where joy and anger, fantasy and politics, the personal and political met, collided, and intertwined, giving life to a show in which everyone was protagonist and spectator at the same time. It was like being on our stage: there was no crisis of continuity between dream and reality, between reality and fantasy, because we had enough of it to excite and emulsify our lives. "Live as if in a dream and don't dream about living" was the phrase that I continued to write with a felt-tip pen on every surface I came across. Even if they were sad, the soul of Piazza Maggiore came out in Claudio Lolli's songs; his "Happy Gypsies" perfectly represented reality and sentiment. Lolli was the soundtrack of the time for all of us. Among his best songs, the one that meant the most to me was "Michel," which was about a very particular relationship between two guys: "Michel, do you remember how special the tenderness that united us was . . ."

Between Class and Gender Consciousness

The whole group that I left Naples with stayed in a house on via Mascarella, very close to where Lorusso was killed. The two-bedroom house was literally invaded by sleeping bags. It remains one of the places where I have felt much discomfort, embarrassment, and frustration. Only when I laid down in my sleeping bag did I realize that those present were equally divided up between men and women; at least that's how it seemed to me! It would have been the prerequisite for the absolute creation of couples without any gap if it were not for me. I didn't dare think what awaited me. I hadn't foreseen it in the least and when I turned to my traveling companion looking for a little complicity, solidarity, or understanding in her gaze, I saw an expression of sensual and improbable expectation in her. These were the situations that terrified me the most because I had not yet reached a condition of tranquility and security so that I could manage the situation, accepting myself as I was. My homosexuality was evident and manifest, but not yet declared. Coming out was not a common thing, so even if someone had openly revealed their orientation, without declaring themselves homosexual, others would have struggled to understand it. The problem was saying it; even in an apparently liberal situation it wasn't easy, and it wasn't easy to admit it to oneself. Today all of this might seem absurd and incomprehensible, but it wasn't then, and you would think that in a movement of that magnitude, made up of thousands of liberated people, there would have been about thirty more or less visible fags.

In hindsight, I{f} am sure and I affirm with certainty that in those two rooms, besides me, there were several{m/f} others{m/f}. Although liberation was in progress it was not yet complete; and having sex or making love remained the first step that one wanted and had to take, but with whom had not yet been clarified. We still had to name and make sense of our desires. At least in Italy, libertarian and liberating practices had been initiated, but they remained exclusive to those of the elite or avant-garde; the bulk of the people were still dealing with two thousand years of repression from which one does not escape in a single moment, much less with awareness of it. Consciousness requires courage, and at that time when it all began, the required dose was double. I imagine that when the lights went out, embarrassment assailed many of those present, because a few years later I found some of them rendered happy and finally out as fehgs. My traveling companion wanted it and I tried to pretend. I went as far as kissing but it was demeaning for me and I think a lot for her too. Subsequently, after having come out and acquired self-confidence, I would have been able to manage straight relationships more calmly, in fact eliminating fear and anxiety, making love with a woman could have happened several times but at that point without any more frustration.

As soon as the movement got back together we departed, but the logic of hitchhiking disrupted the starting lineup, so I found myself at the Bologna highway exit with Gegè, one of the tough guys. We had a sign with "Florence" on it because we had decided to make a stop in that city for a visit to the fabulous building that the Florentine movement had occupied in the center. We arrived in Florence very late and particularly tired, so after eating we decided to go to sleep, and Gegè went searching for a quiet room. No trace of our other traveling companions. Being in the very center of the city, the building was very popular, with assemblies, small groups smoking joints, others who were playing music in the middle of a considerable amount of people in sleeping bags who were sleeping or fucking. My knight found a kind of rather ramshackle space under the stairs, and as usual my atavistic naivety made the meaning of that choice incomprehensible to me, since there were much more welcoming rooms. Gegè didn't have a sleeping bag so we had to share mine and sleep squished together. It was embarrassing for me, especially because he was one of those decisive types, a very common genre of person usually flanked by a woman partner who, in retrospect, I think now served as a cover, or permission to show off. We slipped into the sleeping bag and I{f} very rigidly wished him a good night. It goes without saying that this kind of person does not usually let you sleep, and above all will never say that he is in the mood, so he will never make the first move. From the impulse that emanated from him and from his movements I sensed a certain predisposition, and when I realized that he was very excited I started to move my hand, which he immediately took with his whole arm! Even that time it wasn't exactly my passive skills that he appreciated. The thing that left me{m} perplexed and terrified was that, at the end of the relationship, these people tended to ignore me, pretending not to know me. Often in the end they asked me not to talk about it, and one of them even came to ask me expressly to pretend not to know him. Usually it made me laugh so I nodded and reassured them, an attitude that over the years has guaranteed an inexhaustible supply of self-proclaimed hets to go to bed with. But the male's vision was increasingly compromised!

Something didn't sit right with me, because in all that widespread longing for liberation among the companions there was a hetero sexuality, lived openly, including all its phantasmagoric aspects, and another, the homo or polyform one, which despite being evoked, was lived in secret. When these things happened, I believed that it had always gone on in this way, that the reality was that I was a fag and stayed that way while the macho guys, despite their homo relationships, continued to be straight. Later I thought that these guys had homo relationships by pure chance, because of a series of coincidences and fortuitous situations. Later I began to understand that there were many closeted and repressed fehgs, many more than one imagined because, despite the numbers I do not like and do not believe, based on the percentages that say that 10 percent of the population is gay, I would say that many of the self-proclaimed macho guys I slept with were not het. Even this theory doesn't really convince me now. I believe that gender identity and a possible sexuality related to it are cultural conventions that collapse every time favorable circumstances are created. Two or more bodies that meet, regardless of their sex and gender, can create a special alchemy. Similarly, an encounter between two or more people released from imposed dimensions can create dimensions and situations never imagined before. Sexuality is free and fluid; it follows desire, which is also free and fluid—besides being creative and fantastic—exactly like that fantasy that we would have wanted in power for years. For convenience, opportunism, or tranquility, every one of us chooses to live in only one dimension, and we stay in that dimension all our life even when our heart beats strong elsewhere.

Nomadic Tribes

The next day when I woke up in that Florentine basement, I heard familiar voices; it was the Naples Medicine collective who were camped in the next room. Gegè dressed quickly and disappeared, while I joined that little group that I liked so much. They were soft and sweet, and with them I felt less embarrassment and much more attachment. We hitchhiked again in a southerly direction and, since we adapted to the route of those giving us a ride, we took a detour on the highway because the driver took us to Perugia. We didn't disdain to abandon ourselves to the current because in every city (and therefore also in Perugia) there was a situation to become acquainted with, someone to meet, parts of the movement to discover, especially because its university for foreigners was famous. We stationed ourselves in the central square where we met Kristos and Jorgos, two Greeks who offered us hospitality in a cottage in the Umbrian countryside not far from the center of town. I stayed there for three days because Kristos, who was gorgeous, hosted me in his rattling bed in an old attic where, through a window without a jamb, the flowering branch of a cherry tree was bursting into spring. Seven people lived in the cottage, which could therefore be considered a commune: the two Greek students, two couples of Roman freakazoids, and a queer who worked as a restorer. I remember Kristos's long blonde hair—strange for a Greek— which intertwined with mine at night, the cherry blossom that penetrated the room, and the constellation of Gemini, which has always been present in my life.

At that time classical communes had already gone into crisis mode. The experiment of autonomous microcommunities, based on different forms of coexistence, based on agriculture or crafts, a shared space where everyone contributed according to their abilities, the place that had represented a model of life for me was disappearing, and in its place what would later become a business was taking off.

The others had already left, and after a short stay I took advantage of a ride in the car that the freaky hipster couple gave me to the capital, where they went to sell the leather bags they made. Between joints and smoking pipes aboard a Deux Chevaux Citroën, I found myself in Piazza Navona which, with Campo de' Fiori, Piazza Farnese, and Santa Maria in Trastevere, represented a destination and a stop-over for all the dreamers of the world. The four squares formed a corridor in which one moved from time to time in search of the right situation. By the right situation I mean exactly what one was looking for or needed. Drugs, sex, rock and roll, and I would add politics, colors, flavors, and that inevitable dose of fantasy. That spring was really intense, full of aromas and flavors. Everyone was in the square and you could even meet some more or less well known characters: Julian Beck and Judith Malina, Gregory Corso, Francesco (the singer of Banco del Mutuo Soccorso), a Renato Zero who was known but not yet famous, a distraught but still laughing Gabriella Ferri, Mafalda (the German sorceress), and all that entourage of the more or less famous people who were confused with the alternative universe.

One person who caught my attention was a strange queer who I later learned was called Margherita, made up and disguised in the most absurd ways. Every now and then she appeared in the square with a hallucinated look, leather accessories, often in fake leopard skin, smudged lipstick, and smeared mascara; she wandered around, fitting perfectly into the scenery of the square. I later met her during one of her bestial hangovers in which she felt like the lover of all the nerds on earth and the Holly Woodlawn of Campo de' Fiori. Visible faggolas were few; in all, three or four were noted for their flair and creativity. Among them there was one who struck me particularly for her androgyny and for her look tending toward punk, a trend that hadn't yet taken hold in Italy. When I met her a few years later at the Devo concert, I understood that Ursula—that was her name—was not queer but trans. Nuances, small differences that weren't clear to me yet, perhaps because I was too naive, because there wasn't much knowledge, or because the boundaries were unclear. I saw Ursula more and more often in all those nice situations like concerts, parties, and special clubs. But I found her by my side in a leather miniskirt, stiletto heels, and exaggerated makeup at the premiere of *The Rocky Horror Picture Show*. I don't remember if it was '79 or '80.

Ursula was one of those who didn't disdain various additives to be smoked, ingested, snorted, or shot into a vein. She too would leave us toward the end of the 1980s in a bed in the lodging house for AIDS patients where she had found refuge.

During that time someone's "character" corresponded exactly to her own way of being, a coherence that had a sense, a meaning, and a value; she was not loosened by an experience, a path, and a belonging. Characters were real and original because they didn't need to appear but simply to be. The exterior was a mirror of the interior and aesthetics were a clear sign of belonging, an intimate coherence that linked the person to what she was, did, and looked like.

When you made a choice, you were automatically on a side; aesthetics were a sign that conveyed meaning: long hair, parkas, bracelets, ripped jeans, clogs. A pair of jeans was enough to place you both beyond and against. Today this might seem irrelevant but it isn't because it's enough to compare prices and realize the difference. Everything that was bought secondhand in various markets then fixed or customized is now resold at a high price as vintage or with designer labels that everyone buys not for any particular affiliation but simply for fashion and advertising. Paradoxically, today one can find the right-wing manager or the asshole with dreadlocks, tribal armband tattoo, Che Guevara pendant, and a Celtic cross. In the creation of this jumble, fags, or rather, gays have played a decisive role as aesthetes, stylists, and fashionistas. Perhaps unknowingly they have contributed to creating fashions, trends, "things that go *in*" and "things that go *out*," top, trash, grunge, cults, and various bullshit. If for centuries faguettes, despite the denial of such, have produced culturally, artistically, and politically, giving the best of themselves, yet a few years were enough to be able to give their worst. Liberation's fault?! Has globalization, the limit of democracy or of the system that has incorporated them, made them functional and harmless? It would be enough to recover just a little memory to make things proceed differently and in a slightly more beautiful way.

In a situation like that of the Seventies in which everything was still being experimented, pioneers and adventurers paid a steep price, but the strength they brought out to be themselves automatically consecrated them to characters of great stature. Today, being a character is everyone's dream but few are because it is not understood that one cannot appear inside and outside, otherwise, as Cesarina puts it, "there is a risk of not being seen even by Bernadette."

In the many attics of the historic city center with prices that were still affordable, there were common people, comrades, freaks, artists, and all that rebellious and nonconformist fauna that represented being and not fashion, substance and not form, aspiration and the need to live outside rigidities and patterns. A thousand invisible queers were mixed into that population. Like me many others were looking for quiet and welcoming places to rejoice. And it often happened that we ended up smoking, drinking tea, listening to music at someone's house because there was so much desire to get to know each other. Many, indeed most of the young people and not only them lived alone. They tried to break away from their families. The common and widespread aspiration was to leave home to live independently. Over the years this trend has reversed, perhaps due to the high cost of housing, perhaps because peace has been restored between parents and children, perhaps because there is no longer a strong desire for autonomy and after all it's more comfortable at mom and dad's house.

Between frenzy and delirium, spring sprouted as it approached another fateful date: that of May 12th. Kossiga, then minister of the interior, after the days of March and after the killing of a policeman in April during some clashes that broke out in the San Lorenzo district, had banned any type of demonstration in Rome. The prohibition was absolute and also concerned the Radicals who wanted to celebrate the anniversary of the victory of the referendum on divorce on

May 12th. The Radical Party of that time was very different from today's. Despite its professed nonviolence, it was often in the streets with the whole movement. Its neoliberal orientation was not yet predominant, remaining in any case an ever-present party, especially when rights were violated.

The radicals decided to challenge Kossiga's ban by meeting in Piazza Navona, and with them the entire movement. That day I hitchhiked to Rome. I{m} had returned from a few days in Naples from a long wandering through the bustling and movementist Italian situations, and I found myself on the move again. From the Grande Raccordo Anulare, where they had unloaded me, I took a bus toward the city center. By the time I arrived in the area, the situation had degenerated, and reaching the square was practically impossible. Unlike those days in March, it wasn't raining, it was a beautiful sunny day, the kind in which the famous "Roman Ponentine" made you feel all the aromas of nature, flowers, and hormones.

In Largo Argentina the air was unbreathable due to the tear gas. I managed to change course toward via Arenula but shots were heard from that direction too and many people ran toward me.

I remember that day very well. I remember the uneasiness as acrid as the smoke, my nerves on edge at every bang. I remember the fear and the screams. There was no way to stop for a moment and rest as new shots immediately alarmed you. Suddenly a tear gas stick rolled up a few steps away from me, and I had the unfortunate idea of returning it to its sender, ignoring the fact that it was still hot and I burned my hand.

That day the clashes involved the entire historical center, from Trastevere to the Pantheon. Rumors were circulating (subsequently confirmed by countless photos) that many special policemen had infiltrated and been confused for comrades, with *Lotta Continua* clearly visible in one pocket and a gun under their jacket. For a change (ha ha), I also saw Zanza, in feminist garb, deliriously freaking out along with other crazed faguettes. I would have liked to join them but the situation changed so quickly and violently that immediately after seeing them they had already vanished in the smoke of that big Santa Barbara which was the center of Rome.

Meanwhile there were rumors of a comrade killed and many injured, at which point I realized that the best thing to do was to get out of there. After about three hours on the run, I managed to get to Termini station and take a train, without having bought a ticket, back to Naples, still unaware of exactly what had happened that day.

Giorgiana Masi, a twenty-year-old companion from Lotta Continua, had been killed at Ponte Garibaldi, and that evening when I heard the news, I felt profound sadness rather than anger. It was the first time that a woman, one of us, was killed in the square. Her photo with that sad expression tore my heart apart.

It could have happened to anyone, given the massive use of weapons by the police. In the general stampede that day we had all been targets and potential targets to aim for. No, it was no longer time for joking around. In that period there was no need for appeals or summons: after such an event our comrades met immediately, everywhere. Despite the absence of cell phones and email, communication spread with the important contribution of the hundreds of pirate radio stations scattered throughout the territory. Every city and every reality had their points of reference where we met in certain situations.

With the assassination of Giorgiana the level of confrontation rose further. There were very violent incidents throughout Italy, in particular in Milan and Turin. That famous photo from *Espresso* that portrayed the two opposition movements in a procession, covered by balaclavas, one of them with the P38 leveled, dates back to those days. Compared to that ostentatious violence, the sentiment and stance were not clear, there was a mixture of attraction and repulsion. Although everyone understood the absurdity of that logic, we were unable or unwilling to distance ourselves from it. And in any case the party, the springtime, the boldness, and the rioting went hand in hand.

Every evening there were impromptu parties, concerts, and ring-around-the-rosies in squares and neighborhoods. The days of March and May had left an indelible mark not only within me but throughout that generation. "After Marx April, after April Mao, and after Mao . . . June!" was the title of *Zut A/Traverso*. Assemblies, processions, parties, and sit-ins continued and multiplied but began to take on a different tone. There was an increasingly clear separation: on the one hand the hard-liners convinced that society needed to be changed, power overthrown by force, and the time to do so was ripe; on the other the creative types who questioned everything and everyone, with no other tool than that famous "fantasy" that they wanted in power.

I don't remember the exact date, but sometime between May and June there was a Radical Party demonstration in Piazza Matteotti in Naples; among the guests who took turns on stage was Alfredo Cohen, whose preface to the book *Homosexual: Oppression and Liberation* I had read. I knew little about him and was even less aware that he did theater. Accompanied by a pianist, he sang a queer song, the first I'd heard, which went something like this: "Hello gentlemen,

I'm abnormal, I'm a dirty homosexual, join in, ya' southerner, bada bing bada boom." The performance amused and intrigued me. I looked around trying to grasp the public's mood, but my impression was that most of the more than indifferent public was unaware. The homosexual question was not central, not even centered. Some pulled it toward feminism, others toward transversalism, others still diluted it in fantasy, others inserted it into the more complex class struggle. The fashionistas were still extraneous to the situation, otherwise they would have inserted it into the history of costume or fashion or perhaps they would have launched one on its own.

Continuous Crush

Despite the thousand distractions of the times I was living in, I also tried to study. The first exam I took was the one for Sociology of Art and Literature. The test was about the poetics of Living Theater and its relationship with sociopolitical movements. I was examined by G.P., a famous activist of the MI (Marxist-Leninist) groups with whom I felt calm and at ease enough to report not only on the Living Theater but also on Lukács's Marxist critique, finally perceiving the management of that "knowledge from below" of which he philosophized so much. After that exam, I also easily passed the one in Sociology 1, which was entirely focused on student movements and the very lame theories of Weber and Durkheim. Fortunately the Frankfurt School saved me. Of all those books I studied I no longer remember anything; there are other things that have remained with me.

At the assemblies, the demonstrations, and in the corridors of the occupied university, I often saw a very interesting guy who enraptured me, deeply stimulating my gay imagination, which soon invaded my dreams and my whole heart. He was my ideal type, the one with whom and for whom I would have liked to experience the revolution a thousand times over. Shoulder-length curly hair, round metal glasses of an engaged intellectual, shaggy beard, patched jeans, parka from whose pockets the inevitable *Lotta Continua* popped out, a purple scarf around his neck that remained a color full of particular meanings. Every time our paths casually crossed I noticed in him, too, a certain curiosity toward me, perhaps a vague correspondence of amorous feelings. Then one evening at Lina's house we met. His angelic air, his sweet ways eased all tensions, and therefore I fell madly in love with him.

Calabrian, enrolled at the Polytechnic, sympathizer of Lotta Continua, passionate about Claudio Lolli, boyfriend of Diana, one of the companions of Lina's group. In one of the many nights spent dreaming and planning the revolution, listening to "Gli zingari felici" (Happy gypsies), our minds first and our bodies later intertwined in that famous triangle, a possible alternative to the suffocating couple. In some moments (I would say few) the triangle was equilateral; in many others it was isosceles or rectangular. At the center of the scene there was always the guy who, however liberated and libertarian, could not shake off his armor. I remember that only when Diana fell asleep did he give himself over completely, but a wake-up signal from her was enough to make him stop. And yet all three of us had gone to bed together consciously. At that time there seemed to be a particular predisposition to get involved, to dare, to discover new horizons, to be contaminated. There was the desire and at times the need to go further, to enter deeply into experiences: we wanted to know, get to know, participate, while almost always remaining faithful to our certainties more than to ourselves.

All three of us belonged to the same circle of comrades. There were as many groups and kinds as there are soccer fans today, each one having its own political and cultural connotation, with facets and nuances such as to give everyone a certain transversality. There were neighborhood collectives, and each area had its own: factory collectives, company collectives, university collectives, and each department had one or more of them. In almost every group there was a feminist component. The women companions took center stage. The women involved in the movement were equal if not superior to the men, even if not all of them put their feminism first, not to exclude it but simply because it ran through the movement, was part of it. The compañeras, like the other groups, diversified according to their positioning not only within the movement but within feminism itself. Interpretations, practices, and different readings, but all well aware of the importance of women's liberation, of their conquests, of their struggles, of their presence within the liberating movement, above all a heated and radical criticism of misogyny was still very present and persistent among some companions, whom it was necessary to confront every day. I have witnessed many quarrels and more or less heated discussions between the two genders, deep lacerations over the criticism of the patriarchy still deeply rooted among revolutionaries, confrontations and clashes that have gradually diminished until today, where guys have returned to being the undisputed masters of the scene. In fact, they are almost always the ones to hold the floor in the few assemblies, they get pissed and they piss others off, they who talk on the radio and write in the newspapers, who use a megaphone to shout in the squares against the world and against the war, which is their war. Before the other half of the sky was much more present and participatory, and as far as I'm concerned their contribution was crucial in battles, especially in the gay ones. Today there are so-called antagonistic realities in which the presence of women is so marginal, their voice almost nonexistent, that their contribution seems to stop at a mere side role. Even sadder are those situations, unfortunately many, in which women massacre each other, which they do very well, taking the place of the guys or often defending them. I'm talking about the alternative area, certainly not the Vucciria in Palermo. Today we talk about feminism as a phenomenon and no longer about a feminist as a person. I no longer hear "she's a feminist" but rather "she refers to feminism."

Green Valleys and Blue Lagoons

In July when classes and exams were done, I left for Villavallelonga, a pleasant location in Abruzzo National Park where a gathering of the movement had been organized with music, art, and entertainment. The most beautiful sight was seeing thousands of people in an immense valley surrounded by woods, camped on the meadows and among the trees. Tents, sleeping bags, bonfires, music, naked bodies, acid, singing, war dances, love dances, night howls, stars, somersaults on the grass, guitars, Living Theater. Julian Beck and his company got everyone involved with their show, *Seven Meditations on Sadomasochism*. The actors (and other people too) tranquilly went around naked; between caresses, hugs, and kisses, we seemed to be experiencing magic, if it weren't for that group of people in the opposition movement, who no one really paid attention to, who came out of nowhere like clockwork, making their proclamation and chanting the slogan of the day. As it regularly happened, the food shop was expropriated, which in Villavallelonga was also the only one directly managed by the organizers. Thus, the guarantee of meals was lacking since the nearest shops were in the village, which was about seven kilometers away, and participants, unlike today, were almost all on foot.

In one corner of the valley was a colorful curtain, festooned with veils and draperies that read "Libertarian Homosexual Collective." In front of the tent there was a constant crowd and a continuous coming and going, mainly due to large quantities of grass and various substances sold locally. Intrigued, I approached a fat and hairy fehg with a beard and mustache, blue makeup, naked, and a purple scarf on her head, who was in front of the tent. I{m} was greeted by a tongue-in-mouth kiss that took me by surprise so suddenly that I didn't have time to understand who was giving it to me. It was the fat woman in charge of the welcoming committee who gave the same treatment as a sign of peace and love to all who approached. I don't remember where the group came from, but I think they were Roman because they referred to a university collective in the capital. If I'm not mistaken they were called Crazy Gothic Vampires.

In those days I wasn't well. I was deeply distressed and the kiss of that kind and liberated fehg sent me back into depression, with a strong case of gastritis due to nervous tension. My crises of anguish were periodic and frequent, the result of phobias, insecurity, and shyness—a negative mixture that petrified me, taking away my strength and energy. Only now am I able to interpret that malaise, associating it with the anxieties, the old troubles that were linked to the fact of not being able to live my homosexuality calmly. The awareness of a difficult path together with the awareness of my limitations clouded the horizon; I was still too young to achieve that pride that makes a difference. Or maybe the whole world around me was still too young. I lived that condition common to all crypto faggolas: fear, anxiety, and guilt—a condition unfortunately still very widespread, despite the greater possibility of revealing or unveiling oneself. I still had many doubts and uncertainties, and I had not yet really aligned myself with other faggolas. A bit of healthy self-awareness would come later. I would speak above all of conscience because the gay phenomenon was not clear to me in its dynamics, in its experience, in its sociocultural and political dimensions. The fehgs I knew up to that moment had not inspired me with particular confidence, nor the desire to open up. I think it was a reflection of homophobic culture, a reproduction of it in the form of fear. I kept seeing homosexuals as very focused on their own experience, exclusively on sex, always and in any case crabby, goofy, and ghettoized. The reason for that closure was rather the fear of mirroring me, the nonacceptance of me, the lack of a political awareness of it, the understanding of its profound value in the reality of those years, and above all the fact of not having yet met the right faggola, the one who intrigued me, or rather, someone who intrigued me and declared himself gay.

At Villavallelonga among the bushes, more beautiful than ever, I also saw Mauro, the one with long black hair who I met on the Humanities staircase in February. After showering me with kisses, he invited me to the Living seminar on political sadomasochism, which I attended with a lot of embarrassment because we were naked, touched, kissed, and in all this I was afraid of having to do it with those I didn't like or with a woman, a relationship that I still could not manage with composure.

From there, more or less en masse, we moved to Sardinia, precisely to the Valle della Luna, where, on the occasion of the impending full moon, there was to be another gathering. The Valley of the Moon was truly magical, and anything could happen on moonlit nights, even meeting a Prince

Charming named Gianfranco who catapulted me into the galaxies. I entered into psychedelic harmony with him and, leaving our clothes on earth, we entered naked into a dream. The dawn was even more magical than the night in its orange color that flooded us, illuminating the prince's black Sardinian hair with vermilion reflections. At midday I came down from the trip which began with a frightening drop in energy, the end of the trip and the perception of reality, a deep anguish for the sleeping bag that the prince had taken away, leaving me the memory of the magical night and the whole paranoia of the day, no more prince and no sleeping bag.

The Biggest Piazza Was Too Small

That sweet and restless summer concluded in Bologna, where the movement's convention had been organized for the 23rd through the 25th of September. The decision to meet in Bologna was in response to the repression against our comrades following the events in March, the tanks in the square, and the killing of Lorusso. They wanted to tackle the contradictions on the left, to clarify the relationship with the Communist Party which had set in motion its power of control against the movement in Bologna.

That time I left by myself some time before. Besides the sleeping bag I brought some spare clothes and my omnipresent tape recorder with which I used to store and preserve every sound of the movement, from the speeches in the assembly to the slogans chanted in the processions, to the noises of the riots, to the screams, including those that Mario Mieli would let out on the stage in Piazza VIII Agosto. In the book *Piazza Maggiore Was Too Small*, there is a photo that portrays me with a friend, holding the recorder during the final event in order to collect the voices of the square.

Bologna, which was invaded by thousands of comrades from all over Italy for a week, was immersed in those days in a surreal atmosphere, a kind of Woodstock spread out over the city. The tough guys of the movement were concentrated on fighting each other inside the sports hall. The *nouveaux philosophes*, including Deleuze, Foucault, and Guattari, who had signed the manifesto against the repression, were in Palazzo Re Enzo. In all the university classrooms and in every city center there were assemblies and debates. Hardened feminists, delirious Indians, threatening opposition movement members, angry faggolas in a huge and colorful festival. In every piazza there were concerts and shows, sometimes organized, often improvised.

On one of those days I participated—more excited than ever—in my first gay assembly called by collectives, microcells, and gangs of faguettes in a classroom on campus, in via Zamboni, if I'm not mistaken, in the School of Humanities. In front of the classroom there was a crowd of onlookers, probably many closeted queers (*cryptochecche*) eager to discover new horizons, the classroom overflowing with people. Screams, cries, and jabs came from inside. As soon as I{m} entered, I felt an unstoppable desire to escape, but by then it was too late. Almost immediately a brawl broke out with the various photographers who immortalized the scene. It was enough for the most agitated to seize some photographic films to restore calm, so to speak! There was no agenda, much less an order for the speakers, a political line, or a specific demand: the important thing was to be there. I remember a fehg from Naples, who was less crazy than the bystanders, who persisted in carrying on a more or less serious speech, continually interrupted by the delirium of the others, his words covered by the shouts and clamor of the situation.

One of those present read a long and extensive list of participants: OPF (Organization for Protecting Fags), PFA (Poor Fag Assistance), LSM (Liberated Socialist Mothers), CCE (Collettivo Cule Edili), Collective of Naked Ass Cheeks, Collective of Metropolitan Squaws (against the overwhelming power of the Indians), the Floppy Penis Collective, as well as schizophrenic, obese, and crazy, blow job–giving fehgs . . . concluding the long list with "and then they say that all the different ones are the same." Among the animators of the scene a few stood out: the COP (Paduan Homosexual Collective) which later became Le Pumitrozzole, the COM (Milanese Homosexual Collective), very marginally some from FUORI!, and other small, variously composed groups. Among the people I remember were Cocca from Rome, Silvia from Parma, Rocchia, Valerie, and a really nice faguette named Justine who freaked me out, a special correspondent for *Lotta Continua*. The most intrepid ones decided to set up an anti-male patrol led by a stiff and proud Valerie. In fact, the patrol aimed to find these hypothetical cute guys and then kiss and undress some of them; the signal took place through a flower that Valerie threw to the lucky one. Suddenly she stood right in front of me and began to stare at me, as she had done on other occasions. At first with curiosity and then with a haughty manner, I saw her rise up to her full height and pull up straight, as if to say, "don't bet on me wasting a flower on you." After a while, when Silvia from the COP continued to talk, I don't remember exactly what about, Rocchia, with a flashy prepunk look, performed a striptease that revived the whole scene. I had not yet heard of punk, and Rocchia's safety pin in her cheek was the first I had seen, along with her black, upturned glasses and black lipstick on her lips.

That day, in that gay gathering, we didn't accomplish anything; it all boiled down to a big show, as often happened throughout the movement, perhaps due to the incompatibility between a part that always took itself very seriously (perhaps too seriously) and another that desecrated and questioned everything and even itself. It often happened that when we were seriously discussing something and trying to make important decisions, impromptu groups or even individuals very spontaneously got up from the audience to contest by stripping naked or ranting about whatever. I also witnessed coerced stripteases where small groups of women, fehgs, and various creative types threw themselves on the politician on duty, trying to take off his pants, kissing and caressing him while the unfortunate one tried in every way to hide embarrassment and anger. Due to a sort of modesty linked to being politically correct, one could not get angry with women and creative types because of the risk of being accused of reformism or male chauvinism, but some got angry: the hard and pure opposition movement members, those for whom the revolution was a serious matter. And there we slipped into the dramatic.

The ability and the will to let go and get lost was widespread but not entirely obvious. Then as now there was a category of people for whom the world is colored and another for which it is black and white; some are able to color it and then see it, imagine it like this. For others it remains gray, immobile, static. Personal predisposition, character, chromosomes? How can you know? Though theories don't always manage to translate into practice and dreams don't translate into reality, they still help us to survive in this sea of shit. After all, reality has always been far from how we like to imagine it. Commander Marcos, in one of his letters written from the forest, having taken note of the sad reality, invited everyone to a healthy, sacrosanct delirium. And the city of Bologna observed, thought, and welcomed. Bologna: the same city that from those days would slowly become the Italian punk capital. At night under the porticos there was an endless expanse of sleeping bags, and there was no way to make room for everybody in attendance, no matter the effort. Bivouacking in Piazza Verdi I met Enrico, a twenty-year-old anarchist from Carrara with whom I spent pleasant days of politics and passion. I slept with Enrico, so to speak, at the Faculty of Arts, where we had built our own alcove between the benches of a classroom, let by the university on a free loan. When we made love I perceived a lot of tension in him; I felt that he was attracted and liked it because he was looking for it, but he couldn't relax, let himself go. One morning when we woke up, he—very embarrassed—confided in me about his homosexuality. He was sweating and stammering while he did so, and then disappeared.

The Transvestite Cries Out for Revenge in the Presence of the Phallus

The convention culminated in its final demonstration, a huge procession, thousands and thousands of people winding their way through all the streets of the city center, with the exception of Piazza Maggiore, where the bishop had decided that very day to officiate Mass outdoors. The Ministry of the Interior had set up its entire security apparatus with thousands of policemen and a few tanks surrounding the city. Even the great well-oiled machine of the Communist Party had been set in motion to control the situation. Despite the tension, everyone was calm and relaxed, singing the endless jeers directed at bourgeois and shopaholic Bologna, at the PCI, at Kossiga, and at the police.

There was a gay segment of about forty people in the procession, including many of those I had seen at the university assembly. Among the most beautiful slogans I remember: "The anal route against capital," or "It's time, it's time, make-up for the workers," or even, "We like Paolo Sesto better with a tutu." The gay segment was inside the creative one. With the feminists there was some disagreement due to the outfits that were increasingly rampant among the queers who, according to the patterns of rigid feminism, represented the revival of an ancient female model accomplice of the patriarchy. Among the gay opponents of that thesis was Mario Mieli, who in a famous passage of his *Elements of Homosexual Criticism* reports the controversy very well in the chapter on Gay Communism. Those outfits were very different from today's trans, drag, or transvestite. Rather, they were a casual and creative use of colored scarves, veils, tunics, hats, feathers, and sequins as well as lipsticks, eyeliner, eye shadows with theatrical colors, including the first punk accessories. It was a sign of revolt and a sense of liberation. They were the first forms of queer subversion that paved the way for modern drag, a phenomenon that had existed abroad for some time, while here in Italy it was something limited exclusively to the world of entertainment.

Until then, homosexuals who took part in political demonstrations had done so in a more or less serious way, highlighting some features of their experience without particular aesthetic extravaganzas. It was precisely the movement of 1977 which, by bringing out that fantasy that the generation of 1968 had only theorized, opened the breach of visibility. All forms of exaggeration and provocation found fertile ground, and the queers happily rode this favorable wave. I therefore believe on that day, many closeted fehgs were in the creative segment because it allowed them to put on makeup, cross-dress, and exaggerate without screwing up or questioning themselves.

The real surprise of those days was the ending. After the procession had roared and danced far and wide, but without invading the so-called red zone—as it would be considered today, i.e., the surroundings of Piazza Maggiore in the hands of priests and Communion and Liberation members—we flowed into piazza VIII Agosto, where Dario Fo should have concluded the gathering. I took a seat in the front row, ready with my tape recorder. When the square was full and Dario Fo had started reading various press releases, Mario Mieli took the stage. Accompanying her was Antonia, very shy as always. Mario was wearing an enormous yellow satin skirt, a black lace blouse, necklaces, bracelets and various jewelry, black eyeliner and blue eye shadow, dark, almost black lipstick, and heels. She approached the microphone, asking to speak. Dario Fo ignored her, the security service tried to dissuade her, to get her off the stage. Undaunted, she didn't move until Dario Fo, with an inelegant, mocking air, handed her the microphone and Madame began to speak: "Comrades, we are here in Bologna to demonstrate against the repression that has oppressed us for years. They gave us a route for the procession and we accepted it. Then those who were diverted here to listen to Dario Fo—whose theater work everyone knows—while the bishop is in the square saying Mass to save the city from blasphemers, that's where we have to go." Dario Fo took the microphone back and with a sarcastic laugh, he said not to listen to him, but Mieli regained the microphone while the square overwhelmed him with boos. Then she said, "What a pity, another wasted opportunity, you are used to being sheep and you will continue to bleat." And as the boos increased, she began to bleat, then she turned around, lifted her skirt, and bending over, showed her ass: what a great and fabulous, faggoty provocation, indeed *queer*! "The transvestite cries out for vengeance in front of the phallus," says Mario Mieli in his *Elements*.

Porporino

I returned to Naples for the last three months before moving permanently to Rome. Having no more home, I went to live with Lina, my closest friend, one of the few survivors whom I still see. Today she is a renowned photojournalist who has lived in New York for twenty years. The content of her work is a worthy legacy of those years, in my opinion. We met in court in Naples at the trial of Maria Pia Vianale, an irreducible militant and fascinating person belonging to the NAP (Proletarian Armed Nuclei) who symbolized the rebellion of a generation of many women through her way of acting, angry and sweet at the same time. Her proclamations from the defendants' cage remain famous when, dragged away by her irrepressibility, she kept screaming: "We don't recognize your right to put us on trial, but it will be the proletariat that will put you on trial."

Lina's house was in the university area, therefore very busy, a crossroads of people who stopped there to have coffee, to smoke a joint, to discuss politics. And so we kept meeting many new people.

It was during those last three months in Naples, precisely at Lina's house, that I met Pino Simonelli, a famous and recognized anthropologist affiliated with the chair of cultural anthropology in the Faculty of Sociology. An esteemed intellectual with Pasolinian reflexes, of whom he was a friend and acquaintance, a scholar of Neapolitan culture, popular traditions, specifically magic and its rituals. I owe him so much! He introduced me to Naples and its deep bowels, the most hidden and fascinating parts, its true culture, and its mysteries. He introduced me to the gay scene and to many more or less well known people and characters. He taught me many things that no one else could! Above all, I owe the name Porpora to Pino. In fact, he was the one who renamed me Porporino, from the title of the novel by Dominique Fernandez, a name that would later become Porporina and finally Porpora.

I met Pino in the department at his seminar on "The South and Magic," which he presented with Lombardi Satriani. Only later did he confide in me his attraction toward me, and that at the lessons he always tried to keep me after, to capture my attention, to get to know me, even though I hadn't noticed anything. He would never stop doing it until he found the thread that would lead him to Lina and then to me. I had a short but intense affair with Pino; he fascinated me with his immense culture and profound knowledge. He always took me around to business dinners, study meetings, or to the Neapolitan artistic and cultural salons. He introduced me to many characters, including Goffredo Fofi, Roberto De Simone, Leopoldo Mastelloni, and Peppe Barra. I felt the greatest emotion, which he helped to enrich with suspense, legends, and mess-ups, on attending the premiere of *La Gatta Cenerentola* (Cinderella the Cat), De Simone's great show staged at the San Ferdinando Theater. In fact it wasn't exactly the first, because the previous year, on December 8, 1976, it had been interrupted by the extremely violent clashes over self-reduction policies which broke out in front of the theater. For me that was the first time I went to the theater and it couldn't have been a better occasion. I liked it so much that after that evening I asked Pino to go back, eventually seeing the show four times. What intrigued me, besides the extraordinary beauty of the play, were the actors, several of whom I had learned were gay. Pino had revealed secrets and plots to me, which thrilled me so much. What most enchanted me was the screenplay, which in my opinion was, and still remains, profoundly revolutionary in its way of dealing with the gender issue. In fact, "Cinderella the Cat" stages the eternal dispute between the masculine and the feminine, questioning them, highlighting their nuances and hypothesizing possible alternatives. The opera ends with an extraordinary interpretation by Concetta Barra who, playing the part of the Gypsy, says: "ma io credo ca pe sta' bbuono a 'stu munno o tutte ll'uommene avarriano essere femmene o tutte e femmene, pe ffa' tutta 'na vita cuieta e aggio riito bbuono!" (I believe that in order to live well in today's world all men should be women or all women should be men, or there shouldn't be any men or women, so that we can all live a peaceful life).

A few months later I accompanied Pino on a surprising journey to research funeral lamentations and magical rituals in Lucania and Cilento, in the Basilicata and Campania regions. We made a stop at the Certosa di Padula, at the time still closed to the public, which we managed to access thanks to a special permit that Pino had obtained from the superintendent. It was thrilling to walk together along those paths that had remained untouched for centuries: the prince and the page at court, confused in a dream, enveloped in time, wandering around with the ghosts of that enchanted place.

We then went to Montemurro Lucano, an inland village where Pino had an appointment with an elderly lawyer who owned one of the most important archives of popular culture in the South. In the living room of the lawyer, whose name I don't remember, we met Francesco Rosi who was doing in-depth research for his film *Christ Stopped at Eboli*.

"I would like to live asleep / within the sweet noise of life / You are the only one in the world who knows, of my heart, / what has always been, before any other love." Pen and Pasolini, intertwined and recited by Pino, who taught me to listen, collect the poetics of things, transmitting sensations that I didn't know yet, or allowing me a first and fundamental reconstruction of meaning, gay hermeneutics!

I prepared for the anthropology exam for a long time; I did it before I even met Pino, working on a group research project on popular festivals. After touring the Benevento area for months studying the rite of flagellants at the feast of the Madonna di Guardia Sanframonti, and after studying—really well this time—an unexpected event prevented me from appearing at the roll call for the exam. In fact, that day clashes broke out at the university, if I am not mistaken, for the "suicides" in the Stammheim prison in Germany, of Andreas Baader and other components of the RAF (Rote Armee Fraktion). I had to choose: the exam or the protest. I chose the latter, and months of searching went away in glory. Pino later proposed that I take the exam with him, preparing me on De Martino's text "The South and Magic" and on everything I had learned during our trip to Lucania, therefore on the dirges of the old women of the Basilicata.

The most interesting experience I had thanks to him, whose importance and significance I didn't immediately understand, was attending a dinner to celebrate the wedding of the *femminielli* in the Quartieri Spagnoli. Pino insisted that I attend the *femminielli* parties and rituals, which, despite his stories, did not arouse any interest in me at the time. The dinner took place in an old tavern in the presence of about thirty guests, many of whom were transvestites. I use this definition because, not yet knowing the word "trans," it was the most popular one. Paradoxically, since the introduction of the term "transsexual," the slow and inexorable end of the *femminielli* and their beautiful world has begun; under the pressure of globalization and its blunders, a centuries-old tradition has crumbled. That of the Neapolitan *femminielli* was the oldest cross-dressing trans community in the Mediterranean, and when Pino told me this I did not understand the importance of his invitation, essential to the knowledge of an experience that has now disappeared.

We were among the first to arrive at the pizzeria, so I had the honor of witnessing the entire ceremony that developed upon the arrival of the guests, from the delivery of gifts to the endless treats given to the bride, decked out in a spectacular white dress. I saw the transvestites arrive dressed up for the party, laden with jewels, drenched in perfume, lighting one cigarette after another, transforming the tavern into the branch of the Zolfatara of Pozzuoli. Upon our arrival, the bride greeted us in a loud voice: "He has arrived, professor! Good evening Prufsso', it's a pleasure!" And then, turning to me: "Hey, little one, give me a kiss. Lord, how pretty this little one is! She's all woman, she's a little woman."

Among the people Pino had introduced me to was Paolino, a fellow gay member of the Political Biology collective, very nice and very affectionate with whom I formed a solid friendship. Paolino introduced me to the faggola scene in Piazza Vittoria, a historic meeting place. I have a bad memory of the first evening he took me there, because we were attacked by two plainclothes policemen. We were chatting and chirping on the steps of the monument in the center of the square. Valerie, Antonello, and Tata were there too, when suddenly two guys from the "special force" arrived who began to break our ovaries. They were particularly aggressive and started slapping one of us. Valerie came forward and, to make them stop, she brought out her acting skills by starting to be all saccharine sweet until she dissuaded them. At the time, situations like this had to be taken into account because they happened often, especially when one was visible; one couldn't even ask for help without risking ending up in the police station. Let's say that the possibility of rebelling, responding, fighting back, was not even taken into consideration; they were so strong and we were weak.

After I moved to Rome, I continued to see Pino periodically, until the mid-eighties when the disease that had tormented him for some time took him away. I keep hidden away his "The Ballad of the Shepherds," one of his research studies on Christmas and its legends, and the vinyl record of *Cinderella the Cat* with a dedication.

La Dolce Vita

I settled in Rome permanently in January 1978. My mother found me a room, I must say a very welcoming one, in Piazza Barberini. Three of us lived there together with the owner, an old Roman lady who locked herself in her room at eight in the evening and never came out until the next morning. My roommates were off-campus students. I felt no connection with one of them, while with the other, a Calabrian enrolled in Architecture, a pleasant erotic tryst was soon born: only sex, but equally engaging, especially when I realized that he wanted to have a threesome and with his best friend at that, a very nice Sardinian with whom he delighted in playing the guitar. I lived there in that house, so to speak, for the first six months. In reality, I only went back there when I wanted to see my roommate or his Sardinian friend.

I slept with him or sometimes with them and the next morning I unmade my bed so as not to make the owner suspicious.

As soon as I moved to Rome, Paolino put me in contact with Cocca, the faguette I had met at the gay assembly in Bologna. She was the first Roman fehg I met and was the conduit for all my future acquaintances. Paolino had arranged an appointment for us at the Pantheon where Cocca showed up with great pomp and therefore with perfect visibility: a fiery red velvet jacket, tight black trousers, eyeliner, shiny hair, and a long cigarette holder from which she languidly sucked her cigarette. The meeting was exciting because it was out of the ordinary. The gay scene in which we would later quietly move was still under construction, oscillating between the desire for transgression, the need for visibility, and the fascination of the forbidden, but it was also made up of discretion and caution.

Up to that moment my freaky and comradely belonging had pushed me to other contexts, and I was still not able to combine the two experiences. In the first days of Roman life, while I was eating at the university cafeteria in via De Lollis, I met Carol, a very bizarre and very stoned girl from Terni, who ran away from home and went to Rome in search of herself. Red bobbed hair, freckles, with an evident Venus squint that was accentuated during her frequent and lively hangovers. She was talkative, with the habit of repeating everything aloud, absolutely everything that passed through her noggin, including those things that are not said for politeness' sake. As soon as she saw me she began to woo me with her ways that were so funny that they had the effect of making you die from laughter rather than making you fall in love. Sometime later, when we became inseparable friends, I realized that she regularly lost her head to subjects who sooner or later came out as fehgs. In fact, when she spotted them she would start courting them until she was exhausted and then they ended up in bed with me.

The name Carol came from the Rolling Stones song, but she was soon nicknamed "the Countess" because of her high bourgeois, ladylike manner which concealed her proletarian origin. She lived in a small house in via dei Volsci, where every night there were many who slept over, all those we were able to invite: those who had missed the last bus, the vagabonds in search of hospitality, the adventurers, and all nocturnal creatures. The small house was one floor above the Marani bar, the historic meeting point for companions, located in front of the Radio Onda Rossa headquarters.

Although there was no bathroom, she was always impeccably made up and elegant. She didn't even seem to belong to that environment; she was the only one who wore makeup—well, let's say she tried—and smoked Marlboros or Camels, even though we lived off of begging. She looked in the mirror constantly, and it took hours for her to get ready in the midst of a bunch of freaks, filthy, ragged, and penniless. She had water poured for the bidet by one of them, her hair dried by another, someone asked to make her coffee, someone else rolled her a joint in a ritual that was spread over the whole afternoon or night according to when she got up. After making us wait for hours, she lit her cigarette regularly on the long holder, looked at us, and with a princely way, declared: "I'm going down to get a martini at Marani" and then we all made fun of her. But she, the fatal noblewoman, would go down to Marani, order a martini, two martinis, three martinis, and on the fourth the lady began to give way to the drunken mess who made everyone die of laughter.

Carol always had to have someone to be madly in love with, despite her crushes destroying her and all of us around her. We watched out for her for entire nights under the windows of Campo de' Fiori, Trastevere, Monteverde, and San Lorenzo.

Although she had never met him, she also fell in love with Walter, the companion who owned the apartment, who fled—like everyone in that period—who knows where in order to find himself.

Her retired mother periodically sent her some money for the rent which she spent on herself in a single evening, perhaps inviting the whole cheerful brigade to dinner in some tavern in San Lorenzo. The neighborhood still maintained its homey characteristic and was full of low-cost taverns, those places that offered so-called half portions which were usually whole but still half the price. Or those places that have since disappeared that were called "wines and oils" or "fiaschetterie" where you drank by the minute and ate standing up for a first or second course. Some people had credit, with others we had a standing bill, which at times was discounted by helping out in the kitchen. From the taverns of San Lorenzo we usually left drunk and always in company. It was easy to get together around Marino with a flask and old comrades, people from the area, forced laborers, loser artists, and lost fools. The most popular taverns were the Calabrese, the Bottiglieria del mercato, the Morto in via dei Campani, the Bionda in via dei Sabelli, which we had nicknamed the "De Laurentis" for the spectacular hairstyle of the owner who seemed to come from the set of *Quo Vadis*.

Together with Carol it wasn't difficult to widen friendships or deepen relationships, soon creating a deranged group, which included—in addition to the two of us—some Sardinian comrades and the famous "Calabrian clan," a large group of comrades from Catanzaro, themselves all from collectives and associations. The Sardinians had a house in via dei Campani where I would later go to live. A circuit was created between the two apartments, the bar, the university cafeteria, and the gardens of San Lorenzo. Our group had *new entries* and escapees, but over time a central nucleus stabilized around which a large number of subjects revolved. In fact, the group was considered those who lived more or less permanently in the two apartments: Paolo, Nocciolina, Carol, Lilli, Elia, and Lud.

Paolo was a medical student from Gallura, a perfect double of Antonio Gramsci who psychically manifested all the diseases he studied in anatomy books; his unmanly attitudes led most people to consider him homosexual. We sometimes called him "Stroke" because when he began to relax he began to theorize masturbation to be practiced alone or with other people, as a way to liberation. It often happened, in fact, that even in the presence of unknown guests, intent on chatting or rambling, he, as if he were doing the most normal thing in the world, took out his dick, stroking it and inviting those present to join him in a circle jerk. This was amusing, at times surprising, or embarrassing. Often he did it when there was someone he didn't like or someone who was clueless or particularly rigid.

Paolo had long had a relationship with Nocciolina, who was beautiful, brunette, and dark as only Sardinians know how to be. Taciturn and introverted, she spent entire days without saying a word because she said everything with her coal-black eyes. Her long, wide embroidered skirts, lace, and embroidered blouses recalled Sardinian costumes. Nocciolina went out in the morning around town begging for money, then went to the market in Piazza Vittorio to retrieve fruit and vegetables that the shopkeepers gave away at the end of the morning. When she returned, she socialized her income with all of us.

Lilli—who also went by "Gorilla" because of her deliberately unfeminine and simian movements—was from Calabria, a former activist of Lotta Continua, lover of Walter (the companion in crisis whose house had been occupied by Carol), and loved to flaunt her nudity during the many *happenings* of the movement, whether they took place in the countryside, by the sea, or in a normal public square. I remember several newspaper articles with photos that portrayed her naked, calm, and blissful in the crowd. She was a restless dreamer without political or cultural belongings or possessions, tending to wander in order not to stop and think too much.

Lud

Lud appeared like a bat on a cold and lysergic January night, truly beautiful with his gaze that captivated and bewitched like a Gorgon and a charm that tormented the heart; bat by night, swallow flying around the world by day. Carol clearly fell in love with him; she began to rave deliriously until she was able to drag him into her alcove in via dei Volsci. In that apartment there was only one huge double bed where we all slept passionately together, and that night Carol, after having trapped him, retired to the bathroom to make herself beautiful and spruce herself up while Lud and I began to play with each other. He kidnapped me and in ecstasy I fell in love with him, even though ours was more than just that, a relationship of deep friendship, complicity, and delirium. After about two hours, the time she needed to spruce herself up, Carol came out of the bathroom, and finding us enthralled and happy she made the usual hysterical scene by throwing shoes, books, and whatever was within range, cursing that everyone who she picked up then figured out he was gay.

But it was she herself who immediately laughed at it, also because that evening in the big bed there was another guest from the "Calabrian clan": straight, naked, and eager. Of that night I also remember the screams of the Countess when the embers of the only cigarette that the four of us shared after making love ended up under her ass.

Lud and I had given the group a nice gay blow, both of us{*}, strong{*}, together{*} began to bring out all the super gayness that was compressed and had accumulated in twenty years of waiting. Like volcanoes that, after having slept for a long time, woke up spitting out lava, fire, and lapillus. Lud, like a true Sagittarius—an adventurer who goes fast without looking back—would suddenly disappear only to reappear after a week or a fortnight; he started by letting himself be carried away by the current and ended up three thousand miles away. He traveled, galloped, and the earth burned under his feet. The other Sagittarius of the group was Nocciolina who, like Lud, would disappear and we'd lose track of her for weeks. We didn't worry much about their absences as we knew they would be back. Travel was not an empty word, but a concept and a way of life. It wasn't just a psychedelic experience but a continued departure and an absence of landing. We were deeply convinced that nomadism was the way, a key to access knowledge and other dimensions. Traveling was and remains a detachment from private property, from everything that belongs to us and to which we belong; it is decontextualization, discovery, experimentation. Traveling was a present and constant element, it was, in a word, *movement*.

Given the very high mobility that we all had and the possibility of losing sight of each other, with Lud we decided to make a concrete date in order to socialize with all the people we liked: July 15 in front of the Moulin Rouge in Paris. Not the Latin Quarter, Montmartre, or Montparnasse, but the Moulin Rouge, which was a symbol of sex and perdition in our imaginations.

In a group meeting, we had decided that our two houses would remain open to everyone and therefore continue to be places for meeting and socializing. The fridge was always empty and the beds always full. I often socialized my bed, making parts of me, my body, and my imagination available. The location of the houses in the heart of an original, popular, and truly alternative San Lorenzo neighborhood made them fit into a map, a reference circuit extended to comrades, vagabonds, and alternative folx. People didn't have cars like they do now and it often happened that returning home at night was difficult or unsafe, so we ended up sleeping wherever it happened and it often happened at our house. After midnight and until dawn the doorbell rang so much that the lady in the bar downstairs had nicknamed us "the guys from the registry office." Among the night owls, in addition to wanderers and vagrants of various kinds, there were those who were late to the assemblies of the via dei Volsci collectives, or to the Radio Onda Rossa broadcasts. The "hardasses," as the diehards of Autonomy were defined, who loosened their brakes at night and became decidedly sweeter, were very different in bed from how they were known outside of it. It was there that they expressed the best, the sweet, and the "creative" side of revolution, what others did not know and did not even remotely imagine.

Particular encounters didn't always take place at my house. There it would have been too disgraceful given the traffic and promiscuity of the place, so more discreet places or houses were preferred. It was for this reason that one morning, while I was having breakfast at the Marani right in front of the Radio, one of the leaders and a member of the Supreme Soviets, after having looked around carefully and made sure that there were no prying eyes, called me over, inviting me to eat strawberries and smoke a joint together at his house. Handsome and dark, charming, super macho and also super busy, super serious, and super gifted, or as Zanza used to say, "underdeveloped, that is, developed 'down under.'" In her heart Carol had elevated him to the status of idol, falling madly in love with him to the point that more than once with the most incredible excuses she dragged me to his house, creating absurd and embarrassing situations in which she fearlessly advanced while he remained rigid as a statue of marble, according to her because he was still too much in love with his ex. When he proposed that we go and eat strawberries, I was quite surprised. I didn't expect it. The invitation intrigued me and particularly moved me. Too macho to be true, but I{m} was still too naive to grasp the homosexuality of the subject. All of the opposition movement's male ardor in a bowl of strawberries instead of cream: rather than strawberries and blood, "strawberries and a hand job!" The meetings with him continued over time, always and in any case in great secrecy, despite my having immediately leaked everything to the others in the group, causing Carol to become more and more convinced that all her longed-for principles were not so much blue, but rather pink. He never asked me not to say hi to him in public or not talk about him, but when he saw me in the presence of others he was indifferent and we were like two strangers. I{f} felt like a partner in crime and, all in all, proud of having an unsuspected lover among the extreme fringes.

Our house was always enriched with new inhabitants. Among the more permanent ones I also remember Eusebio, a stoner from the "Calabrian clan" who added a touch of a Tangiers smoking den to the house. All kinds of drugs were enjoyed and shared. Eusebio was the scion of a rich family who supported him in his studies. Everything his parents gave him was invested in drugs to the point that he almost seemed to live on smoke because he was never seen eating. We didn't have any provisions at home; they did not last long, and we all had lunch in the university cafeteria, which at the time cost 300 lire without any need to show your student ID. From time to time Eusebio too, having run out of money and special effects, went down among the people and, like all of us, came to beg for money in order to eat at the cafeteria. It was during the endless queues in the cafeteria that friendships and new stories were born. It was in the ranks of the cafeteria that Lud and I each time chose the prey of the day. We aimed at it and with a brazenly gleeful way we took to courting it. In the square in front of the cafeteria there was an anthill of people who, after eating, chatted and talked, almost always about politics, only to end up having coffee at someone's house, getting a joint from someone else, having tea at Laura's or Nicola's, to take a nap with Isa, Roberto, and Stanislao in that incessant movement in which feelings, passions, discussions, games, and a lot of poetry were born.

There were also different locations inside our group. Me, Lilli, and Paolo were more politically committed. Carol, Lud, and Nocciolina were more creative, or if you like, more bohemian. There were always two hundred liras to buy *Lotta Continua*, so there was always a copy of the newspaper in the house. The radio was synchronized with the modulations of Radio Onda Rossa and Città Futura, and the news came in a continuous and uninterrupted flow. We were always well informed about events, including those that had taken place five minutes earlier. It never happened that there was a police raid, a fascist attack, an occupation, a sudden strike—fairly frequent events—when we didn't know in time to organize a response.

With the Faguettes or with the Chavs

We all became part of CASL (San Lorenzo Opposition Committee), a collective born within the historic one in via dei Volsci. Within this collective there was a consistent female component and, moreover, in that period the presence of women was crucial in all contexts and in all areas. I remember the Polyclinic Collective, one of the strongest in Rome, with a clear female predominance. Inside CASL, but in general in the whole via dei Volsci environment, we were seen as not very reliable since the real *Kompagni* measured their coherence by the length of their mustaches, muscles, seriousness, and the ability to integrate with the proletariat who lived in San Lorenzo. Later it would be that same proletariat who would neutralize the reality of the opposition movement, a proletariat who would later become the petty bourgeoisie of the neighborhood, enriched by illegal means, with house prices that today cost millions of euros in San Lorenzo.

The young proletarians of the neighborhood, better known as "hicks" or "chavs" (*coatti*), had different groups with respective meeting points: in piazza dei Campani, in piazzale Tiburtino, and in via degli Equi at the corner with via dei Volsci. The latter got confused with their companions because they shared the same cross street. Between the two realities there was a *pax* useful for both to continue their more or less licit practices. The comrades nurtured a feeling of solidarity and false understanding toward them because they were proletarians. They never started a criticism or a reflection: they were part of the neighborhood, they were a characteristic of it, so they had to be accepted as they were. Later they would have gained the upper hand, and their tackiness from a defect would have become an asset, to the point of being taken as a model by the so-called alternatives types. A clear example is all that chauvinist and aggressive energy of the various rappers or hip-hop artists who are depopulating the more or less alternative scene. Their distinctive feature is precisely that machismo which, pushed to excess in some contexts such as the Rasta one, has even come to preach violence against gays.

The offices in via dei Volsci, together with the two cafes in front of them, were very popular. The whole movement met there with its important political collectives. I had met an old classmate from the Polyclinic Collective, batshit crazy, who lived not far from my house. Her gay nephew Danilo lived with her, and I hosted him whenever there was the stench of a raid in the air and a consequent search of her house, all things of normal administration. Danilo was a reserved, introverted half artist, half intellectual who never fully integrated into our little group. Once I got a genital infection and, not knowing who to turn to, Danilo accompanied me to FUORI! where people knew that there was some kind of venereal disease doctor who could see me. FUORI! was in via di Torre Argentina, at the Radical Party. We were welcomed by a very nice faguette who directed us to the home of Doriano Galli, a queer impromptu doctor who ran a sort of gay counseling center out of his house which was meant for queers with venereal disease problems. The faguette who had welcomed us at FUORI! took the opportunity to invite us to the group that usually met at Laura Di Nola's house in the Jewish ghetto where, she told us{f}, an interesting experiment in homosexual self-awareness had begun. When I arrived at the improvised consulting room, Doriano invited me to undress, while his little dog named Frocetto (Little Fag) continued to bark at me{m}. Embarrassed, I took off my pants. "Frocetto! Leave the ladies alone," she commanded the dog as she scrutinized my "vaginal redness." He prescribed me an antibiotic ointment and recommended that I be passive for a while and therefore not penetrate anyone in order to make the infection go away. I wasn't really prepared for that direct and blunt talk. Between Frocetto barking, the doctor{f} groping, and Giovannona Coscia Larga, an elderly fat fehg who acted as her assistant by austerely observing my privates, I was sweating like a pig. However, I felt that all the tension that would usually have assailed me was noticeably easing, surely because I was beginning to familiarize myself with the queer environment.

Being Overwhelmed

During the CASL period, one evening when I{m} returned home I found a fellow member of the collective in my room who had missed the bus. He rolled a joint, we smoked together, and I noticed him trying to flirt with me. I absolutely was not attracted to him and to avoid an embarrassing situation I{f} slipped, very stoned, into bed. After a while he came onto my bed and started to stroke himself. I pretended to sleep, and he kept going while I went into total paranoia; I was attacked by a numbness that prevented me from reacting in any way. Perhaps due to the effect of the smoke, the embarrassment, or my physical weakness, because I was exactly half his size, when he threw himself on me I didn't have the strength to resist him. He pulled the covers down, his hands holding my arms, insistently trying to stick his tongue in my mouth as he continued to rub against me. I had turned to ice, I was feeling terrible, I wanted to get him off me but I couldn't until he reached orgasm. After that he lay down on the other mattress and collapsed from exhaustion.

That night I didn't sleep a wink due to the malaise that gripped me. The next day I talked about it with my companions, who got furiously pissed off because it seems that the guy had tried to do the same thing with some of them too. My companions were enraged and for this they urgently called a meeting with the collective. The top leaders also intervened, trying to restore peace, but in what they said, in their attitudes, in their chatter, I found something deeply offensive and politically incorrect. They were all ironic and the gist of the speech was: "Oh come on! Of course Porporino didn't like it, and then he spends the whole day together with that other queer Zanza hanging around San Lorenzo and then complains if some guy jumps on him."

Subsequently my bold partner, to make up for it, for weeks dedicated songs by Lou Reed, the Velvet Underground, and David Bowie to me from the pirate radio stations, which absolutely did not make me reconsider what had happened.

Despite the feared openness, the irrepressible need to do something, to have everything immediately, there were still strong prejudices about everything that were directly or indirectly linked, according to some, to bourgeois power. This is the reason why all foreign rock musicians were considered assholes and servants of the system. Lou Reed, who had sung "Berlin" in a military hat that might have resembled an SS hat, was considered a Nazi; the Velvet Underground singing "Heroin" were bastards. In all of this, only the great martyrs were spared, namely Jimi Hendrix, Janis Joplin, and Jim Morrison, but only because they were dead.

There was a sort of proscription list whereby all artists in the New York entourage were considered degenerate or children of Babylon by the same logic that would later take root among Jamaican Rastas. Many liberation movements began to travel united, on the same path—the Black Panthers were linked to the Gay Liberation Front, for example—but today instead there is an abyss between Angela Davis and those Black rappers who sit at the top of the charts who, with one hand on their cock and the other inciting revolt, feel they are the heirs of that tradition.

I also remember the palpable distrust of young punks. All this belonged to the old logic of morality within the movement, that of order within anarchy, that patriarchal power thanks to which everything we threw out the door came back through the window. If we want to be honest, although the companions' environment was the most livable for us, much remained to be done to eliminate or reduce the macho legacy that everyone carried within. It was a challenge that was never met, the stuff of sissies or hysterical feminists, and the results are now there for all to see. It was much easier to be on the chavs' side than with the queers and feminists, much less demanding, less tiring, perhaps more convenient because there was nothing to question; on the contrary, it was a confirmation of one's male status.

Flora and Fauna

Remembering all the flora and fauna, which were not two transvestites but the colorful and eccentric characters who passed by our house, is almost impossible. Among the many I remember Nicolò, a doppelganger of Joe Dallesandro, a very nice freak who lived by begging and one day was arrested during a proletarian expropriation at the Ricordi shop in via del Tritone. We saw his photo in the newspapers under the big headline, "Arrested [. . .] the son of the President of the [. . .] proletarian expropriation." He disappeared; I saw him a few years later on the bus with a basket full of figs and eggs that he was coming to sell in the city. He told me that he had become a farmer; whims of the righteous bourgeoisie!

But there was also Alessandro, an artist who had just returned from a long trip to India who stopped at home, smiling, his gaze fixed on Bangala. He remained in the same position, playing the same two notes on the sitar he had bought in Benares for nearly two weeks without interruption—a situation that risked sending us to Bengal too. It ended with the intervention of his parents: an idiot father and a talkative, high bourgeois mother who swooped into the house wearing lots of makeup, jeweled like a Madonna full of perfume. She talked nonstop, appreciating our taste and our look, but condemning our lifestyle. Alessandro was taken away and admitted to a nursing home.

Then an absurd guy showed up; I'd already seen him around in Naples among our companions. He always wore the same Saharan shirt and the same safari hat, attended all the alternative initiatives, approached the female companions in a mellifluous manner and tried to kiss them, shamelessly hitting on all of them in a heavy way, a habit for which he often obtained loud slaps. When I found that Lilli had brought him home, I didn't hesitate to kick him out the door; it was the only time I didn't accept someone into the house. We accompanied him to the student house, where we had a sort of pied-à-terre, a room that Paolo had been assigned for merit and where we all used to relax, study, or get some privacy. Among the guests it was almost normal that someone would also happen to be illegal, such as Drago, an old comrade who still hasn't given up today, who remained with us for the entire period of his inactivity. He had been written up for violence and assault, for having only verbally confronted a girl from the PCI. The so-called aggression had been carried out mostly by the companions of the Psychology collective, also assiduous frequenters of the house, but Drago was the only one to pay the consequences, also because he was very well known in our circles. His inaction was almost normal because the level of rebellion and insubordination was so high and widespread that violations of the law were frequent; indeed, the famous mass illegality was an extensive and obsequious practice. Drago didn't work; he was studying sociology, I think, but he didn't give a damn and stayed at home all day. In the evening, however, he needed to go out and he did it in the most absurd way, which is why we called him the "Pink Panther." He had had raven-black curly hair; he had bleached it—or rather, burned it. He wore a pair of dark glasses, a long black leather coat, and cautiously opened the door, looked around, and then walked away. After a few minutes we heard him scream in falsetto, then: "Porporino uuuh, Porporino ooooh." They were the chavs who, seeing him done up like this, mistook him for a transvestite queer, calling him by my name because they were convinced that "Porporino" meant "gay." I understood the association of my name with being gay only after the fact, when the fehggy comings and goings of the Narciso faggolas began the catwalk that painted the San Lorenzo district pink. Whenever the faguettes passed by, highlighting all their gayness, they heard shouts in falsetto: "Purpura uuuh."

That was also the time when psychedelic experimentation reached its peak. Those orange LSD tabs were around (the famous Orange) but they no longer had anything to do with the first magic mushroom that I had bought in Parco Lambro four years earlier. Acid too, like all drugs, had evolved from a use linked to research or the deepening of states of consciousness to a more political and less mystical use, linked to the need to experiment with practices and techniques of estrangement from the system. A few more years and it would become a pure and simple additive at the disco, to be taken without special instructions for use. The instructions for use were mainly cultural, spiritual, and, if you like, political. I have never abused LSD, not out of fear but because I was convinced that behind its use there must be a logic, a path, a search. One of the most popular books at that time was Carlos Castaneda's *The Teachings of Don Juan*, the text of psychedelic travelers, of dreamers in search of the so-called separate reality which guarantees an alternative to what was slowly returning to be the usual reality of the same old shit. In addition to *The Teachings of Don Juan*, in our home libraries there was no shortage of *One Hundred Years of Solitude* by Gabriel Garcia Marquez, *The Master and Margarita* by Bulgakov, *The Art of Loving* by Erich Fromm, *Bury My Heart at Wounded Knee*, texts by Marcuse, Nietzsche, Cooper, Marx's manifesto.

The use of various substances, the research associated with them, and the perceived stages of consciousness were part of a logic consistent with our experience. I remember the nights spent feeling each other, perceiving each other, and penetrating each other in amazing journeys of the mind and heart. You entered into deep harmony; you recovered parts of yourself. With some people you got close, with others you got incurably further away. Acid makes you hypersensitive and activates deep communication channels, so that relationships are decidedly transformed. It must be said that the Campani group was also forged and welded through the psychedelic experience. Some left because they weren't able to tune in, others we lost in the sidereal spaces, some in Kathmandu, and others in Machu Picchu.

I remember Alberto, a companion of the "Calabrian clan" who was always with us: cute, charming, but too masculine and rigid to be able to share a process of liberation with us.

I had slept together with him, in the same single bed, but nothing had happened; he was one of those types who made you dream but who would never be there and he made you understand it. Although he was alternative, he was a Latin lover with pussy printed on his cerebral cortex, a man who had to find a girl to court in any situation: when there was no woman available, he disappeared. These were sensations that were intuited but not explainable because they lacked a tangible confirmation. These were deep vibrations that were created during the *trip* that very naturally separated the cream from the milk, so there was no need to say it because these kinds of people would walk away on their own.

I also remember Paolo, who was particularly entangled with acid to the point of making it his reason for living, a great pleasure, a profound research, so much so that he philosophized about it. During a particularly strong journey he could no longer come out of it. Usually in the waning phase, at a certain time we would go out to taste the dawn, its colors, its flavors, its avian melodies. That morning Paolo claimed to have lost his sight. We headed to Tiber Island, which together with the Orange Garden was our favorite place. We positioned ourselves at the farthest point, under Ponte Garibaldi that splits the Tiber in two, and we abandoned ourselves to coming down. Nocciolina, laughing, strolled on the ledge of the bridge as if to lick the water, Lud touched the strings of his guitar, Lilli drew or dreamed, Carol adjusted her makeup and hair, I dreamed of Lud, whom I liked so much but I could never have completely because in his eyes he had not only me but the whole universe. That time, Paolo's *trip* lasted almost two days, a reason that convinced us all that he would never come out of it.

I had a privileged relationship with Carol, with her madness, but at the same time I was becoming closer and closer to Nocciolina, whom I also called Streghetta (Little Witch). During one *trip* I began to perceive a particular sensation toward her, of charm and transport; I felt something that went beyond simple affection: a real physical attraction. She was very charming, with her Sardinian hair, introverted, silent, almost magical. While doing acid she watched, scrutinized, and her eyes glittered in the candlelight. She made fun of Francesco and his philosophizing, and she would suddenly burst into laughter while we debated the universe and the meaning of life. She had the pride and importance of her people stamped on her face. She often indulged in Sardinian dances that she tried to teach us too. She and Paolo were nicknamed "their own people," I think from the name of a political group. Both of them, like many Sardinians, were of modest origins, of few words, honest, transparent, and faithful.

Good Morning, Night

The morning of March 16, 1978, before returning to San Lorenzo, I went toward the Pantheon to buy one of those glittering purple veil scarves that I adored so much; I had left the house in Piazza Barberini, where I had slept in the company of the Calabrian the previous night. While crossing via del Corso I was shocked to see dozens of armored police vehicles with flashing blue lights that were moving as a whole, while the fast and frenetic passing of many racing cars sped through the center with blaring sirens. There was something strange in the air because I experienced that classic feeling of tension and nervousness that heralds tragedies: it was clear that something big had happened. Having bought the scarf, I headed home in a sea of chaos and tension that infected everyone. I took the first bus available where, among curious and perplexed people, a lady announced that Aldo Moro had been kidnapped. There was still no clear news but the palpable tension seemed to confirm that statement. I realized the gravity of what had happened and instinctively I immediately went to the university, which I found, however, to be deserted; then I went to the bar in via dei Volsci, but the few companions present told me to leave because the situation was so serious that from moment to moment it became more and more unpredictable. Some feared police intervention in San Lorenzo and the university, a closing off of the area, or a coup d'état. The first move had been made and the game had become much more serious. The slogan that hitherto stood out on walls and leaflets—"Bring the attack to the heart of the state"—suddenly became a reality, leaving us all aghast.

Feelings of fear mixed with bewilderment assailed all of us who clearly understood that from that moment on nothing would be as it was before. I started to understand as the days passed: Rome was garrisoned; I felt trapped, watched, under siege. Much more than a sensation, it was reality. One evening while returning home with Carol, Lilli, and Nocciolina, we were stopped by the police. It was a very bad experience because it felt like being in Chile: they put the barrel of the gun in my mouth, telling us that it was over for us, but they didn't just refer to the four of us, it was over for *us* in a broad sense, an enlarged *us*, an *us* who were pieces-of-shit communists, an *us* who were fags and feminists, *we* who were good-for-nothing longhairs.

In the same period in Florence, as happened to many in those days, a very dear friend of mine was unjustly arrested for terrorism. He was accused of setting fire to two police cars, an attack that he had absolutely nothing to do with. I was named a witness because he had been my guest until the night before, when the facts of which he was accused had occurred.

In that period an unprecedented repression was triggered, made up of checks, stops, and searches that, like clockwork, I received in my room in the pension in Piazza Barberini. That was the reason why the owner evicted me and why I permanently moved to via dei Campani 50, my historic home from May 1978 to December 1984. I must say that a certain fear assailed me because my imagination began to show me chains, handcuffs, bars, and the like.

When I was summoned to testify at the trial, I stayed in Florence for a week as a guest of a feminist companion at the Careggi student residence. I met her at the trial, which had received a lot of attention and participation from her comrades due to her strong political acumen and the fact that Red Cross lawyers were working for the defendants. Among these companions was Albertino, who immediately became my fawn during my stay in Florence. Blonde with emerald eyes and two lips as red as cherries, he shone like the sun among all those pissed-off opposition movement guys who crowded the courthouse. He stared at me intently, never taking his eyes off me. He smiled sweetly, and I couldn't understand what enchanted him about me, whether my testimony at the trial, my being gay, or who knows what. Throughout my week in Florence, he followed me step by step, to the point that my hostess—understanding the situation—left us the room. He only stopped staring at me when he slept; otherwise he kept looking at me, amused and amazed as if he had seen a Martian. The day of the trial I arrived late with a sleepless night behind me; emotion and fear made me mess up so much that I contradicted myself to the point that the judge said I gave false testimony. I{f} left for Rome, madly in love with Albertino, but never heard from him again. I tried to look for him. I asked the companion who hosted us. I asked the other companions, but no one had seen him since. Disappeared, dissolved into nothingness.

After May 1st I returned to Rome with Paolo, Carol, and other vagabonds we'd met in Assisi, while Lud, Nocciolina, and Lilli continued to wander. From time to time they reappeared in no particular order and then left again. Postcards and greetings arrived, and sometimes news from the sea, and other times from the mountains; sometimes from the South, sometimes from the North. Despite this euphoria and spring vivacity I felt the weight of my obligations and responsibilities because I also had to study and take exams. But as soon as I got back to the books my mind flew to Lud, with whom I{m} was intimately in love. When he was there I felt less alone, I felt his complicity, after all we{f} were two lost and despised faggolas in an environment that, however liberated, was not yet sufficiently gay.

I began to privilege my relationship with Paolo because we were the only students in our group; therefore we had the same commitments and roughly the same responsibilities. He was studying medicine, was very good at his studies, and, despite being constantly surrounded by a huge mess, he managed to keep up with his exams, maintaining a very high grade point average. He was a hypochondriac and for this I was amused to see him hit the books. Because he was afraid of dying, he felt like he had all the diseases he was studying. He constantly felt his pulse, put his hand on his forehead, touched his glands, and asked everyone present to look at his eyes, skin, ass. He was cringingly depressed, and only Nocciolina understood, but teased him with her cynical jokes.

In mid-May the body of Aldo Moro was found. After two months of anxiety, between the tension and the negotiations, the famous "attack on the heart of the state" had materialized, the hard line had prevailed, everything became heavier and more complicated, and that inexorable low point full of anguish began.

The First of May

In May we all left for Assisi, where the May Day festival was taking place, an ancient ritual of a tradition dating back to the Middle Ages to celebrate the arrival of spring. The festivities would last for three days, during which the whole city sank as if by magic into the Middle Ages: people in period costume, cars banned, public lighting replaced by torches and bonfires, flute and mandola music on every corner of the streets, pages and minstrels who kidnapped our imagination. The taverns were the highlight of the evenings, two ancient cellars in the old city center, one for "the most noble part above" and the other for "the most excellent part below," which were the two opposing factions into which the city had been divided since the Middle Ages. Rivers of wine flowed in the cellars and an air of total anarchy breathed among the old tables. Inside, all the brakes and all the taboos fell away: it must have been the wine, the fire on which the porchetta roasted; it must have been the party, perhaps even the historical period, but it turned into veritable bacchanalia, a large brothel without anyone setting limits. And reality began to merge with fantasy or with the Middle Ages.

I already knew about that festival because I have family roots from Assisi; I had participated several times with my parents, but only experiencing it from the outside. We hitch-hiked a little at a time, forming a kind of caravan with all the people we met along the way. A journey that was thwarted by the infinite checkpoints due to the kidnapping of Aldo Moro, who in those days was in the hands of the Red Brigades.

The meeting point was the central square of Assisi, where competitions, parades, and shows took place. We found hospitality, together with dozens of other people, in the entrance hall of an ancient villa made available by its owner. An intoxicating atmosphere dazed us with spring. Among gentlemen and Madonnas, princes and vassals, there were pages, minstrels, shop-boys, and ragged beggars who roamed among the taverns. From time to time the squawking of the swallows was broken by trumpet calls or drum rolls announcing the passage of some messenger or caravan. At night, in the ancient corners lit only by torches, there were minstrels who sang serenades, playing and praising the spring, while Lud and I were like melted honey, from the present to the Middle Ages.

I believe that every situation lends itself to a particular blend, and in Assisi the festival, spring, fantasy, ecstasy, and exhilaration mixed together. Those days were unrepeatable. It was the year following the fateful '77 and the most succulent fruits were harvested from that year. In the evening in the smoky taverns, drunken pages and minstrels let themselves go and, peering under the planks, their tights revealed swelling and agitation. There was no particular resistance because the times allowed us to defy the rules. Among the joints and flowing wine, brilliant glances and flashes of sensuality snapped. It was like being on the set of the *Decameron*. Every now and then I lost the others who reappeared and disappeared into the smoke; Lud, like me, was part of the scene and went from bench to bench and from table to table chasing visions and turning into a fairy tale. We were both busy dispensing fabulous delights.

In the end we returned to the villa where the camp had been set up and we continued to enjoy ourselves, even if, as in all group situations, the perspective changed, and despite the ecstasy of the place, a certain self-censorship was triggered in defense of rigid guidelines. If in the tavern, thanks to drunkenness, one let oneself go, in the common room we returned to playing our roles and the couples reappeared. More and more I had the feeling that this was a stretch rather than a real desire; it almost seemed that after the orgy one needed reassuring confirmations. In fact, it was the boys who had everything to lose. In the villa in Assisi, as in the occupied house in Florence or behind the scenes in via dei Volsci, many did it but everyone hid it.

We returned to the Calendimaggio festival in Assisi in the following years, but the initial atmosphere was gradually lost. In addition to too much booze, the consumption of hard drugs increased which, together with aggression, broken bottles, and brawls, meant that the hostility of the residents grew to the point of turning into closure and repression.

Among my many sexual memories is what happened quietly in public with a self-proclaimed straight partner. I did it to the rhythm of Rossini's *The Thieving Magpie* which one of those present let out to cover their sighs. During an evening of hanging out in the gardens of San Lorenzo, like so many other times, we ended up at our house to have a cup of tea and a joint. I was sprawled out on the bed with Pietro by my side, a Milanese comrade from Potere Operaio who had come to Rome to meet his fiancée, an independent companion of the Volsci group. I began to feel his hand touching me and caressing me, then he moved on to kisses, and finally we slipped under the covers with a dozen people around. Luckily his girlfriend had already left, but a few days later, seeing her again, she attacked me, calling me a bitch, telling me to screw my ass to the rhythm of the *Thieving Magpie*. The affair with him lasted for a few months, every time he returned to Rome, and having consummated it in the presence of others, remained an exception that I remember with great and revolutionary pleasure. It was like making homosexual intercourse public, showing it to others to give it a political meaning as well as a pleasure, indeed, a personal enjoyment.

At home we had a strange common wardrobe: colorful, motley, eccentric. We went to secondhand markets where you could find everything at bargain prices. The most famous ones that attracted people from all over Italy were in Resina near Naples, the one in Latina, but also those in via Sannio and Porta Portese in Rome. Even bartering was widespread and practiced, so clothes and accessories went around continuously, leaving everyone the opportunity to customize them by cutting them, reducing them, gluing them, all very far from imposed fashions and false styles descended from above. We wore clogs, suede boots, sneakers without any particular brand; there was no brand to make the goods famous. There were the Converse All Stars—I remember them well because I've always worn them—but it wasn't because of the brand but because they were the cheapest. Jeans were always torn, frayed, patched, and worn out by time and experience, but certainly not by stylists. Shirts, which were not yet called T-shirts, were very simple with the exception of the very colorful Indian ones or those with oriental embroidery on the chest. Our preference was always for more or less baggy shirts, with checks, big squares, squares of all colors. I also really liked the white ones. I had one of the Renaissance kinds with sleeves wide up top and tight at the wrist. I usually wore it with a purple velvet waistcoat, a wide-brimmed black hat, and lots and lots of necklaces, bracelets, rings, earrings, and brooches. Piercings weren't in yet. Often with the excellent purchases made at the markets in Resina or Latina we were able to set up a stall in Piazza

Navona in the evening or during the day at the university. That too had become a situation for meeting people and giving birth to new affairs. We lived on little and we still managed. I remember never asking my parents for too much money. They only gave me the rent, which corresponded to about forty thousand lire a month. For the rest I made do with the sale of clothes, costume jewelry, and various handicrafts. For a period I painted empty tin cans, especially those containing Valda pills; in another period I made cloth dolls. When I didn't have anything to sell or barter, I begged for money, which worked very well. Indeed, it was a consolidated practice especially in some places such as the university, Piazza Navona, Trastevere, and the whole center of Rome as in all other cities. Nocciolina had made it a real profession, an excellent means of support. There was also another trade that I occasionally resorted to: that of substances, in particular of local grass and acid. The marijuana was from Avellino, which became famous because it grew spontaneously, allowing an abundant harvest every year that guaranteed consumption at low or zero prices. Later, like all things that become famous and then screwed up, the crops would be destroyed. Every year between August and September many people went to harvest the marijuana near Avellino and Benevento, and since that's where I come from, I also often stayed in my country house.

In that period my smoking crisis also began to manifest, caused by real panic attacks, confusion, and insecurity that assailed me when I smoked weed or hash. During the harvest, no distinction was made between male and female plants, and there was a particularly heavy portion that sent several people to the hospital with panic attacks and tachycardia.

Our economy was fair and supportive, no telephones or cell phones (which didn't exist yet), no television because we still managed to do without it, no discos or clubs because it was still customary to hang out in the square, in collective offices, or in common houses. Even the cost of our bills was halved both because of the various tricks we developed and the self-reduction campaigns promoted by the large collectives of the companies that managed electricity and gas.

Distress and Self-Awareness

I periodically continued to have life crises characterized by anxiety, anguish, and depression. Those crises were closely linked to the degree of my self-acceptance, which at the time was not yet strong or stable; they have been declining as my consciousness has grown and my self-esteem has increased which, translated into political terms, is called "pride."

Crises due to confrontation with that accursed normality, that straight line, too straight, imposed on everyone but that no one can or wants to travel, an introjected straight line, an embodied feeling that tells us what is right and what is wrong, what you can and what you can't, what's good and what's bad, and in the end the good things, the ones that satisfy and make you happy, always turn out to be the ones that hurt. The sense of guilt, the disturbance, the anguish all the more profound the poorer the self-awareness was. Conscience is the necessary basis for a healthy relationship with the world and with oneself: we should start from it for a fabulous coming out. Today the practice of coming out has been emptied of all its revolutionary potential—of its conscience, in fact—becoming a pure aesthetic act, without that philosophical, political, or cultural support that gives it meaning and consistency. The awareness of the relationship between us and them, between diversity and "normality," between liberation and oppression, has completely disappeared. The path that brought us here is almost completely unknown, as is our history, our experience. Many are convinced that our liberation started from some designer who invented a particular line of underwear or that freedom was granted to us by discos, saunas, or happy hour; that *pride* is just a parade of floats or, as a well-known gay TV personality says, that *pride* is a Mardi Gras without any particular political value.

Self-mastery, autonomy, and pride mean conscience, or the clarity to be able to overcome feelings of guilt and self-castration, and to take back one's life. It is not easy in a world bent on the market, massified, submerged by communications that continually refer to that murderous normality. They are the values and meaning of everything around us, from politics to advertising. Today we are no longer able to give meaning to our lives; profit and the market do it for us. It almost seems that being gay coincides with what you wear, with the places you frequent, with the place where you go on vacation.

This is why I find it difficult to establish whether being yourself was more difficult before or now! Surely before it was wrong for some things, today for others. Before it was due to the direct and immediate denial and repression, due to difficulties linked to the troubled beginning of our history, to the fact that we were manifesting ourselves even before to the world. Before, they neutralized us in concentration camps, asylums, and prisons, while today they make sure that we neutralize ourselves. Although there are queers, cross-dressers, and trans people everywhere, the level of prejudice does not seem to have dropped off much. In fact, we continue to be killed because we are trans, beaten because we are gay, raped because we are lesbian, fired because we are weak, mocked because we are different, pointed out, considered abnormal by gentlemen politicians and masters of consciences.

We have a partial view of things, a reflection of the small, particular realities in which we live, perhaps more open and hospitable than the general picture. If it's true that mass communications have transformed, conditioned, and educated, it's not clear why homophobia, prejudice, and racism are still so strong. Rather, I would say that those means show the values of those who manage them, i.e., of the bosses, a word that has gone out of fashion along with many others.

Living in a Dream and Not Dreaming about Living

After the spring explosion, the summer heat made me lose track of Lud. In Paris, where I arrived after several adventures, I remembered our date for the 15th of July in front of the Moulin Rouge. We had made that date months before, letting everyone we met know about it, and who knows how many would have taken it into consideration, especially if Lud was the one to remember it. So I wouldn't make a mistake, I went to the Pigalle Quarter. Perched on the Art Nouveau railing of the metro, I immediately recognized Lud with his long curls. This dazzling encounter was followed by an exhilarating ceremony of hugs, kisses, licks, yells, and leaps. I abandoned the companions with whom I arrived in Paris, continuing the adventure with him. I realized that falling in love had evolved into a deep and particular relationship. We began to wander the boulevards, losing track of time, with no destination, without anything, and that was the goal, and in that moment it was enough for us. When we{f} were tired, we stopped. When we were hungry, Lud played the guitar and I collected the money. We dreamed and Paris was the city of *dreamers.* Ten years before it was May of 1968, even before that there was the Paris Commune, the Revolution, Rimbaud, Verlaine, Jean Genet, Artaud, and then all the currents, thoughts, and ideas that had made our history: the libertarian one, the same one that we basically had brought back there. In Paris, given the context, we decided to call ourselves Juliette and Simone in honor of Juliette Gréco and Simone Signoret, but also of Simone de Beauvoir.

During a rainy afternoon we took shelter by a door in the Latin Quarter where, fantasizing, we said to each other, "What would you think if a nice guy arrived right now and invited us upstairs to have tea . . ." et cetera, et cetera, and then suddenly the guy arrived! Tall, long blonde hair, a hint of a beard, blue eyes behind round metal glasses, torn jeans, and a white shirt. He ran in to escape the rain; he was all wet and particularly agitated because he was trying to keep the records he had tucked under his arm from getting wet. I asked him if he would give us a franc and without skipping a beat he began to speak quickly in French. We immediately understood that there was an opening for us but we did not understand the basics of it, and when we asked him to please speak more slowly he stopped on the stairs, put down the records, and, placing his hands on his hips, repeated slowly: "Je voudrais vous inviter chez mois pour prendre un thé! J'abite ici, au dernier étage" (I would like to invite you to my place for a cup of tea! I live here, on the top floor). Without thinking twice about it, Lud and I took the stairs, we looked at each other and smiled: the guy was also very cute. His name was Bernard, he worked at a pirate radio station and lived in the attic on the top floor of the building where we were fantasizing. We entered a house full of records, books, rugs, roof windows, a cat, and all the clutter of someone who lives alone in Paris. Bernard took off his wet clothes and, in his underwear, put on tea as well as lots of beautiful music. I heard Patti Smith for the first time, which immediately gave me shocks and thrills. Lud began to dance, and, before realizing how much was happening, all three of us were on the bed deshabille, making out, dancing, dreaming, and having fun. The triangle was well proportioned and equilateral; its parts tuned in well and fit together just as well. We stayed *chez* Bernard in rue de Saint Jacques for three days; on the fourth Lud, in the throes of his usual static crises, decided to resume flight, continuing alone.

Like a good Sagittarius, he needed to run, move, and paw at the door; I understood this need of his, so I let him go while I took up my voyage toward the Mediterranean. France held an important part in my adventures, and the affair with Bernard wasn't the first. When we headed for the Isle of Wight with a group of friends we stopped in Lyon, as guests of David and two of his girlfriends we'd met that day in a small street in the city center. We let ourselves go with them in a sort of orgy which at the time was rather defined as "free love."

After summer, returning from vacation, the scene of our Roman houses had changed. The house in via dei Volsci had been occupied by a group of freaks with drums and pipes who did not give the impression of wanting to leave easily. Lud continued his *trips*, and I understood that nomadism was his nature. Nocciolina and Lilli were harvesting grapes and apple picking in Trentino. The summer had dispersed and moved inhabitants and visitors to other places, so in September I found myself with Paolo and Carol: we decided to stay in just one house, which is why we renovated the one in via dei Campani, making it more livable. Projects and good intentions lasted until the end of summer because the arrival of autumn brought almost everyone back to the base.

Lud returned for only a month, the time necessary to get his passport and leave for India. He was one of the last to arrive by land on the *magic bus* route, the one that brought hippies to India starting from Istanbul, via Teheran-Kabul-Delhi, a road interrupted by the war in Iran first, then by that in Afghanistan. Lud left in late November, penniless, and returned six months later slightly transformed. He wore a sari that wrapped him up down to his feet, a series of amulets hanging from his neck, a cloth that covered his head, black kohl rimming his eyes. He told us that he spent a lot of time in a tree meditating. I accompanied him to his compulsory military visit. His release for being homosexual, the famous article 28, was immediate. Soon he planned his transfer to Berlin.

Meanwhile, I had bonded with Zanza, who began to rave uncontrollably in our house and during our days. I hadn't seen her for about a year, exactly since the conflicts on May 12, 1977, when she appeared and disappeared in the smoke of tear gas. I saw her in via dei Volsci at Serafina's, an elderly companion who ran the small bar across the street from the headquarters of the collectives. Serafina was considered the grandmother of all the companions and everyone loved her very much. I remember that every time a companion was arrested, which was quite usual at the time, she would start to cry and get depressed. She was one of the typical characters who lived in the San Lorenzo district of the people, that of her companions, and was still a true alternative type. San Lorenzo was a refuge, a place where you felt safe and at home, a place where the fascists and police did not go because if they did, it was at their own risk.

The only drawback, compared to the tranquility, remained the chavs, although taken individually with some of them, nice relationships were created from different points of view. The problem was coming across them in a group, because each one had to prove to himself and to the others how much he was a bully, how cool he was, and, when I passed by, also how macho he was, indeed the most macho. And it takes patience! With many of them I was able to deepen friendships to the point that some of them were a great revelation in bed, giving me great satisfaction. There was a basic difference between the hicks and the comrades, which was sought to be bridged through that understanding-compassion—entirely Catholic—on the part of the comrades. The former were proletarians and the latter sought to be; the former had to maintain a role that was required of them by the group's codes, while the latter proposed it again to feel closer to them. The chavs represented the local, the comrades were supposed to represent the international—or as they say now, the global—but they ended up being absorbed by their ambiguous "particular." And when it happened one day that with Zanza we were insulted by the hicks to whom we opposed a gay resistance, the dear boys of the collective took the side of the chavs because, according to them, the proletariat is always right. Zanza and I were considered provocative{f} and were invited to leave the bar. Let's just say that we decided to leave because there was nothing more to be done: machismo masquerading as the proletariat had won.

This passage must have taken place in 1979, so a year after the events I am talking about, and fortunately, the revolution—like the whole universe, being in continuous evolution, not static but fluid—assumed other aspects, new contours. It took unknown paths by moving toward new dimensions, a trend that escaped many, all those who couldn't see the forest for the trees.

～ 3 ～

Extravagance (1978–1982)

No, I'm not where you're looking for me,
But here where I'm looking at you, laughing.
—Michel Foucault

Zanza

Zanza began to hang out at our place. I don't know if this was pleasing or problematic. Zanza was crazy, but so crazy that even in psychiatry textbooks you couldn't find a case like hers. You couldn't tell when she was joking and when she was serious, when she was telling the truth and when she was delusional, when she was acting or was being herself. Apparently, he was a very normal boy, rather ugly, with a pock-marked face, thick glasses, short priest's hair, and shabby and unrefined clothes. Let's also say that this description refers to his first morning outing; then, little by little, he transformed throughout the day. Everyone in San Lorenzo knew her and she frequented everyone, inhabitants, artisans, traders, which allowed him to slip into houses or shops, snatch things that struck her at that moment—which usually transformed into something exaggeratedly scandalous—wear them, and never give them back. In fact, her stuff was scattered all over Rome, because she came in somewhere else, left what she had before, and took what tickled her fancy at that moment. People knew him and many refused to lend him things because they would never see them again. He began to insist and then, remembering his bad reputation, he took everything and ran away. It was a common occurrence to see Zanza on the run being chased by someone: "Help! He wants to rape me, help me quickly! Get him!" Our house was a sort of storage and changing room where he left the old stuff and dressed in the new stuff. She usually wore clothes, ornaments, and accessories, distorting their meaning and use, such as a lace petticoat worn over her brown polyester pants, a hat with a veil over a parka, or a pair of stiletto heels with pants rolled up to her knees. As soon as he put on his adored silvery things he seemed to receive a rush of adrenaline, giving free rein to all his whimsical, fanciful flair. Even now when I think about it, I get emotional and start laughing. Wearing a blue dressing gown with pink polka dots, like the kitschiest American ladies, she began to sing at the top of her voice, "We are like fireflies," or chant particularly heartfelt slogans such as "Pasolini is alive and will be seen in every man who dies." This performance was the same at home or on the street, in San Lorenzo or in the Garbatella neighborhood.

During the period in which he lived in the squatted houses in via dei Volsci, during a search the police entered his room and instead of subversive material they found substantial quantities of lipsticks, various makeup products, and fishnet stockings, and the joke came out that instead of a den they had discovered a brothel. While our angry and worried companions watched from a distance, Zanza continued in his usual delirium: "How ever will my mouth do without those lipsticks?! Rather than subversives, the queers lived there!"—jokes that made our male companions even more nervous.

Every time he left the house it was like going onstage. At times it amused me but at others it made me paranoid because I didn't know how people would react. Every once in a while we took the bus, which at rush hour was packed, and Zanza with his priestly face began to ask all the guys on board, especially the outwardly more rigid ones, if they had a lipstick to lend him because having lost his, he could not present himself in that state to his husband. Or when the cover of *Il Messaggero* reported in large print the news of an old American lady raped in the pine forest of Ostia: showing the newspaper, in a marked American accent, she asked if the bus was going to the pine forest of Ostia. Since he went to the university often, his other pastime was to enter the classrooms where lessons were held, approach the professor, and ask questions like "But Love, what are you teaching them? Star of the firmament, do you like the lipstick I put on this morning?" He made quick attacks, shocking the professors and sending the students into raptures; before running away he dispensed kisses soaked in lipstick with which he often wrote slogans and phrases on the walls. His favorite target was machismo, and in fact he had a sixth sense in choosing his victims. One of these was Pifano, the leader of the Roman opposition movement with whom, among other things, he was linked by deep friendship. He often stole the rag dolls I had in my room and, simulating the desperation of a mother with her sick children in her arms, stood under Radio Onda Rossa and began to scream in despair, asking for Lady Pifana's help because her little girls were sick. She asked him for help because he was an active member of the powerful collective of the hospital.

Zanza made our house her home for about two years, until her wandering took her to Bologna and later to Sicily, where she is said to have ended up in a nursing home. Every trace of her has been lost. Despite her simple middle school diploma, she was highly educated, cultured, and knowledgeable. Nothing about Italian politics escaped him. In fact, every morning he was at the Marani bar reading the newspapers, and then spent some time making fun of some political exponent, imitating and ridiculing him. He was particularly successful in the role of Professor Branca Sbuccellato, a candidate for the MSI known as "Rubber Band." She started with all her delirium against the communists, railing in the same way whether she was at home, at the bar, at the cafeteria, or in the fierce movement assemblies of which we{f} were both assiduous frequenters. Each time she aroused different reactions according to the climate of the context or the topic of the discussion, but she was unstoppable, and her provocations were like cheese on macaroni. When a very close friend of Peppino Impastato—with whom she said she had worked in the same collective—was killed, she was particularly vexed and continued to scream, denouncing the mafia. She also knew well the Sicilian comrades who were editors of *Evil*, a newspaper of political satire famous in those years, thanks to which for a period she was a guest in the house of a senator, where she invited me to lunch as if she were the hostess. I accepted the invitation out of curiosity because I couldn't understand why Zanza had ended up as a guest in the senator's house, and since he was a republican, at the dinner table Zanza played the part of the inveterate monarchist accusing communists and republicans of having ruined Italy. I was very embarrassed, but I understood that the hosts reacted with tranquility, knowing the ironic inspiration of their dear guest{f}.

Our house continued to be very busy, much more like Campo de' Fiori than a normal home away from home. My bed was also very busy, and when I wasn't hosting anyone it was Carol who wanted to sleep with me. In our homes, as in our lives, there was a lot of traffic, exchange, meetings: many people moved, met each other, socializing time, space, dreams, and sexuality! We weren't worried about how it would turn out, or if there was a sequel to these affairs: Would we like it? Would we succeed? Everything was motivated by an extraordinary desire to do everything, to discover, to leave nothing, because, as they say, every missed opportunity is a lost opportunity.

After the Moro kidnapping, many things had begun to change, and the air we breathed was decidedly different: there was much more tension, especially more distrust because a ferocious repression that affected everyone without distinction had taken place. In addition to specific people and situations, the repression was aimed at the entire opposition movement area. The movement was disoriented, swaying and squeezed between a rock and a hard place. It was really difficult to stay in the middle, between the armed struggle on the one hand and the more peaceful rebellion on the other, between political commitment and repression; all those spaces we had become accustomed to gradually began to shrink. Many hesitated because there seemed to be no choice: either you were on one side or the other. Either you sympathized with the extremist left-wing Frontline (Prima

Linea) or you were with the state. The game had gotten tough. Many felt the need to relax, to get out of the high stakes they had entered. The system had put in place its repressive strategy, which we all came out of very exhausted. I{f} have often wondered, never managing to understand, if those so-called comrades who make mistakes have understood and deepened this point. I have never understood how and why to break down one power just to replace it with another.

As far as I'm concerned, I don't think a better world can be built with the same tools as the one you want to tear down. The violence that we have always suffered is a component of the bourgeois system and that system cannot be overcome by adopting its own weapons. I have often confused rebellion and violence, and only later did I understand that the two do not necessarily go together. It can happen—and sometimes it has happened—that in order to rebel you become violent, but this is not an axiom, and considering violence as a necessary tool for change has been one of the biggest piles of trash. Violence can sometimes serve as a defense, often as resistance, but it cannot and should not become a program. In that season it frequently happened that we were involved in some investigation because someone's address was in the notebook of someone who in turn had been brought up by another intertwined second notebook that made us all conspirators, all terrorists, and all our houses were considered dens. Not a day went by without the news reporting the discovery of a hideout and the arrest of terrorists or the dismantling of the various columns. If all the people under investigation had been guilty, I believe that all European prisons would not have been enough to hold them all. When someone sensed something, a series of events could lead to him if, out of fear and without clarifying, he was hiding. I also remember that several homosexuals—I knew some of them—were arrested because they were considered supporters: the truth was that homosexuals were considered weaker people from whom they could more easily extract information.

For about two months I hosted one of these many people at home, with whom I also shared my bed, falling madly in love with him. I felt like Angela Davis, the passionate one of the movement, days and nights of spasms, and in the end he abandoned me; he fled to Paris suddenly. Before leaving he cleaned out the colored wooden box—at the time I didn't have a purse—where I kept my few pennies.

Valentina Sanna Cortese

In the winter of 1979, the fascists attacked Radio Città Futura and wounded some female feminist comrades who were live on the show. The headquarters of that radio station were also in San Lorenzo, not far from my house. There was an immediate reaction from our comrades, who quickly left in procession toward the fascist headquarters in Piazza Bologna and its surroundings. In that muscular procession I met Cocca in the company of Marco Sanna with Cocò, his always loyal companion. Between the tension and tragedy that characterized that procession, I found a touch of color and fantasy—it wasn't joy, because that wasn't the right time, but gaiety. Marco was shortish and plump, with huge green eyes under the classic glasses of a committed intellectual. Like a good Sardinian, he had big, long black curls, a keffiyeh, a round Tolfa bag with the ever-present *Lotta Continua* inside. He took off a flower he had in the buttonhole of his reindeer jacket and stuck it in my hair, kissing me tenderly on the lips. Before the police raided, I had time to leave him my address, and the next day he came to see me, showing up with a sweet jar of honey that his mother made. He lived in the countryside in Aprilia, which is why everyone knew him as "Marco di Aprilia." Later she was nicknamed Valentina Sanna Cortese, from the name she gave herself when, dressed as a bride, she met Vetere who was mayor of Rome then. What struck you about Marco was his infinite sweetness, his effusive joy, the overwhelming and contagious laughter that did not leave you indifferent; his caresses of infinite affection managed to color even the darkest moments. I vividly remember the one he gave me the last time we met, just after his mother died. One evening he came to see me on the corner where I was selling flowers. He didn't say anything. He looked at me, squeezing my hands tightly, and his eyes were veiled by a deep, infinite, and abysmal sadness. He could only say "hello," the only word that escaped his lips, and then he walked away. At that moment I still didn't know anything about his illness, but instinct made me gather everything that wasn't said during that meeting.

He was enrolled in the Humanities program; being a commuter, he often stayed at our house, where he almost immediately got along with all the other inhabitants. And slowly that house at 50 via Campani became more and more cheerful. Lud occasionally appeared between stops in Berlin, London, and Bombay; Zanza raged like a cyclone over the house, over San Lorenzo, and over all of Rome; Marco always gave us poems, novels, stories, and intriguing gay adventures. Together we confided in each other the claustrophobia we felt inside the opposition movement and the same intolerance toward FUORI! We talked about these things when he stayed over for the night; we spoke of love and revolution, of Rosa Luxemburg, and Malcolm X, comrades and faggots. We talked, we cried, we laughed, and we made love. It was something that came spontaneously; indeed, it was our own powerful means of communication. Certainly, Marco didn't correspond to my classic model of lover, but it was a very natural thing to sexualize the relationship: in that period it was a frequent and active practice that we often applied with immense pleasure. I liked having sex and I did it happily whenever the opportunity presented itself, when I was happy with a person, regardless of whether or not they appealed to me. Sex was had, seen, used, and wanted in all its forms and in all its extraordinary creative and communicative power. Marco thought exactly the same way, and sexualizing relationships became a socialized practice throughout our environment. Marco shared the same political and cultural path, which is why one fine day we thought it would be nice to create a gay collective in the opposition movement.

Narciso

We made an announcement in *Lotta Continua* and prepared various flyers with marker which we put up in the university area: "We are a group of gay revolutionaries who would like to form an autonomous collective within the movement. We're meeting at 4 P.M. on ** in Classroom 6 in the Humanities building." It was spring of 1979. We were aware that there were other gays in the movement (and not only there) who wanted and needed to meet up. I honestly didn't think there were so many! After the first phase that had seen the birth of FUORI!, we needed to take it a step further, to open it up to a wider political area, to relate the gay experience to the revolutionary movement. We needed to get out of the parameters that placed the homosexual question at the center of one's struggles, and to open it up to the social aspect, combining one's experience with a wider struggle for rights. I often speak of homosexuality and revolution because in that period it was spontaneous to do so, let's say even taken for granted. The denial of gays came from the conservative right, from the bourgeois against whom not only the queer movement was lined up but all the great opposition movements that were still alive, strong, and viable. The fear for that first meeting was represented by Zanza, who with his delirious provocations would have frightened any shy and embarrassed primroses. On the first date, there was me, Marco, Zanza, Cocca, and two newbies. A poor result, but we had noticed in front of the classroom a strange coming and going of markedly indifferent and at the same time curious students who peeked into the classroom. We decided to try again, and at the second meeting there were ten of us, including Marco Melchiorri (Nocciola), Enrico Giordani (Aunt Henrietta), Emanuele, and Danilo, while the announcements continued in *Lotta Continua*. At the third meeting there were fifteen of us, and Felix (Aunt Felicity) also arrived from Turin, who at that time was publishing *Lambda*, the only movement publication that maintained its periodicity.

Marco arrived from Aprilia with a bouquet of roses which he distributed to those present, and Zanza continued his provocations while stationed outside the classroom. He approached all those who stopped or tried to find the courage to enter and said to them: "But you too hang out with the faggolas? And what do you faggolas do, touch each other, kiss each other? Why don't you let me try that too? I want to really understand what you feel!" Then he would disappear for a few minutes before returning to his spot. He would enter the courtroom perhaps when we had managed to break the ice. He would slowly open the door, popping his face like a priest and with his Sicilian accent: "Are you all faggots?

And aren't you ashamed?" Marco would get angry and throw the first thing he could find at him.

The situation wasn't quite as calm and relaxed as it could be today; queers weren't liberated yet. They were insecure, anxious. There was no single unifying situation but only one that was in the process of formation. Throughout Italy, in addition to FUORI!, with its offices in Rome, there was Turin, Florence, Milan, and Naples; there were very few other homosexual associations. They could be counted on the fingers of one hand: the COM (Milanese Homosexual Collective), the COP (Paduan Homosexual Collective), the Faggy Collective of Bologna, and Lambda in Turin. All these associations together managed to count on the presence of about fifty people, the same people who moved about far and wide throughout the country, enlivening a scene that was still quite sparse. There weren't even all those nightclub circuits that would later flesh out the scene. I remember that in Rome there was the Super Star which was a large cellar open all night behind the Trevi fountain, frequented by transsexuals and hustlers; the Ompos in Testaccio; a primitive and shy Alibi; as well as a few cinemas that we used to frequent. We picked up soldiers in public places like the Circus Maximus, the Colosseum, and Monte Caprino where there was cruising, but all very *underground*. Each city had its circuit that was still under construction, but despite innumerable obstacles, the situation was extremely exciting, everything was yet to be discovered, and the novel, which appeared day by day, intoxicated us and gave us euphoria and courage. Nothing was taken for granted, except that we had centuries and centuries of oppression behind us, where we had nothing to lose but our chains holding us back. The meetings continued and the collective slowly grew and took shape. We decided to move to a more functional place, so we asked for hospitality from the anarchists who had an office in via Campani, right in front of my house. We even thought about giving ourselves a name, and thus we baptized ourselves Narciso Collective at the Anarchist Club of San Lorenzo at 71 via Campani. This was the ad that appeared in *Lotta Continua* with the addition, "If you can't find anyone, contact number 50 (across the street) and ring the doorbell marked Cannas and ask for Porporino."

The Narciso Collective, which was officially born in May 1979, was nested for all intents and purposes within the opposition movement. Unlike FUORI!, which focused all its attention on the specifics of the homosexual experience—sometimes estranging it from the social, cultural, and political context—Narciso tried to combine the homosexual experience with that of the opposition movement, in the belief that liberation and emancipation were common, the objectives were common, and the enemy was common, which we identified above all in bourgeois and capitalist society. If for FUORI! homosexual liberation could march on its own, for Narciso and for the many collectives born in that period it had to be inserted into a more general process of liberation that concerned not only gays and lesbians but all the oppressed of the world. It was above all the affiliation of FUORI! to the Radical Party which many of us{f} did not like. In the beginning Narciso was made up of about fifteen people, among whom I remember (in addition to Marco and Zanza) Marco Melchiorri, Pino P., Enrico Giordani (Aunt Henrietta), Emanuele, Gianni M., Raffaele, Danilo, Carlo, Cocca, Enzo (Roscio), as well as Anna (Ugenio) and Liviana, who were the only two lesbians. Although we had only one social meeting a week, we saw each other every day because we had established deep friendships. Relations also began to be built with other realities of the movement such as the Collettivo del Tufello, one of the historical collectives of the capital, in whose headquarters we organized several very queer and regenerating parties. A few years later the Narciso became the Mario Mieli Club.

In that spring the phase of true gay militancy began for me. My political activity had a shift, together with my attendance that decreased in the opposition movement environment. But seeing as though I still lived in San Lorenzo and shared a house with other comrades, I continued to maintain a strong bond with that area. I was discovering new experiences, new ways of doing things and being together. We got into the habit of gathering every evening at the Pantheon fountain around which there had always been a veiled gay presence, which gradually began to become less and less veiled, while our visibility took on unexpected colors and tones. Those steps, together with the place in Piazza Navona (the enclosure of the fountain), were strongly unifying. In the evenings the fehgs often met up in those places that were subsequently passed on to the collective. However, those places transformed over time. The Piazza del Pantheon became the meeting place for all of the snobby faguettes who began to appear, only to be displaced in turn by the disco faguettes who invaded everything and everyone in the second half of the 1980s. It often happened that those nice places, initially frequented by groups due to particular characteristics, over time became distorted, becoming unrecognizable. San Lorenzo for example, which today has become a fashionable place with the consequent rise in prices. Before San Lorenzo it was Trastevere's turn, or Campo de' Fiori. Thus the Pantheon—where at the beginning there were crazy faggots, half artists, half intellectuals—then suffered the invasion of that shapeless, uniform, and conforming mass who stopped discussing Pasolini, Verlaine, Jean Genet, and started talking about Versace or Dolce & Gabbana. The colors of our rags were replaced by brand names, the colorful and wild hair by the mass-produced patinas of boring and gooey *gay fashion*. And then we began to cross-dress and stopped undressing! The queers stopped singing or cackling and started going to the gym. At the beginning all this seemed rather like a liberating process, as many queers as they had never seen before, the more time passed the more they increased. But the more they increased and the more their talent decreased, the more they spoke and the less they said. The market would make them its best users. In New York, where they call them "the ones{f} from Chelsea," they say that when *fashion victims* arrive, you have to run away because the market takes notice and prices increase.

The Poets' Festival at Castelporziano

Summer was approaching and I{m} was completely absorbed in the new gay scene. There was always the usual coming and going at home, but definitely more gay than before. Me, Paolo, and Nocciolina were the permanent inhabitants; Carol had moved to Vivi's house; and Lud and Lilli continued to wander. Nocciolina spoke little but was always present in everything I did, often joining in frolicking with us faggolas, but she was depressed. She was in crisis with Paolo, but above all with herself and with life. After a heated quarrel with Paolo she disappeared. At the end of June we moved en masse to the beach of Castelporziano near Ostia where the first Poets' Festival took place. It was a gathering of poetry, music, and entertainment in which many poets of the Beat Generation participated: Ginsberg, Orlovsky, Ferlinghetti, and Gregory Corso. On the beach I met the small group of the Naples Collective of Medicine too, and my heart began to beat strongly for Osaio, who slept with me in my sleeping bag because he didn't have one. The festival lasted a week.

There were a lot of people even if the vibes were no longer as entrancing as they used to be. There was also widespread and palpable tension, a sort of collective dissatisfaction of tiredness. Everything was contested and nothing was proposed. Often groups of people occupied the stage, hindering recitation of the poems. Some demonstrated, others rebelled, some argued, others got high. Everyone was naked: sun, sea, poetry, and love. One day the stage broke under the weight of the crowd, causing fear for the worst. Luckily there was no one underneath. On that occasion someone took a photo of me that was later published in various newspapers, which portrayed me together with the Neapolitan group with flowers in my hair and a white dove in my hand in a scene of poetry and idyll.

I returned to Rome to take my last exam before our vacation, which we had decided would be a trip to Turkey with my sister and Peppe, one of my companions in our circle of friends. As soon as I got home I was struck by a sudden and unmotivated anguish, a feeling of panic; indeed, a perception of death. I hadn't heard anything from Nocciolina and it made me sad. After a few days, I saw her in the gardens of San Lorenzo and I was very surprised to find her serene and relaxed. I hugged her and kissed her, happy to have found her again. She confided in me that she was calm because she had finally managed to make a decision. Being one of very few words, I didn't ask her what the decision was because she never spoke before about the things she was going to do. I took her by the hand and together we went home to Paolo with whom she spent three intense and sweet days. She had an energy, a desire to do, to see, to go around that she had never had before. She finally also allowed a photographer friend of ours to take her picture after years of vain requests on his part. Her vitality amazed us. On the third day, just as she had arrived, she left.

After my last exam, preparations for the trip to the East began. Everything was ready, but on the eve of our departure a cruel phone call arrived from Rome: Nocciolina had kept her word. She had left for Faleria, a small town north of Rome where our friends had a house, leaving behind her things, all of us, and her life. I will never forget her! A piece of me and of all of us had gone away, disappeared in an odd way. I took the news coldly. I was silent, deciding to leave anyway, and when the ship bound for Greece left Brindisi I burst into a violent, deep cry. Tears as salty as that sea seemed to gush endlessly from the Adriatic! Peppe held me, caressed me, and cried with me. Death always leaves you dumbfounded, sudden death even more so, and what about suicide? And the oddities of life never end because at the time of the first draft of *AntoloGaia* a few years ago my phone rang and it was Paolo, who had gotten my number from Enrica. After twenty-five years he called me just as my attention was focused on the part dealing with his relationship with Nocciolina. Paolo told me roughly these words on the phone: "What happened then was beautiful because it was authentic. My relationship with Nocciolina was a great and important love story, authentic even in its tragedy because we lived things to the fullest. Today on the other hand hypocrisy and the nonsensical deprive us of the importance of love stories, if any, by making everything go away as if it were nothing."

The journey to Turkey was beautiful and full of emotions. We disembarked at Igoumenitsa, hitchhiked across northern Greece to Thessaloniki where we caught a train that arrived in Istanbul twenty-seven hours later. Turkey had not yet joined NATO, so what appeared to our eyes was a virgin and uncontaminated country, not yet a destination for mass tourism, all to be discovered, known, and, above all, understood. As we wandered through the crowded streets of Byzantium I was constantly under the eye of the "natives" who smiled at me interestedly and courted me with frequent and surprising butt squeezes. After some initial embarrassment and surprise, I got used to that all-too-normal ceremony on their part. Gay tourism did not yet have its various agencies which over time would debase those authentic traits. Those behaviors were part of a millennial tradition, original but not yet artificial, offered and not yet sold off. We were staying in Sultanahmet, the old part of the city, the destination of all those thousands of hippies who headed for India from the West. In fact, the legendary *magic buses* departed from there, following the route of Ankara, Tehran, Kabul, and Delhi. From Istanbul we headed south, where we met some Kurds who warmly welcomed us into their village. They were very hospitable, welcoming us with dances and songs, and then inviting us to reciprocate. They performed frenetic belly dances and I liberated tarantellas.

The journey ended on the island of Samos in Greece where we stayed for the last ten days as guests, so to speak, of a transvestite named Jorgos. Victims of severe seasickness after a terribly rough crossing, as soon as we landed we camped in a field which the next day we discovered was owned by Jorgos, a transgender/transvestite woman who had retired to be a peasant on that fabulous island after having lived in Athens for years. She raised chickens, rabbits, pigeons, goats, pigs, and a donkey with which she got around in the village. Tight flared pants, sixties shoes with very high wedges, tight satin blouses, dark glasses, a cute hat to hide the baldness that she defied with a flashy ringlet of hair on her forehead. The land on which we had pitched our tent bordered a military camp that Jorgos advised me to avoid; indeed he said to be wary of trusting the military—a warning that I immediately violated. I met Costas who was in the military there and I had a very sweet adventure with him. He was beautiful. Although he was from Athens he seemed to be from Stockholm because of his big blue eyes and his blonde hair.

Capo Rizzuto and Gay Camping

That same summer I spent the days around the national summer holiday, Ferragosto, at the town of Isola Capo Rizzuto, an alternative campsite where the first gay camping experiment took place. I met friends and acquaintances, I got to know other faggots, some of whom would repopulate the Narciso Collective in September. There was a good energy to the commune, an oasis where one lived in a sort of enlarged, experimental, anarchist republic. You would eat outside the tent with people you had just met, join in collective tokes of local weed with the addition of good wine and many other delicacies. There wasn't a clear demarcation between day and night. Everything flowed peacefully without limits of time, space, and the usual rules. With the same ease with which we got together for lunch, group smokes, tea or coffee ceremonies, we made love in quite simply healthy couples or group sex, in a tent, in a sleeping bag, or on the sand by the sea. The most apt description of the commune is the one given by Zanza, who called herself Mariolina Cannoli, since during the evening shows she offered herself as presenter: "Friendlette, this is paradise: we eat, drink, fuck, and do drugs without needing any money! And then the sea, the sun, and nudism; this is communism." Zanza raved about in the open, between the tents, at the canteen at any hour of the day or night, constantly cross-dressed or half\-undressed with veils or drapes on top of her and naked from the waist down.

Beautiful sea, wild nature, and in a corner of the beach there was even a clay quarry where we covered our bodies to cure them, beautify them, purify them. Several priestesses were stationed around the quarry; they were in charge of diving for the clay, slathering it on, and the final massage, more or less what many faggots would discover years later in distant Thailand. There are many photos documenting those mud masks and the naked bodies playing and rejoicing on the beach. One of these reported by a right-wing newspaper portrays Nichi Vendola in an Adamic pose. Many other models portrayed in that scene are no longer here today.

It was the first gay campsite in Italy; it was the summer of 1979. There had been an experiment the year before in Greece, a sort of itinerant campsite between the Peloponnese and the Cyclades islands, in which queers from all over Europe had participated. Camping usually took place after August 15th and lasted from fifteen to twenty days, organized in special structures previously booked and constructed for the reception of hundreds of crazy faggolas.

Vacationers were usually warned in advance and informed of the particular fabulousness of the scenes, which were recommended to be viewed by an adulterous public.

It was an important moment of queer sociality, during which the level of liberation was experienced and new ones were put into place, where the meaning of gaiety was truly deepened away from moral, disciplinary, strategic, and power traps. Fifteen days of delirium and ecstasy, during which there was no longer any difference between day and night, between rules and transgression, between reality and fantasy.

Thanks to the sun, the sea, and nudism, inhibitions were loosened and the campers condensed all that they could not and would rather have wanted to do throughout the year in that period. Theater, circus, and entertainment intertwined with love, sex, and freedom in a nonstop cycle that led to real and liberating catharsis, after which we were no longer the same. Tents, bungalows, and cars became dressing rooms or real stages where everything and then some happened.

In the campsites there was an internal geography made up of bungalows, itinerant sleeping bags, tents, shacks (in every sense), among which some were distinguished by fantasy, delirium, and queerness. Carmelina, a queer with a lost and out-of-tune look, an elementary teacher in a small town in the South, arrived punctually every year at the campsites in her old Fiat 127 with a trailer overloaded with her tent, provisions, decorations, furnishings, and a collection of hats of all shapes that she usually wore while nude to highlight their originality. Out of her trunks came an infinite number of colored rags that enriched the already charged sets; they functioned as stage and brothel costumes, for the numerous ceremonies that had to be presided over during those delirious stays.

At dawn, when the campsite seemed to acquire a little quiet, the silence was broken by Carmelina's shrill, shrill cry: "Viva le recchie" (long live the fehgs), and from all the nooks and crannies of the campsite, a thousand happy voices responded to the call as if to the mythical horn of Bacchus.

Another reference tent was that of the Foggia women, a cheerful and lighthearted group of elderly Apulian queers who were also assiduous campers. It was the group with which a very young and rebellious Vladimir-not-yet-Luxuria made her appearance on the scene. Among them was Francesca Foggiana Coluzzi (her stage name), perfect imitator of

Moira Orfei. Nardina, mustachioed and unscrupulous, who once at six in the morning woke up the whole campsite that had just fallen asleep, yelling: "My jewels, they stole my jewels! Thieves, give me back my precious stones!" This hysterical scene was in response to another delirium, the one now full of the Cecagnola, a great Neapolitan actress who, punctually, when it was time to settle the bill with management, bewildered and surprised, asserted aloud that her wallet had been stolen. The Sardinians' tent, on the other hand, was very popular with "committed" queers, those who by nature politicized the holiday, a mix between a political headquarters and a summer brothel. Meetings, debates, assemblies, seminars, and self-confidence took place there; delirious miniparades set off from there and crossed the campsite singing, shouting, and inviting everyone to engage in mass immorality. Ilaria and Tina, the two Sardinian mothers, were real stalwarts not only in the campsites but in all the ever more frequent meetings of the movement.

In the last few days there was the famous wedding ceremony in which the love affairs born in the campsite were celebrated. A great, desecrating ceremony, to keep in mind for today's "PACs and same-sex marriages," complete with clothes, makeup, rituals, and final buzz. Usually, after the theatrical ceremony, the wedding party took place outside the campsite in some restaurant in the area, thus becoming a moment of socialization with the local citizens.

The last one I attended took place in a restaurant booked for three hundred crazed faggots in the central square of Palinuro. A square room with glass walls, outside which all the curious and above all amazed citizens had taken their seats. Inside the restaurant, mothers, daughters, aunts, cousins of the bride and groom, queens, princesses, and duchesses convened, all with noble titles. Following them, common women, grooms with family jewels, bags full of face powders, drugs, and condoms did their utmost for the ceremony. Already during the *aperitivo* the outburst was at a medium-high degree of vivacity, and when the waiters began to serve the first course the room had changed in appearance, and it was much more like a bacchanal of the Suburra than a normal restaurant. The table where I had taken a seat with the whole royal family was close to the only wall, which we soon discovered was made of plasterboard, bordering the toilets which could be accessed from the outside, and therefore also accessible to strangers to the banquet. Aware of the thin wall that separated us from dozens of eager boys who had gathered in the toilets, with forks and knives we pierced the walls at the right height, creating a graceful and comfortable *glorywall* from which protruded tools of all sizes that delighted the afternoon meal of the austere countesses. Some even used them as coat hangers. When the second course was served at the table, the atmosphere—thanks to the delirious cocktail of drugs, alcohol, sex, and rock and roll—was completely degenerate, which is why the waiters thought it best to abandon the field, while from the outset the more and more astonished citizens savored the spectacle. Carmelina la Seggiara, stoned and naked, climbed onto the table, grabbed a mullet from the plate, and shouted in Neapolitan dialect: "You wanted fish!? So here it is," and threw the first mullet, which was followed by a messy, greasy, general throwing of fish. The ladies saw their most beautiful dresses getting dirty and therefore began to take them off. Everything was scattered around the room, on the tables, on the floor: wigs, bras and fake breasts, skirts, fishnet stockings, slips of all shapes, mouths full of tongues, members wrapped in lips, drag queens dancing the cancan, addicted faggots who sang marches by

Mina and Patty Pravo, while an endless line of young men took turns at the glorywall, which had been opened up at that point to the rest of the guests.

Organizing dinners and parties of that kind was completely normal; there was one every evening organized in turn by a group, a collective, a family. On the beach, in front of the tents, outside the bungalow, at the campsite bar or restaurant, those dinners usually turned into jarring bacchanals that lasted until dawn.

There were also the gay Olympics, complete with purse toss, stiletto heel jump, lad's tug, wig dive, and the ever-present cheerleading squad of which I was a part.

Among the most delirious performances I remember the Madonna ones, where each tent or bungalow represented a Madonna complete with an altar, liturgy, and final procession. Among these the Madonna of the Scabies stood out (protectress of broken, sick queers in bad shape), Porka Madonna (protector of trans and transvestites), the Black Madonna of Bruises and Malice, the fuchsia, checkered Madonna. Veronica Ciccone luckily hadn't appeared yet! Of course there were a thousand improvised shows on the beach, on the campsite trails, and in the squares of the surrounding villages, like when we went en masse to Anna Oxa's open-air concert in a small village in the Gargano. At one point we realized that the audience was no longer watching Oxa but Mark and Bepy, two exhilarating Dutch drags who, unknowingly and suddenly, appeared on a pedestal placed in a corner of the square and, when the public turned around in that direction, it seemed nice to them to raise their arms in triumph, and triumph it was, because the square began to applaud them, all the while forgetting about Oxa. I also remember Ciro Cascina's show in the square in Sant'Elpidio (AP), organized by the local left-wing junta as a moment of encounter with the citizens, a real artistic, cultural, and political success.

At the campsites we went around naked, not out of obligation but out of virtue. You communicate better when naked, you are more direct, more natural, and more free. This was a trend that was much stronger at the first campsites and which gradually faded at the last ones. In the former, the political dimension was also stronger with assemblies, debates, and a lively confrontation with the opposing movement. Even cross-dressing was not sophisticated but spontaneous, improvised with the first rags at hand, liberating and desecrating. Degeneration, not perfection, was sought in order to understand each other and everything that was forbidden outside. On the beach you saw naked people in fishnet stockings, or with stiletto heels instead of slippers, or with veils in their hair and nothing else on.

Perhaps the quietest moment was in the morning when, returning from a wild night, many were sleeping. Wandering around the camp, scrutinizing the rags and accessories discarded outside the tents, we figured out what the night's couplings had been. In the afternoon the beach was repopulated, gradually increasing in pace, and the carousel continued. Usually, before gay camping began, quiet families already staying in the campsites were warned of our barbaric descent, which triggered violent reactions, quarrels with the management, or real insurrections. Some left the campsite with their wives and children; others stayed and usually didn't regret it. On the contrary, they were fascinated because entertainment was guaranteed; they just needed to put aside false modesty and preconceived ideas. Over the years, many of those families have kept in touch with the faggolas they met at the campsite, Having developed lasting friendships.

Once the communist mayor of a small village in the surrounding area invited us to the local festival as guests of honor, in which the faguettes wanted to participate, giving their best in terms of costumes and scenography. The village was perched on a hilltop, so it was necessary to leave our cars at the entrance to the town packed with people, many of whom were represented by emigrants who had returned for the festival. The procession of queers, many cross-dressed for the occasion, went up the streets that led toward the central square where the band and the grand reception were. Suddenly, panic began to spread. There was a rumor that the first ones to arrive in the square had been attacked, so a stampede began along the downhill streets, hysterical queers screaming, some falling off their exaggeratedly high heels, others in fits of panic, all under the wide-open eyes of the unsuspecting villagers who, enraptured by so much scenography, were amazed by that daring escape which they thought was part of the show. It had happened that some local guys, excited by the situation, believing themselves to be cute, had bestowed slaps on the asses of the first lady adventurers who, coincidentally, were the most feminist of all! Open up heaven! "How dare you, shitty chauvinist," and then the feminist fehg slapped the guy. The queers who followed, blinded by mascara and the spotlights in the confusion of the crowd, instead saw the guy punching the queer. "Help, they're attacking us!" The ruckus echoed from the dozens and dozens of faggots who went back toward the square, and the distorted news that spread was: "Save yourselves, the crowd wants to lynch us!" We retreated to the campsite with broken heels, disheveled wigs, runny makeup, and the next day there was a large bouquet of red roses from the mayor and citizens apologizing for what had happened.

The first two camps in 1979 and 1980 were organized at Capo Rizzuto, the third in 1981 at Orgona (CH), in 1982 at

Vieste del Gargano, in 1983 at Sant'Elpidio (AP), in 1984 at Rodi Garganico. In 1985 there was the turbulent experience of Rocca Imperiale (CS), where homophobia fueled by the first absurd AIDS campaigns had its most visible effects. Chased out, indeed, chased away even with stones, we then took refuge in a nearby town, welcomed by the left-wing junta. However, problems with the citizenry were almost always created by local bishops or priests and then usually echoed by the fascists. The last two camps, then in full crisis due to the AIDS emergency, were in Sardinia in 1986 and in Sapri in 1987. Let's just say that everything went very well up until the one in Vieste. Then an inexorable crisis began which led to the end of that exhilarating experience.

The arrival of AIDS had dealt a big blow to our gay open-mindedness. Its disastrous effects on health and above all on public opinion began to manifest violently in the second half of the 1980s.

Gay Activism and Its First Conference

After the summer, the gay, metropolitan activities started up again. September and October were usually the busiest months for activism, because we were fresh and relaxed from the summer break and wanted to do things again. Narciso had established itself permanently in the anarchist head-quarters in Via Campani where today the Anomalia book-shop is located. Since the previous spring we had already been thinking of organizing a conference because we felt the need to meet up face to face, to get to know each other and pick each other up. During the summer—and especially at the campsite—we understood that different groups, collectives, and experiences had been created around Italy. The so-called gay galaxy was quite consistent, therefore it was necessary to find a glue, a moment of encounter that would give form and substance to that experience.

We rolled up our sleeves and organized the first conference of the "Revolutionary Gay Movement." To tell the truth, there had already been a conference the previous year in Bologna organized by the Faggy Collective, a conference I hadn't attended because I didn't yet frequent the gay scene.

In the collective organization of the conference, in addition to Narciso, the Collettivo Orfeo of Pisa, the Faggy Collective, and others, there was also Lambda, the Turin collective led by Felix, Gigi Malaroda, and others who at the time published *Lambda*, the first magazine. Or it might be better to say the first handout—which took its name from the Greek letter and symbol of homosexuality—that would subsequently be transformed into *Babilonia*, the gay newspaper with the largest circulation.

Internal communications took place through *Lambda*, announcements in *Lotta Continua*, through trips, letters, and postcards. Computers and all electronic communication were not yet widespread and neither were cell phones. Communication was premodern, much closer to carrier pigeons than to the Uranus satellite.

The conference took place in Rome in the first days of November at the Convento Occupato, an old, deconsecrated convent from the fourteenth century, occupied by our companions in Stella Rossa who had turned it into a political laboratory. The convent was in via del Colosseo. In addition to the normal and frequent political meetings, there was a popular canteen which served as an alternative restaurant, the forerunner of the modern kitchens of social centers. A series of initiatives was held there, such as a theater, a gym, a film club, cultural meetings, the most famous and popular of which was the weekly meeting of Psychoanalysis Against, the Freudian group led by Sandro Gindro who theorized a free and natural homosexuality. The Psychoanalysis Against seminar was a fixed appointment frequented by extravagant intellectuals, companions in crisis, emerging homosexuals, and various forms of humanity where interesting encounters often took place.

The preparations for the conference, including meetings, debates, preparations, and hunting trips, continued briskly until its first day. Teresa and I had the responsibility of managing the refreshments, so we prepared sandwiches and various delicacies in the kitchens of the Pinzimonio, a bed-and-breakfast wine bar run by a lighthearted group of companions, all very nice, and above all crazy, able to tune in well with our growing and exaggerated madness. Because it was downtown, Pinzimonio became a popular alternative gay hangout, partly because of its clientele and partly because of its managers, some of whom soon came out. It was located in Borgo Pio in a small square behind Saint Peter's, which also became a meeting point and above all a pickup joint. We met, upset and drunk, at the long tables where everything went on, from the committed speech to the joke, from the kiss on the lips to the one with the tongue, from the foot under the table to the blow job inside the bathroom. I remember well the preparations for the buffet for the conference because it was a Wednesday, the traditional day of papal audiences. In fact, that morning, going partially cross-dressed to Pinzimonio, we crossed Saint Peter's Square at the moment when the Polish pope was meeting his faithful flock. He had not yet reached the pinnacle of success and, as there had not yet been an attempt on his life, there was little security. By chance we found ourselves a meter away from the pope, who, submerged by the cheering crowd, was struggling to make his way through it. Teresa and I then began to yell, amused: "Let her get through, you'll ruin her dress!" A lady close to us, realizing our irony, with anger, acidity, and hysteria severely called us out to the police, at which point Teresa, putting her hands on her waist like a sugar bowl, replied angrily: "Hey lady, what I meant was: let her pass . . . your holiness!"

The conference was the first of the newborn movement and therefore after a long pause of inactivity it was intriguing and interesting; for this reason all the gay people made plans to come to Rome. Groups, delegations, singles and singulars, queens, princesses, the common women, the crazy ones, the mustachioed, and the fabulous began to arrive. I was at the reception desk at the top of the entrance stairway making the ID badges, so nothing and no one escaped me. At my side Marco Sanna in great pomp with multicolored dungarees was adorned with brooches, bracelets, scarves, earrings, his bag full of newspapers, books, papers, *Lotta Continua*, and the ever-present bouquet of flowers. All of Narciso did the honors of the house, doing its utmost in organizing and dispensing pecks and kisses.

Felix arrived, curly haired and pale, with the Turin delegation; I was particularly struck by a handsome Calabrian Moor named Giuseppe, with whom I had an affair during the days of the conference. Very blonde, superb, and fierce Ivan Teobaldelli, known as Ivana, another historical pillar of the movement. The Trapanate from Trapani, the Tarantolate from Taranto, the Trentine, the Pisane dell'Orfeo, among which a very young and intrepid Andrea Pini shone. In large numbers, the Faggy Collective from Bologna was led by Beppe Ramina, charming and intriguing like few others. And then the various queens who arrived in no particular order, as well as the princesses and courtesans. The inevitable Massimo Consoli, an intrigued and critical Bruno

Di Donato, charming and even majestic Mario Mieli. Dario Bellezza also arrived, but he immediately got into an altercation with Marco Sanna over an ill-digested article on the new movement, which is why he left in a huff. What struck me most of all was the arrival of Valerie, fascinating and shocking: under a long fluorescent duster coat she wore a ruby-red bodysuit, fishnet stockings and stiletto heels, a black ostrich boa around her neck, and a huge studded belt. Her hands were long and shapely, adorned with dozens, I mean hundreds of rings. She flaunted forward and arrived first, announcing her entrance. For the first time I met her in a more equal position, where I too was an active protagonist of the scene and, despite her classic haughtiness, I received her with a smile. It was the first time she deigned to greet me, a great recognition for me.

Mario Mieli

Mario Mieli arrived in the late afternoon. Wrapped in a long dark cloak, he wore trousers tucked into high-heeled boots and a pompous oriental silver necklace around his neck. He advanced slowly with his hieratic smile and a gaze that went beyond me, beyond everyone, beyond everything, beyond the meeting, beyond the known horizon. He went up the convent staircase and stood still on the reception landing as if he were contemplating. There was an emptiness around him, an emptiness that is created out of respect or fear for an important person. He kept smiling and, despite greeting everyone, he remained distant. His was not the distance of those who push themselves but rather that of those who, having traveled too fast, stop to wait for the others to arrive, and who knows when they will arrive, or even if they will arrive!

Before that I had already seen him during the three days in Bologna on the stage occupied by Dario Fo and another time in Trastevere. I had met him one evening while he was walking alone in Santa Maria in Trastevere, wearing his usual cloak; I remember following him because he intrigued and fascinated me at the same time. I had also involved Carol in that chase, who didn't quite understand, and not knowing who he was, went around staring at him, smiling at him, shocked. Mario didn't understand what she wanted; she, with her classic savoir faire, believing he was someone I wanted to pick up, said: "But you know . . . he likes you," pointing at me, who meanwhile ran away, embarrassed.

I had read his articles in FUORI! but, despite having bought it, I had not yet read his *Elements of Homosexual Criticism* because it was difficult for me to understand. How difficult his articles in *Re Nudo* had seemed to me. I had tried to interpret them years earlier, in my room back at home. I was still working through some theoretical passages, the link between sexuality and revolution, that queer framework that Mario had already been proposing for years, as a reading, interpretation, and upheaval of our lives.

Many stories were told about him, among which the most common was that of coprophagia, which intrigued me a lot, to the point that I thought it appropriate to have it clarified directly by him, given that he continued to remain alone on the landing of the occupied convent. I approached and introduced myself. I don't remember all the preliminaries, including the appreciation for his necklace which he explained to me was an Afghan prayer holder. Once we had broken the ice, I got to the point, asking him, with a whole series of preambles, for explanations about the famous shit and his coprophagia, convinced that it was just a tall tale. He, without saying a word, opened the prayer holder, took out a lipstick tube with an ancient silver wrapper, took off the cap, and with a finger began to spread the dark-colored contents that was in place of the lipstick on his lips. After having smeared a little and licked and rubbed his lips, as one does when putting on lipstick, he said more or less these words to me: "You see . . . a little is enough! The important thing is that a part of what comes out comes back, so as not to interrupt the circle!" I did not understand the meaning of his words, which became clearer to me some time later, when I read his second book, *The Awakening of the Pharaohs*, which allowed me to associate that speech with profound research of his, which I believe is linked to an alchemical practice.

While I was chatting with Mario, an infernal hustle and bustle was coming from the conference room. As in all movement assemblies, even in the gay one, everything had to be questioned, contradicted, rejected, and the tussle that followed was merely infernal. Mario took leave of me with an elegant nod of the head and entered the arena. At that moment at the speaker's table there was a Black faggola from San Francisco in a tight-fitting T-shirt, a shaved head, mustache, a large gold ring in her ear: one of the first stereotypes to arrive from overseas. The Black American was unable to continue because of the many arguments and screams, while Mieli, without saying anything or asking permission, leaned over the table facing the public. As soon as he positioned himself, that infernal clamor began to subside, and when silence fell, Mario, smiling and raising his index finger toward the audience, began in French: "Ça c'est la verité" (This is the truth), referring I think to the big mess and above all to the difficulty of communicating. I don't remember what followed, but I think Mario didn't continue further, limiting himself to that observation which contained everything in itself, admirably expressing the sign of the times. Looking back, I think he was already working on the *Awakening of the Pharaohs*. He perceived the ebb, the exhaustion of a phase, the sunset of the collective—of all that experience the contents of which were magnificently expressed in *Elements of Homosexual Criticism*—and he celebrated its end. Wrapped in his cloak, looking away, prophet and priestess, he seemed to clearly foresee all that was to come.

The after-party took place partly outdoors, between the Pantheon and Piazza Navona, partly at the Pinzimonio where people dined, partly at Monte Caprino where they hooked up, and mostly, above all, in the beds of hospitable landladies.

For the occasion of the conference we had also organized a demonstration in the center of the capital, which was, however, forbidden by the police. It was therefore decided not to give up on the idea and to organize another one in Pisa at the end of November. We also decided to organize the first gay pride for June 28 of the following year. The idea was launched by the Faggy Collective of Bologna, who for the occasion wanted to start negotiations with the Municipality of Bologna to have a seat assigned. A real document did not come out of the conference but a series of ideas and positions that reaffirmed the position of the gay movement within the antagonistic one. A communiqué was also issued in solidarity with the workers of the Fiat company on strike, and it was decided to ask *Lotta Continua* for a page of queer information on a weekly basis. Immediately afterward, in fact, the Fag Page began to appear every Thursday with articles, information, and documents, a very interesting experiment which coagulated various subjects representing the voice of the whole revolutionary gay area around itself. Several photos published on the Fag Page had been taken at my birthday party and portrayed the crazy founders of Narciso. I too wrote an article entitled "From the Mass Fag to the Social Fag," riffing on the title of Toni Negri's text "From the Mass Worker to the Social Worker," which at the time I had chosen as the text for my exam in history of philosophy. In the article I analyzed the relationship between homosexuals and partners or between homosexual partners and castrating male partners.

The Royal Family and Self-Defense Techniques

In the meantime, a small group of particularly interesting queers had joined the Narciso Collective, which really made a difference. Later they became my group, an incomparable presence of the gay scene of those years. The common thread that brought me to them was, as always, Cocca. In fact, it was with him that I had previously met Albertina, Teresa, Mario, and Cristina. The meeting took place at the Suburra, which was an enormous cellar in the Rione Monti used as a tavern, a famous meeting place for comrades and various alternative types. The name was derived from its location in what was once the infamous district of imperial Rome called precisely "la Suburra." Up to that moment, with members of the strange group I had limited myself to a few chats; I wasn't yet ready to immerse myself in openly and shamelessly gay relationships. The little group did not go unnoticed: in addition to Cocca with her kohl-rimmed eyes, her light blue eye shadow, veils and scarves, which generally speaking came within the gay outfit, the others{m}, or rather, the others{f} were visibly and provocatively dressed as women. Albertina, whose diminutive nickname was associated with her well below average height, petite and all pepper, an unpleasant baldness (which she skillfully hid) represented her biggest problem, which she never acknowledged. She had her eyebrows redone, face powdered, very little masculine clothes in bright colors that never matched, rigorously heeled shoes that she flaunted in her very cheesy way of walking. Usually she had to enter first: whether you went to the theater or to a party, to a demonstration or to a fashion show, the entrée was always hers, skillful, with a walking stick in her right hand which she repeatedly tapped on her left to emphasize her presence, and her languid and queer "Hello . . . and who are you!?" Her swaying gait consisted of three phases that were not always synchronized with each other: her legs with well-fitting, size-five feet made short but quick steps like a supermodel's; her torso swaying like a gondola on the Grand Canal in Venice had another speed; her head that seemed not to be subject to the law of gravity instead moved in all directions dispensing smiles, sweet and at the same time poisonous glances. She had a strong, fiery personality—sometimes ferocious and with a tendency to fight—which she persisted in considering political practice. Albertina did not accept provocations, responding in kind to all those who felt entitled to make fun of us, in a period in which widespread opinion was that a queer could and should be made fun of, accept the joke, and keep quiet. Let's say that with Albertina this situation was reversed, and the resulting surprise effect was all in our favor.

One evening, while I was strolling fabulously with her in a small street in the center, we met a classic couple, the kind in which she thinks: "bella figa ce l'ho solo io" (I'm the only one with a nice pussy), and the supermale thinks: "sono er mejo de tutti" (I'm better than everyone), with a German Shepherd at their feet. The bully, in order to demonstrate his virility to her and to all of us, tried to scare us by unleashing his dog on us, but the dog wouldn't attack. He tried to make the dog play by throwing stones at us while we continued our stroll without a care, but since the dog's intelligence did not catch his master's exaggerated intelligence, *er bullo* (the bully) began to run around us, trying to excite him. While playing, the dog bit his ankles, causing him to crash fearfully on the ground, with his skull landing on the hood of his car. The guy had made a bad impression and seemed worn out, but Albertina, swaying more than ever, turned around sharply: "Ah, Porporì, let's go back!," and when she found the beautiful pussy and the poor idiot still on the ground, after looking at him condescendingly, she turned to the woman, laughing: "Ah, Bella, watch out for your husband. He's gonna kill himself!"

Monte Caprino

We usually ended the evening in Monte Caprino, a historic gay meeting and cruising place where, rather than to hook up, we went to hang out with our other girlfriends. Gatherings between us girlfriends usually took place in Piazza Beatrice "Ciuuenci," with the added and prolonged *u* as we had renamed it from its original Cenci. It was the only place in the entire historic area that was a little brighter. Every place on Monte Caprino had been renamed with a gay version. Therefore, there was the Orgy Room, Sunset Avenue, er Passetto der Vaticano—a narrow and bumpy passage that led to the Ravine of the Orgies, above a cliff—named that because more than once some faggolas have fallen from here which, taken to the emergency room, turned out to be Vatican priests—the Rupe Tarpea, which overlooked the gardens, from the top of which, one evening, a group of zealous Roman chavs decided, as often happened, to break the ovaries of us fehgs. In an instant Monte Caprino became deserted. Let's say that we tried to reverse the trend, and when the assholes arrived we went toward them because we had decided that the best defense is a direct attack. And so it was that evening!

Usually the withdrawal of the faguettes was announced by Godezia, an old Roman fehg, a fish seller at the Campo de' Fiori market, a regular visitor to the place, who shouted: "Nnamo belle, su su tutte a casa che so' arrivate 'e donne e cominciano i casini" (Come on, girls, everyone home! The women [referring to us] have arrived and the trouble begins!). The swashbucklers threw stones from the cliff, and they laughed at the top of their lungs, satisfied that they had put hundreds of queers to flight, but certainly not we who were waiting for them at the exit. Albertina's walk was more sinuous than usual, and her walking stick nervously beating everywhere did not bode well. The thugs, satisfied with the stunt, approached the exit where they unexpectedly found five queers who hadn't fled. They kept raising their voices, ranting as a threat and an invitation to flee, but I, Albertina, Lucy, Teresa, and Cocca stayed there quietly, without having planned a specific action. When they came within range, Albertina, like a wild cat, clung to what seemed to be the leader, climbing from his legs up the shoulders and chest until she reached his head, giving him an infinite number of blows with her stick while she screamed and scratched. The fool, suddenly caught, began to scream, trying to get Albertina off of him. His two accomplices, surprised and frightened, ran away, chased by us, while the guy in Albertina's clutches shouted: "Aiuto! Lassame perde' che c'ho precendenti!" (Help! Lemme go! I have priors on my record!). Thinking that he had run into a gang of other thugs, he tried to explain: "But I'm a guy, I don't have anything to do with this!";

and while she massacred him with scratches, bites, and punches Albertina answered: ". . . and I'm a woommmmmaaaaan."

That was a sweet and languid revenge: having an asshole in your hands who paid for all those who had always done it to us. And he wasn't the only one. We had decided that nothing, absolutely nothing, would go unpunished.

One evening there was a bunch of us sitting in Piazza Navona all made up or cross-dressed, when the classic Roman bully approached us and said: "You certainly are strong ugly girls!"; and Albertina responded: "You are beautiful!"; and he: "Nun c'ho bisogno d'esse' bello, perché c'ho 23 centimetri sotto infatti me chiameno er banana!" (I don't need to be beautiful, because I've got 23 centimeters down there, in fact they call me Banana!); and Albertina: "And they call me Strawberry." And in a fraction of a second she got up, took an empty beer bottle, and smashed it on his head.

I remember so many actions of this kind but here I'll report only the tastiest ones, those that in the end made us feel better, more satisfied, because in those actions we felt we had avenged thousands and thousands of queers who had had to suffer and remain silent. Like that time at the Capo Rizzuto campsite when a group of local assholes watched from the top of the cliff laughing and throwing stones, convinced that the faggolas would keep quiet. We went up the cliff, and while the group had disappeared, only one asshole in a tractor was left to hold up male pride, and he did it by brandishing a pistol. This triggered the wrath of Merdaiola—another legendary entertainer and brawler who passed away a few years ago—who, with a sudden leap, mounted the vehicle, punched the hero of the foul masses, took away his pistol, and threw it into the fields. With a burst of applause, she unkindly but very hastily led the naive hero out of our orbit.

Another day at Capo Rizzuto, we decided to go to the village as a group to do our laundry in the public fountain. While we{f} were cheerfully displaying our lingerie, a crowd that didn't bode well had gathered on the other side of the square. Suddenly a moped detached from the crowd carrying the two heroes on duty who were heading toward us at high speed. Arriving close, nearly running us over, Valerie pulled out her slender hand, embroidering the face of the improvised Batman with her five long nails. Of course our escape was daring, but at least we{f} returned victorious and not defeated. Long live LGBTQIA+ pride!

Teresa, whose name was taken from the film *Teresa the Thief* for her spasmodic need for proletarian shopping, was a tall, blonde fehg with a mustache and eyeliner, strictly tight-fitting trousers to highlight her very sleazy gait, with an irrepressible tendency to laugh and the impossibility to shut up every time someone said one word too many! Subsequently, Teresa, having abandoned the mustache, would become my "transition" friend: in fact, with her I began my first hormonal treatments and all the relative trans experiments.

Mario, on the other hand, was an old, alcoholic, agora-phobic fag who had a huge house in Piazza San Giovanni where, in addition to dogs, cats, and canaries, faguettes with no fixed abode or fixed identity slumbered, cross-dressed, homeless and boobless, in addition to his provocative, young, and particularly favorite sex workers. Cristina was the only cis woman, despite having all the physical and psychologi-cal characteristics of a transvestite: charming, above all very sensitive, a former prostitute, she survived on hustling and working as an extra in Cinecittà. She was, in fact, one of those bizarre and extravagant characters who worked with

Fellini. When I met the small group at the Suburra or around the Roman nightlife, they attracted me, but I was unable to establish a regular relationship with them. At Narciso I seized the opportunity and slowly insinuated myself into that small group, which began to welcome other queers in addition to me, all rigorously and absolutely insane. Albertina confessed to me that her way of surviving was to prostitute herself, that sooner or later she would become trans to finally be able to hit the streets and earn enough money to be able to afford the good life in spite of the system and right-wing thinking. If one has to walk the streets, better do it well and make it a tool beyond mere survival. She asserted that since she invested in her body with waxing, makeup, and wigs, it was right and proper to get paid well. This surprised me. I had never thought about it before. I thought that prostitution meant scraping together a few coins and not as much money as Albertina claimed; I thought you needed to do it with slobbering old men and not with bold and above all charming young men willing to pay. "Ah, Porpora, wake up! Can't you see how pretty you are? Don't you know much money you would make!?" she often repeated to me.

When Albertina spoke of her prostitution projects, the other sisters kept silent and listened, more astonished than attentive. At the time, being trans coincided only and exclusively with being a prostitute; in fact, we said "being trans" to mean "turning a trick." After all, I think it was the only alternative for those who decided to embark on that path of reappropriation of their lives.

Narciso now had about twenty permanent members and just as many part-timers. Characters, couples, and small groups including Ugenio and Liviana, the first two lesbians who broke open the gay monochrome. Ugenio was the name with which we had all baptized her, an authentic butch, an eighteen-year-old student in a Roman high school, coming from a small town in the hinterland. Dressed up with chains, studs, brooches, shaved and colored hair: the most authentic punk look. She always walked around with a knife in her pocket, always ready to fight, especially when it came to defending her pride and responding to chauvinist provocations, a very real risk when she walked around with us brazen and provocative queers. We had decided not to lower our heads, not to submit. We all had a path of political militancy on our side, with all the desire to assert our gay pride that had been repressed for centuries, an issue that motivated us, never allowing us to retreat when it was necessary to affirm our pride. Clearly we were careful not to go shopping in Parioli, Balduina, or in all those bloody black areas.

In the collective, and in general in the queer scene, it was customary to rebaptize the new girls by giving them a gay name, and I was infallible in coining the nicknames. Many of the most famous names in fact, such as Cesarina, Nocciola, Teresa the thief, Agata—all strictly female—I had picked them out. The feminization of names was a gay practice; everything was declined in the feminine and when something was already feminine, *essa* was added as an augmentative, so that the cigarette became the cigarett*essa*, the handbag the handbag*essa*, Porpora the Porpor*essa*.

Interesting relationships and deep friendships prompted us to create meeting places and moments. So, in addition to the regular Thursday meeting, we met during the day in San Lorenzo and on the university lawns, in the evening at the Pantheon, Santa Maria in Trastevere, Piazza Navona: all places that would become fixed points of reference of the gay scene.

One evening at Pinzimonio I met Valeria, a somewhat hipster companion who began to court me, and I, having accepted the courtship, ended up at her and her companion's house, a hipster who sold necklaces and bracelets in Piazza Navona. The three of us got into the same bed, and while he pretended to sleep, she and I started making out and finally made love. For me it was the first time I'd done it with a woman, and after the first time, that same night, there was also the second time because I liked it. When she and I, exhausted, tried to sleep, the boyfriend secretly began to make out with me, but as soon as Valeria seemed to wake up, he withdrew. This story lasted all night until the morning when she left to go to work, leaving us alone. At that point he felt calm and let himself go. Although he was also a nice guy, I wanted to keep from that night the cute story I had with her, Valeria, and not his hypocrisy and sexist subterfuges. For once I wanted to tell male addiction to fuck off, and proudly own up to a healthy transgression. Before getting up and leaving, however, I wanted to have fun. I waited (pretending to sleep) for him to get very aroused, while he hugged me and rubbed me, pressing his dick on my ass, and when I felt he was just at the right point I pretended to wake up, I turned toward him who had the expression of, "Finally, feel how horny I am and what a nice hard cock I have," I gave him a peck on the cheek and left. I remember that story with pleasure because it had an important meaning for me. I had finally managed to overcome the fears and obstacles that limited me. I felt my revolution was more complete as I had deepened or re-established a relationship with women, or rather with femininity, with that universe which before then was incomplete for me.

In addition to our merry gang, the Pinzi also hosted the "San Giovanni guys," a group of highly stoned alternative twenty-year-olds, all guys, very cute from all points of view. There was only one woman among them, nicknamed "the

Witch." We shared the pleasure of wine, drugs, music, and the reckless life with them.

We often formed one large group that met in the gardens of San Giovanni during the day, when those places were still controlled by our comrades. San Giovanni represented an area wrested from the fascists, which had some of their most dangerous locations, such as that of Piazza Tuscolo, right nearby. The square was a sort of frontier, but still considered ours for all intents and purposes, even if at night it became dangerous because the fascists went around with the objective of attacking and sowing panic. Me, René, and Lucy paid the price when, having left a party cross-dressed, drunk, and eager for pleasure, ran into a thicket with four bastards armed with rods who attacked us. René and I managed to escape, but Lucy, due to a very tight dress that was not very functional for escape, saw the worst of it. When we saw her on the ground, with those bastards lifting their metal rods, René and I on the other side of the square began yelling at the top of our lungs, setting them to flight. Lucy got away with a few bruises and a lot of fear. There have been others of these bad encounters, one again while I was with Lucy in front of the Colosseum. They arrived on big Vespas in broad daylight. I remember the shitty face of one of them who, after punching Lucy with contempt and disgust, told us that people like us should be shredded up and thrown in the garbage. I also remember the attack on the entire Narciso group during a Sunday walk in Villa Borghese, when we were surrounded by a group who wanted to recreate the deeds of the fascist blackshirts. They formed a corridor in which we were forced to pass in single file while they spat at us, kicked us, and called us "ugly fags." Luckily, they didn't go further because there were lots of people walking around. But if the situation had allowed it, I think they would have really hurt us.

I intertwined with the boys of San Giovanni in tantalizing affairs; they were all so wonderfully cute that the risk of falling in love was always lurking. Even among the Pinzimonio managers I enjoyed pleasant entertainment. After all, in that period everyone, absolutely everyone, was open and available for further developments. It was as if there was a desire to know, to challenge taboos, to do what we had always been told not to do, to get to know others and through them ourselves and the world. Stories of just sex, little love stories, various mess-ups were widespread, very widespread; they were a fact.

I often wonder if it was just my particular propensity, a coincidence, or if it was the times, because the beds I've{m} been in, the toilets in which I've consumed, the difficulties I've gotten myself into at that time were truly innumerable. There was a widespread propensity for adventure, beyond the rules, sexes, genders, and all the mega bullshit that would later take hold again. Today there seems to be a widespread opinion that there is a lot more sex, like never before, but I have many doubts about this. Now we have sex that is different in its forms and modalities, which doesn't necessarily mean doing a lot of it and doing it well. Rather, I believe that the overabundant and often distorted media communication creates and transforms reality according to need. What we receive does not correspond to reality but rather to people's dreams or needs, more or less induced. Let's just say they show us the classic misunderstanding. All you need to do is access the internet, surf, chat, link, tune into your cell phone, send a text message, watch a DVD, but all on a virtual level that is far removed from the reality of the body and the senses. There is no sweat, there is no smell, there are no moods, the body no longer exists in its entirety but rather in individual, disconnected parts. We don't realize it because it almost seems like science fiction, but our bodies are super controlled, caged, predefined, sterilized. We live in a society of prevention, planning, and sterilization. We are passing or perhaps have already passed into a dimension in which the body is only a heavy burden, where the triumph of its substitutes is absolute. Only those who have managed to maintain a memory that is not only psychic but above all physical can be aware of this passage, those who still manage to remember the smells, the flavors, the colors, and the sensuality of the real body, its fatigue, the throbbing of its bleeding.

Evidently one no longer remembers or doesn't know what happened before the tsunami that would soon hit our lives. The black wave of AIDS erased everything, including that little-considered physical memory made up of the senses. Many of us thought, "every woman for herself," and in order to do so, we preferred to forget. The reality that was beginning to open up was too heavy to think about bringing our things to safety. It is very important, essential really, to understand what happened, what that so-called sexual revolution was and what the arrival of what was initially considered the "gay plague" and later "the plague of 2000" meant. The plague almost always marks the end of eras, cultures, and civilizations. Its exploitation has meant that messages are conveyed through it and policies are passed because its effects and its very meaning are destabilizing. In the future, when things will hopefully be clearer, we will perhaps be able to better understand what happened, how politics, institutions, and knowledge have positioned themselves, what role the Church has had, which was offered a greater weapon than the atom bomb, both for its physical and media effects. But I'll talk about this again; now there's more to tell, our fabulous story!

Extravaganza

Lucy was added to the group, which was beginning to take on a certain solidity. Lucy, with her mouth, her little black curls, her big eyes, and her "attributes"; super Roman and slummy, coming from the collectives of Centocelle. Subsequently René, slender like a reed, sinuous like a gazelle, refined in ways and practices, descended from the ancient Scaliger Angevin Bourbon d'Orleans nobility. I, Teresa, Lucy, and René represented the ram's head of the approach, pickup joints, gay and militant cruising.

Several days before the conference at the end of October, we were joined by Ilaria and Tina, the two Sardinian queers we met at the campsites who, tired of being in the military in Barbagia, moved to the mainland. Ilaria was teaching in an elementary school that she had to leave when a photo of her was published showing her both gay and militant at the campsite. Tall, thin, bony, Sardinian in the color of her skin and hair, she came from years of political militancy, which she transferred and concentrated verbatim into the gay world; for this reason, she was recognized as one of the peak leaders of the movement in that period. Ilaria put a lot of passion—sometimes too much—into everything she did, immersing herself in the experiences of struggle without sparing herself. She felt like the great Sardinian mother; she wanted to impersonate the primordial goddess. She was considered the mother of all the faggots that she wrapped in big and warm hugs that moved her. After the initial hug in fact, she stared as if to convey all the gay liberation that brooded inside her while her eyes, black as Sardinia, became shiny with emotion. One day she chained herself in protest in Piazza San Silvestro because, having fallen in love with a beautiful boy and unable to love him for a matter that she considered political (since it was associated with prejudice and homophobia), she remained bound to fast all day and night. We all joined in her delirium rather than her protest, while Albertina continued to shout: "Ilà, Ilariaaaa, are you done yet? He doesn't want you because you're dry and lanky, not because you're a fag, wake up. Maybe put on some makeup, put on a wig and get yourself paid!"

Tino was her twin sister, her shadow, who followed her into exile when they realized that Sardinia was not livable, and the great revolution awaited them on the mainland.

When she arrived, Ilaria decided to make her revolution by fighting and protesting in all places where there was injustice, especially when it was directed at gays and women. She managed to alternate or combine a great seriousness, dignity, and morality with exquisite irony and queerness. Often, when she got drunk, she would have a mystical *trip* and start singing sacred songs, giving rise to processions in which we all joined, always turning them into amusing bacchanalia which, depending on the place, could end in orgies, processions, or group catharsis.

Almost always our hangovers were collective and delirium reached exaggerated and unexpected levels. Like that evening when we ran into a group of pilgrims who, getting off the bus, unfortunately added a few comments to the initial surprise at seeing us. Albertina, always ready with her usual stick in her hands, without saying a word, got on the bus and began walking up and down the aisle; Tina, who felt like a hen that time, also went up repeating, "cluck cluck"; Ilaria began to sing hymns to the Virgin Mary; me, Teresa, and Lucy, not knowing what else to add, danced and laughed out loud. The pilgrims were petrified, as if Our Lady had really appeared to them.

Immediately after the conference we went to spend a few days at Teresa's house in a mountain village in Abruzzo, along with Albertina, Cocca, and Ilaria. Those were unforgettable days, and for the first time I experienced communal gay life. Walks in the woods, raids in the surrounding villages, an evening in front of the fireplace, even venturing into an experiment of collective self-awareness in which each of us tried to open up and tell everything, absolutely everything: anxieties, fears, desires, and secrets. One evening I remember we played a game in which everyone undressed and tried to describe their body, confessing what was good and what they would like to change. That same evening Giacomo, a Roman boy on vacation nearby, had joined us. During our reflection on the body, he and I began to make out and ended up immediately in bed, where Cocca joined us too. In that situation Giacomo, who in addition to being very cute was also apparently very male, took a pair of thigh-high stockings that he had stolen from his mother out of his bag, put them on, then painted his eyes and mouth with black eyeliner. He reminded me a lot of Lou Reed and I think he wanted to imitate him because in that period on the punk wave, Lou Lou was starting to have considerable success here in Italy too. I continued an affair with Giacomo and, as usual, I fell in love, but his very strict and conservative parents, given his bad habits, made him disappear.

One evening during that vacation, Albertina took some amphetamines, which aroused great excitement in her. She wanted at all costs to go to Tagliacozzo, the largest center nearby, to pick someone up. It was one o'clock in the morning, and in the month of November you only find wolves in those parts, but she was stubborn. She was made up and polished and she convinced me to accompany her. Out of curiosity, I let myself go on that expedition, which seemed doomed to me. We arrived in the deserted square of Tagliacozzo while she kept repeating that she wouldn't go home if she didn't do shit. I let her talk, thinking that sooner or later she would surrender to the evidence. As we continued to wander in the car we saw shadows in the distance. Albertina pricked up her antennae and aimed straight at two rustic and ingenuous boys who were talking among themselves. I, who was driving, stopped the car and she opened the window: "Hey guys, are you from here?" and they, as amazed as if they had seen a Martian, nodded. "Do you happen to know where the transvestites hang out around here?" "Ma veramende ge ne sdà gualguna verzo Avezzano" (I guess there's a few near Avezzano). "And how do you usually manage?" The two, a little confused, could not connect. Albertina astutely asked them if they knew of a quiet place and in the end, we followed them to an old abandoned quarry. As soon as the car stopped, she darted out for the cutest one while the other one approached me. I tried to act indifferent because I didn't even remotely like him. After some delay he asked me to do something, but I, as if falling from the clouds, said that he was wrong because I was straight and homo relationships didn't interest me. "But how did I even tell my friend that he was going to be with a brunette and I a blonde!" "Too bad! You misunderstood." Disappointed, he got out of the car, waiting for Albertina, who was satisfied and wanted to go home, but he, who wanted her, began to pull her by her arm, causing her to end up with one foot in a puddle of motor oil. Her screams were heard all the way up to the Gran Sasso; she screamed, cursed, and howled worse than a Marsican she-wolf as the two guys ran away, distraught. She got back into the car with her usual confidence and calmness, took out her mirror, adjusted her lipstick, and, turning toward me, said, "We can go!" Albertina asserted that it was necessary to externalize one's madness not only to live better but to defend oneself, because when people think you are crazy, they become afraid and leave you alone.

Pisa

At the November conference we decided to hold a gay demonstration outside the capital, organized by the sisters of the Orpheus Collective of Pisa. The event, the first in Pisa and one of the first in Italy, took place at the end of November. A procession of about 500 people was opened by a banner that read, "We are mothers, we have gay children and we are proud of it." Ilaria, Anastasia, Albertina, and Valerie carried the banner dressed or cross-dressed as respectable ladies. In addition to being militant, the procession was above all amusing. It crossed the center of Pisa on a crowded Saturday afternoon, among incredulous rather than curious people and a large police service. At a certain point some fascists also threw eggs, which only made us more determined. At first we were all a bit tense, which was normal for most of us who took to the streets for the first time to reclaim our gaiety. Some had put on masks to disguise themselves, others enormous goggles, turbans, hats, and scarves. Then, as we proceeded, we relaxed and uncovered ourselves, as we understood that to free ourselves we had to walk with our faces uncovered and heads held high. The procession ended with a beautiful party in Piazza dei Miracoli, with dances and roundabouts around the Leaning Tower to make it "stand erect," as the cheerful girls shouted, simulating coitus and embraces.

Even though I was completely immersed in gay life, I hadn't detached myself from the reality of my companions and I maintained a profound relationship with it that allowed me to attend both the gay scene and the opposition movements at the same time. The two realities remained distant; between them there was a void that I perceived very strongly. My comrades seemed to live according to a tradition made up of established rules, codes, systems of thought, and ways of acting. They took many things for granted, including their liberation, which wasn't so obvious. Relationships had settled on roles and behaviors that deep down reproposed the paradigm that we had been fighting for years.

For many of them, knowing how to chant harsh slogans or throwing a cobblestone or a Molotov cocktail was enough to convince themselves that they were perfect revolutionaries, that they understood everything, that they knew who the class enemy was and for the rest they were set. Often, indeed almost always, they forgot about the most dangerous enemy, the bourgeoisie or the fascist (according to Pasolini) that everyone carried within. The mechanisms of reproduction of power were not clear to everyone, a reflection that the matter was still far away. Mechanisms unclear to those who screamed in the streets, to those who kidnapped Aldo Moro, to those who organized themselves for the great revolution, to all those who filled the squares and the world at the time. What a pity! If the mechanism of poetry had been clear, maybe today . . . who knows! I realize that with *ifs* you don't make the revolution, and history proceeds despite our mistakes, but it is also made up of those *ifs*. Knowing the mechanism, perhaps we could have better channeled all that energy which would soon be dispersed in a thousand rivulets. I stopped licking my wounds. In recent years, in addition to Foucault and Nietzsche, I have read and reread Pasolini, his theory on homologation and that on the "fascist we carry within us," to which I would also add, "the male chauvinist we carry within us," not to be confused with the male (self-proclaimed) that comes inside it!

At that time in Montesacro the fascists had killed Valerio Verbano, and those of us from Narciso participated together in the demonstrations and funerals when the police launched violent raids inside and outside the Verano cemetery. Between shouts and gay slogans, we ran away among the graves, while the tear gas—as always—dissolved all our makeup. That was the first time we participated as a collective in a movement demonstration.

In that demonstration more than once we were laughed at and made fun of by the squats of the Worker's Collective, whose attitude as usual was: "What do fags have to do with it here? This is a serious matter!" Twenty years or so later, the survivors of those sides would ask me how I endured that situation. Among these there were several closeted queers or, as they were called at the time, "cryptoqueers" who, as victims of that climate, could not come out. Twenty years later, after the storm, they would confide in me all the discomfort they had in playing parts that were not theirs, in wearing clothes that were not theirs, in remaining silent in an environment considered liberated, but given the assumptions, was not very liberating.

Desiring

During our vacation in Abruzzo we had made great plans for our lives, plans for a more congenial, less hostile world, a gay, fabulous, and fantastic world, a world very far from reality; but we, smart and creative, still managed to adapt that reality to our world.

We{f} were convinced—and above all had decided—to live our lives to the fullest. Never ever would we have adapted to something that did not belong to us. We wanted everything and we wanted it right away, we wanted to take our life back, live it proudly without asking for anything but taking everything. We were queers, daughters of the times, nonconformists, adventurers, communists, libertarians, sinners, and proud to be such. The group had a reinforcing effect on all of us; it produced a great motivation that translated into conscience, self-esteem, vitality.

We used feminine adjectives more and more often, which was a choice even before it was a need. The group was always present, decisive, and driven to the point that it was awarded the high honor of "royal family," due to the presence within it of queens, duchesses, and princesses. It was our eccentric and provocative way of mocking or demolishing the power that had always been hostile to us: Albertina was the Queen of Rome, Teresa the Duchess of Abruzzi, Ilaria the Queen Mother or Empress of East and West, Tina Archduchess of Sardinia; myself and René, we{f} were daughters of the empress and therefore princesses, respectively of the West and of the East.

Immediately after the conference, from the distant lands of Russia, between the Urals and Vesuvius, another great figure joined the family, Her Highness Anastasia Romanov (alias Ciro Cascina), who with her performances and her theater would become a recognized actor of the movement. A nomadic artist, a bit of a sorcerer, a bit of a holy man, a bit of a flaneur, a bit of a pimp, with the alternating ways of a noblewoman and a commoner. Ciro had nothing that belonged to him and nothing to which he belonged; his anarchy was real rather than theoretical. He didn't have a home because he lived in all the houses, usually in the prettiest ones where there was good energy; he had no money, and when he had it, he gave it away; his life was the theater that he gave to others, and the others in gratitude offered him home, food, clothing, holidays, and all the delights of life. Having no wardrobe, he dressed in the things he liked best that he picked up in the houses where he was a guest, abandoning the old and taking up the new. Thus, he lived around Italy in a delirious and endless theatrical tour. Usually, his shows were not planned but improvised where he deemed it appropriate, so he happened to participate in a two-day show without interruption, or attend a two-minute speech in the square, a birthday party, a demonstration, a dinner. His shows were born in the moment and were the staging of reality, where provocation exposed actors and spectators. His most famous show was *The Madonna of Pompeii*, a subtle and profound satire of Catholic bigotry and its relationship with sexuality, a play which, given the position of the Catholic Church, would have been very topical today. The show could invariably last an hour, two, three, or go on all night with no continuity crisis and no decline in attendance. Anastasia involved those present in a game of roles in which she played to overturn them to bring out the characteristics of each one. Although she acted in Neapolitan dialect, her language was understandable everywhere in the South as in the North, in Italy and abroad. His most famous performances were those in Piazza del Nettuno in Bologna from 1980 to 1982, during all the demonstrations for the taking of the Cassero. His last performance in 1982 caused much discussion: an unwelcome provocation that came when the scene, despite the taking of Cassero, was already changing. The taking of the Cassero was celebrated with a party-show in a town hall in Piazza Maggiore where the tourist office is today. During the show, Anastasia took a guy from the audience, pulled down his pants, and gave him a blow job. Then she turned to the audience and with a sincerity I'd never seen before, she said: "I did mine, now you do yours. Goodbye and thanks." The silence and embarrassment highlighted all the disagreement of the nascent political leadership.

Bologna and the Grand Duchy of Pistoia

The royal family followed Anastasia in her constant wanderings, in turn becoming an extremely nomadic subject. In about two years various residences followed one another, the most famous of which was Pistoia where the royal residence was established.

Albertina continued her trans research. She felt like a woman and pursued the desire to walk the streets in order to become economically independent. Her problem was to find a place where she could work the streets, which was not easy. At that time, in fact, streetwalking was a difficult undertaking, since all the areas were controlled by the various trans clans who did not allow others in the area where they had created their reliable circle of customers, who, after so many vicissitudes, did not like to share with others.

Albertina's opportunity presented itself at the Rome conference when she strengthened her friendship with Valerie who, despite her young age, was already selling flowers in Bologna, the city considered by many to be the best square in Italy. She pandered to Madame and after a few weeks Albertina got all of us to go to Bologna to find Valerie. We organized the pilgrimage in Agata's van together with Marco Sanna, Teresa, Ugenio, and Cocca.

In Bologna, some of us were hosted by Valerie and some by Cocò, Marco Sanna's partner, a feminist who worked and lived in an AIED counseling clinic, located in a charming little villa in via Masserenti. Valerie, on the other hand, lived in a squat in Via Clavature, known as the "Traumfabrik," the same one where Andrea Pazienza and many of the alternative Bologna entourage lived.

Bologna the red, the gay, the nonconformist; Bologna the alternative, the punk, the libertine; for some Sodom, for others Stalingrad, for all of us{f} an oasis where we could relax and rave about, unlike that violent and dangerous Rome from which I came. There we moved around calmly even among the comrades as in the whole alternative scene, merged and intertwined with that creative area which expressed its highest point in Bologna. Bologna shone with its own light for its history, a political tradition, for the Resistance and its red junta, for the legacy of '77, for Radio Alice and the transversalists, because it was the Italian capital of punk, for the university that it filled with energy, for its gay ferment, for all this and so much more, Bologna has occupied a very important place in my life and in the gay experience in general.

We returned to Rome without Albertina, the first who decided to transplant to Bologna, and to do so she had to take up residence there and gain the trust of the transsexuals. Residence was essential to be protected from possible—and at the time frequent—threats from the police, which in addition to tarnishing one's criminal record, risked prison. Obtaining residency was not easy because you had to have a domicile and demonstrate that you had a job, similar to what happens to non-EU citizens today. Then there was the risk of the trans patrol which controlled and did not allow new people to work the streets in its territory. Let's say that, through Valerie, Albertina managed to do all of this, settling in the Rocchia house: a place more insane than that you couldn't find. La Rocchia was a very stoned, very punky, very Bolognese queer, a real character from alternative Bologna; with Antonia, now an operator at Lila, they would become the most famous DJ couple of that scene. In the meantime, Valerie too had become part of the royal family with the title of "Queen of the Two Sicilies," thus opening the realm of Bologna to the group as a third residence, together with those of Rome and Pistoia.

Ilaria and Anastasia had settled in the Grand Duchy of Pistoia, guests of some sensitive and open companions who we met at the Capo Rizzuto campsite. It was headed by three large apartments located in the historic center a few steps from the Piazza del Duomo, which soon became the most popular gay hangout in Tuscany. The comrades from Pistoia all belonged to the Lotta Continua area, and the relationship with them opened up a sphere of collaboration and communication with all the local alternative reality, from Florence to Pisa, from Prato to Carrara. Pistoia became the reference point not only for the royal family but for the entire creative side of the entire LGBT movement; it was the seat of so-called crazy people. In one of the three apartments the sanctuary of the "Madonna of the Scabies, protector of sick, broken-down, and badly damaged faggolas" was also born. A mannequin dressed as a nun was venerated which was supposed to attract the various infections that our promiscuity exposed us to: scabies, syphilis, crabs, discharge, etc. Ceremonies were improvised, between the sacred and the profane, with vestments, rituals, choreography, songs, and dance. Propitiatory processions were set up which, after having passed through the rooms of the sanctuary, continued in the street up to Piazza del Duomo, where the people had by now become accustomed to our delirious performances. The Queen mother and the other sisters, strengthened by their madness, thought of organizing another national convention of the gay movement right there.

The conference took place from the 1st to the 4th of May 1981 on the premises of the former Breda, an abandoned factory, part of which was destined for cultural initiatives. In those days a small town like Pistoia filled up with queers. The city was colored in fuchsia, marked far and wide by stiletto heels, enlivened by leafleting, songs, dances, and processions. The conference, of which I have really fond memories, had a surprise ending. In fact, it ended with a great collective orgy in which, in addition to the queers gathered in the city, a substantial representation of the healthy and curious local youth participated. For the final party we had been given an old, vacant theater; the main floor free of seats was reserved for dancing while delirious faggolas performed onstage. But it was under the stage that the joyous party continued; in its dressing rooms similar to niches, the crime was consummated. In the hall we danced, drank, and fought. Intrigued by the event, many young men were eager to enter. In the beginning, a dispute arose between the irreducible feminist queers who wanted the party to be only gay, and to remain so, and those who, instead, wanted it open to everyone. The second position also prevailed because the curious guys were kind, calm, and promising.

Me and my sister, the Princess of the East, started the dance. Gussied up and cross-dressed, we had picked up two guys with whom we hid ourselves under the stage: the spark that many of the guests were waiting for. Most of those present converged under the stage where the absence of light helped to transform everything into a large *dark room*. I also remember that the relationship with the guy with whom I had descended into hell became a triangle. He lit up his lighter and in the glow I recognized Aunt Felicity next to me. In those days the three apartments had been transformed into "hostels of gayness," where anything and everything went on.

Lesbians and/or Feminists

The almost complete absence of lesbians was evident, not only in Pistoia but in all areas of the gay movement. The only lesbians present were Ugenio, Liviana, Sandra, and two or three others. I can't say exactly what the cause of that absence was. I believe that in that period most of the lesbians referred to the feminist movement in which they perhaps had more reasons to recognize themselves. I knew many lesbian companions, all members of feminist collectives or groups, and all of them spoke of the gay movement as something interesting but essentially different from their path, an experience that did not directly interest them and above all did not completely convince them.

For a while I believed that the lesbian experience was an integral part of feminism. Indeed, I thought that the two experiences overlapped, becoming the same thing. I{m} was convinced that lesbianism was more a passage of feminism than a choice. I thought this because the practice of coming out was not yet very widespread and therefore I saw very few lesbians who were out. For being naive, I still didn't grasp a precise dimension of the consistency of the lesbian experience; this naivety was not only mine but widespread, given that all of us needed a bigger movement that would welcome us rather than cover us up. If my ingenuity made me only give in as gay to those who shamelessly manifested it, the same thing was true for lesbians, with the difference that an effeminate fehg was recognizable while a woman was less masculinized: I didn't consider her a lesbian because many women, and the majority of feminists, rejecting the forms of classical femininity, were more masculine, that's all!

Lucia, a lesbian companion of the Psychology Collective with whom I had become a very good friend, one day asked me to accompany her to the Old Government, the building occupied by women. I knew I{f} wouldn't be able to enter but she tried anyway by dragging me into the internal courtyard where, however, I{f} was escorted outside by the patrol. The Old Government was an important reference point for all women without distinction because in there, together with the meetings, parties, and various activities, there was also a consulting room and a legal service. I often happened to accompany friends and companions for the most varied matters, always assuming that for me that place was inaccessible.

The whole gay movement consisted of no more than two hundred people, whose small number allows me to recall the names of almost all the participants. The usual reckless, daring vagabonds and vagablondes who animated demonstrations and events. Usually, the number of participants grew gradually after the departure of the processions, enlarging them, in the same way it worked within the movement, passing, after the initial departure, from a few hundred to the thousands of today. We expected the others to come forward and then jump into the fray and blend in. And slowly we increased in number until June 1980, when we organized the first pride celebration in Bologna. From there began a journey that two years later would lead to the assignment of the Cassero by the Municipality. The Faggy Collective and to a certain extent all of us grew up on that experience: the battle for the assignment of the Cassero was common, deeply felt by all of us without distinction.

That pride celebration was born, grew, and matured in our hearts and consciences. All the commitment and militancy converged in a unitary and harmonious way toward the deadline of June 28, 1980, in the same days as the Ustica massacre. While we shouted our *pride* in Piazza Maggiore, yet another Italian massacre was taking place in the skies between Bologna and Palermo, with no guilty parties, and, once again, Bologna was paying the highest price in terms of human lives.

I left for the Bolognese pride festival with René, first stopping at the Bob Marley concert at the San Siro stadium in Milan: one of the most engaging concerts I've ever seen. Thousands and thousands of people dancing happily in a stadium that looked like Rio during carnival. The homophobic wave that would later spread among the Rastas had not yet manifested itself, so the Milanese event proved to be engaging and shocking from all points of view.

My house at that time was a real gay center, both for its location in San Lorenzo and because it was in front of Anomalia, the headquarters of Narciso. That house had always seen a great coming and going of people, at first comrades, freaks, artists, poets, stoners, and later gays, lesbians, transvestites, and transsexuals. The two targets (if they can be defined that way) met, intertwined, amalgamated; we were still a collective born within the opposition movement!

Every now and then Lud returned from his travels, and seeing him again was always exciting because he brought new things and surprises every time. From travels in the East, he had passed to those in the West, alternating periods in London with others in Berlin. Often when he stopped in Italy, I went to spend a few days at his house in the Castelli Romani, where an intriguing situation had arisen between companions, local faggolas, and some quiet and relatively nice little chavs. During the day, hanging out in the municipal park (the usual meeting place for alternatives) oscillated with long walks in the woods surrounding the lake. Between the green of the forest and the blue of the lake, our blunders were joined by considerable quantities of drugs, usually weed and various hallucinogens which accentuated the extraordinary beauty of the place. Then little by little, from the more or less light drugs we began to move on to something much more demanding. In addition to Lud, the group included Biscia, a crazy, fat, comical, and bold girly queer, and Brama, a quieter, sweeter, but just as crazy queer, both with a decided tendency to get upset. Every day we fell in love with someone and always lost our temper with sighs, screams, and melodrama. It was Lud himself, returning from a trip to London, who was one of the first to inaugurate that fabulous punk phase with absurd lewks, from the cut and color of his hair, to clothes and accessories.

Punk

When punk exploded, or rather when I noticed it in the late seventies, it was like an electric shock. The out-of-tune notes of the Sex Pistols, the catchier Clash, Dead Kennedys, and Ramones, up to the local Bloody Riot brought us back on track, in the mix, exactly where it was right and above all nice to be. A completely new revolutionary and revolutionized scene in which certain rigidities staggered, because that screamed more than longed-for anarchy rejected and destroyed power relations, of any kind: man-woman, rich-poor, good-bad, beautiful-ugly. Everything was in that experience, even what we had never dared to do; after all, at that point we had nothing left to lose. That critical conscience that had accompanied us for a decade was tired and fatigued, perhaps because it had run at a sustained speed, much faster than the one at which reality traveled. Disenchantment and disappointment for our dreams, for that fantasy that had not destroyed power but had let itself be destroyed by it, becoming fashion, merchandise, marketing. We were pissed off at the answers we didn't get, at that reality that had started to make us cold again. Punk was the last scream that broke the silence. Someone called it the "funeral ceremony." Inside it, homosexuality, or rather queerness, was absolutely not a problem; indeed, it seemed to be a part of it. Its strong point was the music with its bands, those hallucinatory concerts made up of exciting banging in which, while moshing, anything happened and, drunk or stoned, amidst spitting, sweat, and dust, one made out with the many Sid Viciouses who crowded the dance floors. Some concerts are unforgettable, such as those by the Ramones in Castel Sant'Angelo, the Clash in Florence, or Devo in Piazza Maggiore in Bologna, all events that did not leave anyone indifferent. One of the first local punk concerts I attended, the ones in which people spat while they moshed, was that of the Candegina Gang with Jo Squillo in a cinema in the San Lorenzo district, where formations of various Roman bands were also visible.

From My Generation to the Blank Generation, from the Who to the Sex Pistols—punk was not just an aesthetic fact; it was a sign and meaning of rebellion, dissatisfaction, irreducible insubordination. Even if it might seem the opposite, it was a desire and a need to live. In the last outpost to be overwhelmed by the bulldozer of the eighties, under the screeching crawlers of Reaganism, Craxism, and Wojtyłism, one could hear "Anarchy in the UK." I too had the black leather jacket that I called my "second skin" because it held out for decades: I wore it until a few years ago, always the same. I kept a thousand pins attached to it, meanings and signifiers of my rebellion. Tight black trousers ripped and held together by dozens of safety pins, my inseparable All Stars, the piebald shoes that let me travel the world until they appeared in shop windows at fivefold prices. The power of Fashion!

Local punk descended directly from London, even if I had already perceived the signs of that experience in the words of Lou Reed, of the Velvet Underground, of Iggy Pop, and of all that New York scene which had already been fermenting for some time. However, not everything that happened in New York was known; above all, fashion or aesthetic reflections reached us, while little or nothing was known about its struggles and its radicalism. Everything that had happened on the evening of June 28, 1969, for example, I didn't know about. I knew there had been a riot, that crazy queers had done it, but Sylvia Rivera, her drag friends, transvestites, transsexuals, rioted proudly and fabulously that night in front of a Stonewall I had never heard of. I was able to find out more during my first stay in New York, in 1989, when Lina, who had been living there for a few years, told me about the *veterans*, the protagonists of the revolt who lived through it. Later I was able to contact them and invite Sylvia Rivera with her partner Julia Murray to the 2000 World Pride in Rome. Paradoxically she was not allowed to go onstage to greet that important demonstration. Precisely the one who, by throwing a bottle, had triggered the revolt that about a million people were celebrating that day; only a blitz from me, Marcella, and Valerie allowed Sylvia to greet everyone. As they say: history repeats itself!

I had received a distorted and incomplete image of New York. In fact, I believed that the crazy queers who turned against the police were the same ones who roamed Andy Warhol's Factory, friends and perhaps lovers of Lou Reed, Iggy Pop, or of super cool Joe Dallesandro. Later I would read their interviews that categorically denied their homosexuality, dismissing it all with a cut-and-dried "It was just fashion": a cheap artistic license, including David Bowie with his "Queen Bitch" (notoriously dedicated to Lou Reed), who made me believe it. The revolt had been made by real people, by those on the street, by the oppressed. It was bare life expressed in the throwing of a bottle at the policemen and not the exuberance of the artists. It was the latter who attracted and drew inspiration from that naked life and not the other way around. Years later I became a friend of Penny Arcade, protagonist of *Women in Revolt* and denizen of the Factory who revealed to me many backgrounds of that experience that opened doors to the postmodern, trampling precisely on that very naked life.

The '80s Began

Lud, Biscia, and Brama moved to London. Lud, after a mystical and celestial vision, chose a spiritual retreat, a personal journey of profound research. Today with the long beard of an old wise man he lives in the quiet of the Roman countryside; he creates and paints beautiful icons and writes verses. Biscia was among the first people that AIDS snatched from us, and we lost track of Brama, probably within one of the many communities that were beginning to swarm our universe.

It's difficult for me to maintain a chronological order in the succession of events, many and extraordinary. Telling them takes me far away; every time I have to pick up the thread of the conversation where I left off and it's practically impossible.

Our travels intensified, and the most traveled axis was the Rome-Bologna one, the city where everything seemed to converge in that period. But also, all those places where our gaiety found enjoyment. We managed to dye purple—the color of transgression—even the Carnival of Venice, the party that intrigued us, mirrored us, belonged to us. We rejoiced in dressing up and paradoxically, just at carnival, we threw off our masks.

During one of our sojourns in Bologna (March 8, 1980, to be precise), romance blossomed between me and Valerie. It all happened at the home of Cocò, Marco's partner, while her birthday was being celebrated; Marco, Raffa (nicknamed "the feminist"), Ugenio, Liviana, and Valerie of course were there. At that time, I self-financed by selling orange micro-tips (LSD pills), sales of which in any case were associated with experimentation. That time we took one collectively, we danced to the rhythm of Patti Smith, Lou Reed, Iggy Pop, we had fun, and a strange feeling developed between Valerie and me. It must have been the acid, the party, or International Women's Day, but it was the first time I was able to establish a deeper and less conventional form of communication with her. I had always seen her as full of herself, haughty, serious, not inclined to communicate, but this time she seemed different, relaxed and smiling. A strange thing happened, because Ugenio, who was deeply in love with Liviana, was suddenly saddened by our behavior. Because of that attitude she led us to the room where Liviana and Carletto, a handsome hetero companion, were making love on a double bed. Carletto was perhaps the only guy in that slew of crazy girls. I don't know exactly what each of us thought but we were all enchanted, standing at the door observing the scene. I don't remember exactly how long that strange moment lasted because acid distorts your knowledge of time, but I remember that Valerie suddenly took matters into her own hands: lying down on the bed between the two, she invited us to do the same. Those two meters that separated me from the thalamus seemed like kilometers; I was finally profaning that ritual from which I had always felt excluded.

Liviana and Carletto were embarrassed and petrified, in the middle of an invaded and violated bed. The acid mounted violently, sending strange, intense, sometimes disturbing emotions despite Valerie reassuring me, telling me that nothing had happened, that everything was going well, very well indeed. We had succeeded in desecrating the bed of privilege, the heterosexual *castra castrorum*!

At the end of the party, Valerie invited me to her house, which was not far away. As I left, I realized that she had a new attitude that she had never had before toward me: I felt that she was protective and available. Once we got there, however, my *trip* began to falter. It was going badly; it was the first time I had a bad trip, a distressing feeling because it seemed I would never leave that impressive dimension. The walls seemed to squeeze and oppress me; I had the sensation that there was garbage in the bed, my jaws locked, and I could no longer speak, while Valerie reproached me by repeatedly telling me to stop pretending to be queen bee and to get off the pedestal on which I had perched. I looked at her, trying to communicate my discomfort, my helplessness in managing my *trip*, but she didn't seem to understand. As soon as day broke, I ran away in anguish and fortunately met Raffa, with whom I took the train to Rome. I wanted to go home, I needed to be calm in my own place; I still couldn't speak and luckily Raffa understood everything and she supported me. Raffa, known as "the feminist" for her way of dressing, was a seventeen-year-old boy: sweet, calm, and so effeminate that I only realized after some time of hanging around with her that she wasn't a ciswoman. Raffa came to stay at my house when he confessed to his parents that he was gay, a difficult choice at that time that many of us were slowly beginning to make. The reaction was always the same: screams, curses, phone calls to relatives, psychiatrists . . . until being locked in your bedroom or, in the worst-case scenario, thrown out of the house . . . because you were homosexual!

After a few days of cohabitation Raffa fell in love with me, which often happened in that period. When others fell in love with me, I took it lightly and above all with imagination. I didn't see any problem with it; on the contrary I found it interesting for interpersonal communication and, since in that period sex was the panacea, I let myself go, but I realized later that in doing so I made the situation worse, especially for those who were truly in love. It happened again with Max, Roberto, Marco, Alberto, and many others up to Marc André, a Parisian dancer who continued to write to me until recently.

The important event of 1980 was the beginning of my love story with Valerie, but that same year there were other events that directly or indirectly touched me. The royal family consolidated and I began my first transformation experiments, at first only aesthetic but gradually also physical. The idea of being able to transform my body was gaining more and more ground. I saw it as research, an in-depth study, a challenge. Being a woman, the deep and ancient desire that had always accompanied me, began to seem less arcane and more and more possible. A new and fantastic path was beginning to open up for me, not that of becoming a woman but that of being trans: it was a real lightning bolt moment!

The thing that frightened me about all this was not so much the steep path as the health risk to which hormone treatments would expose me; at the time they weren't supported by any tests or medical care at all.

My comings and goings with Bologna were intense and it so happened that I took the train back to Rome exactly two days before the Bologna station was blown up. The fascist attack on August 2 shocked me because of the many deaths, the damage, and because it could have happened to me too. I remember the phone calls where Valerie told me about the gruesome scenery of the station; she was among the volunteers who offered to help out. Then there was that violent earthquake that struck the area where I'm from, devastating it at the same time I was intent on kissing a sweet flower on Lake Bracciano, which, illuminated by the moon, suddenly rippled under the impact of the distant and violent shock. And in December of the same year on a cold and snowy Bolognese evening, in black leather trousers, leopard-print fur, and a blonde wig, I went out to beat the streets cross-dressed for the first time, while in Catania at the same time Lapillo dell'Open Mind was born, which, twenty-three years later in 2003, as an objector in civil service at MIT, would completely blow my mind.

Valerie

A few days after that unforgettable *bad trip*, Albertina burst into the house, excited and amused; she confided in me that Valerie had fallen in love with me. I{m} was surprised; I didn't think that the "hallucinating" night had the opposite effect for her. Albertina incited me; she urged me to make a decision. She saw my probable affair with Valerie as a very nice thing that would have strengthened the relationships within the royal family, between Rome and Bologna, between the fehgs of the movement, between the fehgs and the transsexuals. In short, she saw it as a strategically rather than sexually important relationship. I didn't even have the time to think about it when the intercom rang, the door opened, and the house was infiltrated by an enormous bouquet of red roses held by the highly jeweled and slender hand of Valerie, who, with attached suitcases, handbags, trays of pastries, and bottles of champagne, invaded our home. In reality, she had announced her arrival with a telegram which I had not interpreted literally. I{m} let myself go, fascinated and intrigued by that strange new adventure.

Meetings, reunions, and exchanges increased, becoming a cheerful daily practice. We needed to talk to each other, see each other, meet each other, touch each other, be certain that we were a physical entity as well as a cultural and political one.

In Rome at Narciso or in all those places where there were interesting appointments, friends met with sisters from other cities, from other collectives. Physical places were like modern chat lines or mailing lists, where you could meet, explore, discuss, and even pick someone up. Regardless of their political and cultural significance, those places had the function that discos or bathhouses have today. Not already established on the scene, emerging gay people had not created those circuits which today are normal and all in all taken for granted. The Bolognese Faggy Collective was active in the Emilian capital and soon became a catalyst for a series of initiatives and battles. The soul of the collective was Lola Pugnales, a Chilean queer who escaped from Pinochet; Beppe Ramina who was slaying hearts among all of us; Prussi, as tall as the Asinelli Tower and DJ of the emerging Bolognese punk scene; Medusa; Nessa; and Antonio Frainer.

Mixed and well tuned, there were also several trans that I began to get to know better right in Bologna. Perhaps because it was smaller or perhaps because it was freer, perhaps because I was with Valerie, but in that city, transsexuals were closer than elsewhere. I had the sensation that they were part of the city's fabric. I perceived a greater acceptance, and above all a more rooted and widespread education and respect. The close encounter with them thrilled me. Until that moment I had seen transsexuality as an experience far from me, unattainable, and in many ways impossible. Yet the more I got to know the trans world and the more I felt it was mine, the more I discovered that path and the more I understood that I could follow it too. Seeing those who were considered divine in those times up close, being able to touch them and talk to them, was different from having to observe them from the window of a speeding car.

One night we were eating hot croissants at the Lurido—a bakery that was open at night in via Borgonuovo where all the Bolognese night owls came to refresh themselves—when Eva showed up. I{m} was literally shocked by her beauty. The myth had already been created around her, but she was not yet a public figure. A reverential silence fell inside the oven as "Venus in furs" passed by who, half-naked under a very long white fur coat, dispensed smiles and greetings. At the Lurido you could meet everyone, from the old school Bolognese such as Griaffa, Cocis, Moselli, and Nadia, up to the fabulous newborns like Massimina, Erika, and Messalina. Bologna hosted not only divinities or trans who were more or less defined and definable in their journey but a varied range of characters and personalities who made that scene the most exhilarating of the time: cross-dressing queers, actresses looking for an audience, queers eager for emotions, intellectuals looking for insights, artists looking for inspiration, activists hoping for revolution. Eccentric characters who had transformed Bolognese nights into a lively local festival, and the Fiera, a historic night meeting place, into a sort of cheerful parlor-brothel.

Being trans then was a completely different thing than it is today. There was still no law 164 which recognized and allowed sex change operations, transitioning was not yet supported by specialists and consultants, there was no work other than prostitution, there was no legal assistance, there were only so many roundups and constantly being stopped by the police. Often from the Lurido or in other trans places, news arrived of someone who had been arrested or warned with an order of expulsion, fined for cross-dressing or obscene acts. At night when you were on the street, police raids were a nightmare. Taking that path was like taking a leap in the dark; the almost automatic loss of rights, often of documents and drivers' licenses, was recognized only by the numerous customers who populated the streets at night and covered you in gold. It may be that hunger sharpens one's ingenuity, but despite all those limitations, those trans queens were fabulous.

One of my most beautiful memories of Bologna remains that of Piazza Maggiore. Its size was unique, the destination of all the movement. Its colors, sounds, flavors, emotions, and the air we breathed are imprinted on me! From a distance I had dreamed of it through the songs of Francesco Guccini and Claudio Lolli, and being inside it was like beating with the heart of the movement in rhythm with my imagination.

It began to fill up in the early afternoon, and as evening fell it filled up entirely, overflowing with humanity and many beautiful people. We used to sit on the steps of San Petronio, on those of the Podestà, lying on the Crescentone in the center of the square, walking around them, through and inside a very colorful, precious embroidery. There were those who played, those who sang or recited poetry, those who danced or did theater, those who got high and those who were tripping; assemblies were improvised, debates with related quarrels, spats and fuck yous. Improvised games involved many of those present. Choirs, jokes, and slogans among those sitting by San Petronio and those opposite under the Pavaglione, ring-around-the-rosies, conga lines, tag, and simply chasing each other, all seemed to recall that big laughter that was supposed to bury the world. In addition to being beautiful, the people were calm, including the old communist or anarchist comrades with whom we had passionate and often heated chats; the old Bolognese shared spaces only on condition that we debated politically. Many of them struggled to understand some of our lifestyles so we all lit up passionately and ended up in front of a nice bottle of Lambrusco.

I was staying a few meters away as Valerie's guest in the occupied house in via Clavature. That house was an integral part of that great embroidery, an extension of the square, but over time it separated from the square. Indeed, it separated itself from Bologna and from reality. Thinking about it, even the square began to separate slowly and inexorably from reality, from the city, from history. Many were beginning to feel that great laughter would not continue because of the reality that was beginning to open up, and we had very little to laugh about.

The one in via Clavature was a building with some apartments occupied inside. When I got there, its parabola was at its maximum, but a little later it began an inexorable descent, and the signs of decline began to manifest themselves. Valerie, along with a couple of crackpots, occupied a first-floor apartment at the entrance to which was a heap of used clothes thrown on the floor whose provenance was never made clear to me. Dozens of posters, flyers, and punk fanzines of concerts, get-togethers, and events were tacked to the walls. In Valerie's room the scenography changed completely and instead of the Sex Pistols fanzines there were huge posters of Marilyn, Greta Garbo, and Marlene Dietrich; instead of used clothes there were wigs, stiletto heels, leopard miniskirts, fishnet stockings, and the ever-present soundtrack by Edith Piaf while, when the doors were open, the voices of Nico, Lou Reed, or the Ramones could be heard. On the first floor there were two other apartments in addition to Valerie's, and two more upstairs. The people who lived there knew each other and the interchange was continuous and lively. Two other queers lived in the apartments on the second floor: Denny and Rica, both very pretty and distraught as snakes.

The house in via Clavature felt the same rhythms as the square, and in fact there was a constant coming and going of people. I later understood that it was mainly due to the sale of all kinds of substances, which is why police raids became more and more frequent. In about two years of attendance, that coming and going was completely transformed, from the gay and creative catwalk to an increasingly nervous and agitated one that hinted at the by now obvious relationship with a certain type of substance, an increasingly devastating relationship.

On the stairs among the many writings there was one that struck me because I found it on the walls all over Bologna: "Raf Punk against heroin." It was Giampi Velena's anarchist punk band who today has become Helena. The Bolognese apartment, like mine in Rome and those in Pistoia, was a veritable seaport frequented by gays, trans people, transvestites, queens, and princesses. In reality, there were many other logistical bases where one settled according to need: houses by the sea, in the mountains, in historic centers, and in all those places where life became more pleasant and interesting. After all, wanting everything at once and being extremely nomadic and untethered by ties or commitments, like gypsies with the wind in our sails we headed toward the lands of fabulousness.

It often happened that we camped somewhere in a group: a tribe of delirious sciroccos who confused spectacle and reality. In the company of the Duchess Romanov, the rooms became stages and houses, film sets into which actresses, prima donnas, and extras entered—all absolutely protagonists in any case. From the via Clavature apartment, the royal family made its entrance into the square where, despite the very crowded dance floor, they never went unnoticed.

Usually, the procession was led by Her Highness Albertina, Queen of Rome, one and a half meters tall: bald, heavily made up to the nape of her neck, with overalls in indecipherable colors and the ever-present walking stick. Her short and quick gait, synchronized with the undulation of her hips and the sway of her head, rotating 360 degrees, kept everything under control, especially the beautiful boys or the bad guys. Then came Teresa, the Duchess of Abruzzo, who experimented with her first outfits as a permanent couple with Tina, the Duchess of the two Sardinias; eternally made up and stoned, they infected each other, often bursting into loud laughter. For them everything became a cheerful and light-hearted game. Every now and then one of the two could be heard calling the other: "Run! Come and see what this one's is like!" I saw them lost in their delirium, laughing and making out with someone they met randomly. We followed, hand in hand, Valerie and I: me a bit Amelie, a bit Alice in Wonderland, and Valerie, proud and impeccable, very similar to Sophia Loren. With her Angela Davis hairdo, she sported her sixties eyewear collection and all her eye-catching costume jewelry. To close the procession was Ilaria, our proud and austere Queen Mother with her turbans made of rags improvised in the moment and the soft makeup of a true lady. At her side Anastasia Romanov, always barefoot, who wore the most precious clothes borrowed from other more or less truthful duchesses, dresses that she wore with a mixture of royalty and slovenliness. Ilaria and Anastasia held hands with René, the Princess of the East, who remained the most convinced of all. For this particular inclination of hers, Anastasia had dedicated one of her shows to them entitled *They Looked at Me*.

Several courtesans joined the "family stroll," and the procession continued making its way through the festive crowd, squandering itself in bows, hugs, kisses, screams, and songs. From time to time, it assumed the characteristics of a circus, a political procession, of a parade or a popular festival. Much depended on the quantity of drugs we had ingested, their type and quality, but also on a robust alcoholic base since flasks of Sangiovese circulated in the square like candy. The cheerful gang had the ability to involve and transform the scene into theater and political action. While Tina and Teresa entertained the bystanders with groping and laughter, Ilaria let herself go in her suffragette rallies, and the rest of us arranged ourselves in a choreographic way to give life to the scene in which Anastasia entered and surprised everyone. She invented dialogue on the spot starting from the situation, and in the show she directed she managed to involve everyone present, in a spectator-actor role exchange game. I still have many newspaper articles featuring the royal family in frenzied action. I would have found many of her deeds in poetic form in *Altri Libertini*, the beautiful book by Pier Vittorio Tondelli, one of the narrators of that time and place in Bologna.

Within the gay scene we were considered crazy; we were given the nickname "the Girls in Stiletto Heels." Many were those who followed and flanked us, while others saw us in a poor light: they were the serious ones whom we called "the Mustaches," who asserted that our behavior and our attitudes sent a misleading message, a bad example. We were, according to them, the usual transvestites who drew attention to themselves by diverting from far more important things. This divergence was particularly emphasized in an assembly in the headquarters of the then PCI in via de' Giubbonari in Rome; the meeting was also attended by a young but always skeletal Piero Fassino at the beginning of his political career. On that occasion I met Vanni Piccolo for the first time, later renamed Messalina due to her marked propensity for prostitution which made her resemble Nero's famous mistress. It was one of the first assemblies considered serious, the prelude to a new course. "The Girls in Stiletto Heels" had by now had their day. There was a need for programs, strategies, and campaigns that only the seriousness of "The Mustaches" could support.

At a national assembly in Rome held at the Convento Occupato where the two factions were quite evident, we gave birth to a blasphemous procession that crossed the length and breadth of the hall. Ilaria felt like Our Lady of Sorrows; she opened the procession by singing her sacred songs and improbable rosaries, followed by all of us heartbroken as in a sad Good Friday ritual. "The Mustaches" were pissed off because our performance disturbed them by preventing them from discussing serious programs and things. A new way of being gay and of doing politics was emerging more and more. That dividing line between serious and crazy, macho and transvestite, between realists and dreamers, became more and more marked. Since history repeats itself, as always the first ones won, who over time would claim the creation and history of the entire queer experience, according to some closely connected to the construction of a gay accessibility network. Let's just say that the 1980s marked the end of one phase and the beginning of another. I can't define which is better and which is worse. Perhaps they were the consequence of each other but, speaking with the heart and not with the head, I claim the very high value of the first, of that movement of mad and deranged women who, with their madness and their visibility, blew up the jambs of power, opened the gap through which everyone then passed. It is a passage from the eighties that I find very well represented in one of the most beautiful works of gay culture, *The Rocky Horror Picture Show* with Tim Curry, in the final scene in which the protagonist, betrayed and disappointed after her delirious experience, between tears that dissolve her makeup, says: "It's time to go home." Craxi, Reagan, Wojtyła, heroin, and AIDS were pressing us; we could only go home. But having destroyed our home and family, we were disoriented.

Theater

I don't want to make a mistake, but it was precisely in that assembly in via de' Giubbonari that Albertina made a good speech, and one of those present, if I'm not mistaken Maurizio A., exclaimed: "How nice, even transvestites can talk." At that point Romanov jumped up and gave life to the show entitled *How Nice, Even Transvestites Can Talk*, in the spirit of *Pertini's Secretary* and the famous *Madonna of Pompeii* which had consecrated him as an actor of the movement. The leitmotif of the work was always the same, which was the suffering and eventful story of a Neapolitan gay man and his mother who decides to ask for grace from the Madonna of Pompeii. The length of the show varied according to the context; I remember when it went on and on until the following morning. Once in Piazza Maggiore three distinguished, elegant, and curious ladies who had stopped were involved in the show to involuntarily play the part of three prostitutes and an equally distinguished gentleman was hired to play the part of a transvestite. Ciro, being on a continuous tour, created hilarious situations around him in which I was often involved, all around Italy but also abroad, like that time on a beautiful Greek island where we stayed for almost two months, guests in houses on the island in exchange for entertainment and liveliness. That holiday was beautiful because we got rid of our ballast by letting ourselves go to the sea and the Greek wind through fairy tales and magic.

Romanov's career ended in Bologna on June 28, 1982, with her famous public blow job.

In addition to Anastasia in the gay movement there were other very good actors who made committed and delirious theater. Mario Sucic—with whom I{f} would later go live— staged *Molly*, a shadow woman of other times, indeed a timeless woman, who retraced all of contemporary history by intertwining it with the gay one. The character en travesti, despite her grim seriousness, made us die laughing. Molly, like so many others, abandoned the stage, closing a parenthesis that we could define as the gay theater experience. Then there was Cassandra, a cross-dressing queer from the experimental laboratories born around Basaglia's experience in Trieste. And Luana, a queer from Salerno who did mime and dance. Before that there had been Mario Mieli's COM (Homosexual Milanese Collective) with their famous *Traviata Norma*, the COP (Homosexual Paduan Collective), which later became Pumitrozzole from which Platinette also descends. Some of the COPs managed the Wizard of Oz in Rome, a well-known alternative bistro in Trastevere where exhibitions, debates, and shows were held. That place was the scene of a lively quarrel between me, my partner, and Gabriella Ferri during the period in which we were dating. We were there at dinner, drinking and smoking too much until Gabriella went into a rage. She wanted to make out with me, but due to her drunkenness she did it in an aggressive and violent way, arousing the jealousy of my partner. A fight broke out between us and Ferri, who began to throw plates and glasses on the floor. Upon the arrival of the police called by bystanders, I quickly fled.

Among the great actors of gay theater, certainly a place of excellence is occupied by Alfredo Cohen, one of the founders of FUORI!, of which today I know all traces are lost. His show entitled *Mezza femmena e za' Camilla* (Half a Woman and Aunt Camilla) was a real text of gay liberation. The show toured throughout Italy for a long time and was revived at the Trastevere theater for years. It was the story of a transvestite queer named Mezza Femmena (Half Woman) in a small town in Abruzzo, with her dreams, her nightmares, her desires, and her madness in a crescendo of rhythm that toward the end of the show became a real trance in which Alfredo rolled on the ground and, writhing in simulated labor pains and orgasms, he cried, laughed, and raved. The first time I attended one of his shows was in 1977 in Naples at a demonstration by the Radical Party to remember Giorgiana Masi, killed shortly before. I hung out with Alfredo Cohen for the entire period I was with Valerie because there was a deep friendship between them as witnessed by the song "Valery" that Alfredo dedicated to her, later taken up by Milva who changed the name to "Alexanderplatz" and made it a great success.

There was also a more cultured theater, less politicized but still insertable in a poetics of homosexual liberation. Erio Masina with his *All in Black with No Make-Up*, or *Jennifer's Five Roses* by Annibale Ruccello whom I had the pleasure of seeing at the Convento Occupato in Rome. It was on that occasion that Felice, a Neapolitan friend of mine who worked in the company, introduced me to Ruccello. One of the theatrical shows that struck me most at the time was Lindsay Kemp's *Flowers*, based on Jean Genet's *Our Lady of the Flowers*. We interviewed Lindsay Kemp in the dressing rooms of the Elysée as the Narciso Collective; the interview was later published in *Lambda*.

Another place where it was possible to see little shows from a cultured and busy theater was at Dominò's bistro near via de' Coronari in the very center of Rome. Dominò was a particular character belonging to a previous generation and therefore no longer very young; she was someone who experimented with forms of cross-dressing and I don't know to what extent also with transsexualism . . . today we would say queer!

The theater was not the only artistic expression of the movement: poets and writers offered their vision of the world and their ideas, including Francesco Gnerre, the shy and charming protagonist of that gay scene. There was also a sort of experimental cinema. I remember the filming of *Il Moretto*, the film directed by a Swiss queer who wanted to document the antics of the gay movement in Italy. The scenes were almost always shot in the evening, usually in the queer areas of the capital such as Piazza dei Cinquecento, Monte Caprino, Circus Maximus, Piazza Navona, and Castelporziano beach. In the delirium of becoming cinema divas, we presented ourselves to a call for extras as queers in a hotel on the Aventine Hill for a film with Enrico Montesano. Responsible for the selection was Marcellona, who at the time had not yet become a woman. It was the first meeting with the person with whom in the years to come I would share perhaps the most important experience not only for the two of us, but for all transgender people: the epic story of MIT. When we introduced ourselves, she scrutinized us from head to toe and succinctly said: "We're looking for faggots, not trannies."

1981 and the First Gay New Year

1981 entailed a series of events in which I was involved in various ways: civil service, my father's death, and the prison experience. I was among those who preferred civil service—which was still called "conscientious objection"—rather than the exemption under article 28, i.e., the one that was assigned for homosexuality. At that time article 28 was not yet a widespread practice. I therefore preferred to opt for civil service which, according to the times established by the law in force and its implementation, was reduced to six months, which I carried out at the Roman headquarters of Italia Nostra, the body for the protection of cultural, artistic, and environmental heritage. During that time my father was diagnosed with cancer and was gone within a few months.

On November 19 (the date that has remained fixed in my memory) they arrested me for indecency in a public place, an incredible and shocking experience that marked me deeply. It all happened around 7 P.M. in Piazza dei Cinquecento at the exit from the teaching office, where I had gone to attend a lesson that would have facilitated the last exam of my degree course. I was with René when we stopped for two guys who had asked us for information. I was already wearing clothes that were whimsical enough to be defined as unisex and even a light touch of makeup. We were sitting on a bench chatting with the two when a guy, whose shitty-ass face I'll never forget, came up to ask if he could sit there with us. When we refused, that ugly thug took out a whistle from his pocket, sending the signal to the team hidden in the hedges. A beam of powerful headlights was aimed at us and in a fraction of a second we found ourselves on the famous cart with the ugly thug telling us about all sorts of things. They took us to the Third Precinct, an infamous place where transgender people and transvestites were taken. After being locked up in a cell for about two hours, they made us sign a paper, handcuffed us, and took us to the station where we{f} were processed. From the station in via Genova, still in handcuffs, we were transferred to the Regina Coeli prison where, after more paperwork, we were locked up in solitary confinement cells. It was all incredibly absurd and terrifying. My cell, measuring one meter by two, dirty, cold, and dark, had—unlike René's—a peephole in the door from which, with a little acrobatics, I was able to stick my head out to look into the corridor. I heard René crying. After a while a voice from the corridor began to call: "Number eight! Bella!" Amazed and intrigued, I stuck my head out and in the next cell was Fiorella, a transsexual I later became friends with. She asked me why I was there, and I said I didn't know. She explained to me that this was solitary confinement, the famous holding cells where, in addition to the worst criminals, there were three cells reserved for transvestites. "Look at the door and you'll see it," she told me. I could barely see the posted card that had my full name, student number, and the words "transvestite{m}." After the initial shock we recovered our humor, thanks also to Fiorella who had been there for twenty days by that point. We recited the parts of Anna Magnani and Giulietta Masina in the film *Nella città l'inferno* (Behind closed shutters; known in English as . . . *and the Wild Wild Women*) to while away the time and desperation. We stayed at the Mantellate three days and three nights; in the end they gave us a fast-track trial, and the ugly thug who had blown the whistle declared to the judge that René and I "sucked with our mouths"—these are the exact words of that infamous asshole—"***'s penis." I wish we had! At least there would have been a reason for three days of isolation in Regina Coeli!

In that cell I was able to observe the prolonged presence of transsexuals in solitary confinement. In fact, on the walls there were many writings made with cutlery, including a series of notches that marked the days of their stay: Massimina 43,

Bruna 35, Roberta 38, and so on. This was the treatment meted out to us, and from my experience, I could imagine the offenses. Insulting a public official, obscene acts, noncompliance with a warning, cumulative arrests after which another was triggered. All this was confirmed by Fiorella and a few years later by all the transsexuals I was to meet. All this happened in 1981, not in the nineteenth century.

Upon leaving, I gave myself three days in Naples with Valerie and Alfredo Cohen, who were there for a show. It was difficult to recover from that nightmare, to process that situation that would remain inside me forever.

We celebrated the end of 1981 in Milan at the gay New Year's Eve in Babylon where Romanov would perform. Before New Year's Eve we camped for a few days in the fiefdom of the Duchess of Sardinia in Modena, the city where Tina had settled. I celebrated New Year's without Valerie; our relationship was definitely in crisis. The cracks were due to my urgent need for space and the claustrophobia that a couple's relationship created in me. Valerie tended to cast me into the difficult and very embarrassing role of husband. She continued to speak of me as her man, arousing much perplexity and hilarity in all those who knew me. Despite the role assigned to me, Valerie advised me in dressing (or rather in cross-dressing), she helped me put on my makeup, she lent me her clothes, she moved me to action rather than stasis.

Arriving in Milan under a thick and romantic snowfall, we{f} looked for accommodation in separate estates. René and I—with the young princesses in need of human warmth more than domestic warmth—settled into a small but pretty house on the Navigli canals, close to the place where the grand ball would be held, a former cinema converted into a ballroom. A very nice situation, lively and gay in the right place. The audience consisted mostly of mad queers, transvestites, and militurds, along with sympathizers, friends, accomplices, and various "cryptoqueers"—closeted gays who weren't publicly out. The parties, like all the other gay situations, weren't very crowded, mostly frequented by people who shared a liberating path with us, who therefore felt close and supportive; there weren't yet those overflowing masses that crowd parties and clubs today. Many fehgs were hesitant; they didn't want to expose or compromise themselves. They were waiting for the fray to throw themselves in the middle and hide out there. The club industry, with its huge gay amusement park, hadn't yet discovered the gold vein that millions of faggolas around the world were offering. The circuit, if it could be defined as that, was concentrated in the big cities and limited to one or two clubs at the most. In Rome there was the Cage aux Folles near the Spanish Steps, the Saint James at Porta Pinciana, a secluded and dubious Super Star, at the time in an alley behind the Trevi Fountain; we were starting to talk about the Alibi, the Blue Angel, and the Easy Going, venues that became famous in the following years. I would say that from there that famous "trend" began to take hold, a word and concept that over the years would become an analytical tool, so to speak, for millions of faguettes to look at the world and interpret it. From there, a miserable, gooey, dull gay culture began to develop, let's say globalized because it was the fucking same in every corner of the planet, characterized by the ephemeral and the superficial, completely flattened on fashion and consumption. And I{f} am convinced that the worst thing is not so much the denial of our rights, but the lack of awareness of it.

Underground queer Rome had its own geography which included, in addition to its many gardens and monuments, the Ompos and the Gay House in Testaccio, historic meeting places whose experience is closely linked to Massimo Consoli.

Even if the war had never ended, and indeed a new one had begun, we entered a sort of postwar period where commitment and militancy were put behind us and the categorical imperative was to have fun, to take back everything that for centuries had been denied to us. An understandable and sacrosanct need which, however, did not escape the logic of profit that manages lives, experiences, and needs by transforming everything into goods. And after a while the goods are no longer enough, they don't satisfy us anymore and must be changed. Let's say that millions of fehgs all over the world, if they didn't represent a slice of the market, could have been destructive, perhaps dangerous for the structure of the system, so they had to be neutralized. What better weapon than ourselves!

The Milanese gay New Year was enlivened by nice music with the ever-present Patty Pravo, Mina, Loredana Bertè, sandwiched by the Police, who were all the rage with "Message in a Bottle," and the unsurpassed Clash, the most popular punk group in our area. I was just moshing to the rhythm of "Police on My Back" when I began jostling and doing so happily with a bunch of ugly, dirty, and bad punks from Bovisa. To tell the truth, they weren't ugly at all, and once you got to know them well, they weren't even bad. That evening, thanks to the party, alcohol, and drugs, a funny and very sensual feeling broke out between us which shortly after led us to the toilet of the club where, like good friends, we took out our stocks of various drugs for a year-end cocktail: weed, amphetamines, and the "white lady," the sweetening and numbing powder that increasingly took hold in our lives. We wanted to have fun, to forget the physical and above all our psychological discomfort. For this reason, the anesthetic was fine, to the point that in the times to come it would anesthetize us from everything: from reality, from life, from physical pain, but absolutely not from the inner one.

Although the people outside kept knocking, we stayed in that toilet for a long time. Between the majolica tiles and the white bathroom fixtures, the cheerfulness of the buzz and the languor of the anesthetic mixed beautifully. Sweet kisses, tender caresses, warm hugs, and, despite the Milanese cold, T-shirts and trousers flew, but they didn't come off because of those tight combat boots, and on that floor we celebrated the beginning of 1982 with a punk-flavored orgiastic rite. There were six of us in that bathroom, in an orgy that involved everyone present more or less equally. At first, I was the center of attention, but immediately after that amused and lighthearted gang leveled the situation and everyone touched everyone, everyone kissed everyone, a joyful and liberating masturbation session involved the defendants who, however, due to all that we had already swallowed, did not reach orgasm. Only among punks was sexuality experienced that way, without barriers, fears, or prejudices. Punks better than many others reflected an anarchist, liberating, and truly rebellious spirit; they better understood where power needed to be unhinged.

I ended New Year's Eve in the van of the punk band that I invited to warm up a bit in the house where I was a guest. But shortly after the group had warmed up, the mistress came home, a quiet and homely queer, who absolutely did not like that kind of presence, demonstrating all her disappointment that the punks collected with zeal, indulging in an animated battle of corn that was decorating a basket on the table. The queer screamed and was afraid to see the house ransacked. I{f} was then shown the door and sheltered by Robertino, a queer from the Milanese collective with whom

I had a worthy affair that lasted a few months. I remember on the evening of January 1st there was a theatrical performance of *The Rocky Horror Picture Show*, a real blast. As already in London, New York, San Francisco, the screening of the film took place with theatrical animation and the involvement of the whole audience, a tradition that was repeated regularly for some time.

Meanwhile my life flowed, sometimes like a river in full flow, sometimes like a stream in spring. I tried to study for the few exams I still needed for my degree and I also kept going to Narciso, which in the meantime had grown and been given a more serious structure. My house was always overcrowded and frequented by all the queers in the world. There was also Zanza, who in the meantime had become Giada and was weeping with joy at her newfound femininity. La Merdaiola, after an African exile, had moved to my house. Ugenio didn't live there but, having the keys to the house, he often arrived with punks, shockers, and sweet damsels he had picked up in Trastevere. Valerie also had the keys to the house, and often, when I woke up, I found her next to me. Paolo returned to Sardinia after graduating, but once a month he returned to Rome offering free medical visits to all the queers at home; Albertina in a thick nurse's coat acted as his assistant. It was a sort of "Faggola Grand Hotel" where drag queens, transvestites{f}, transsexuals, lesbians, artists, and bohemians came and went.

I wore makeup and cross-dressed more and more often, beating the streets far and wide all over Italy, but above all in the capital with my best friends, with whom I experimented with new and fascinating dimensions. Pleasant and sensual encounters increased in proportion to my release and the healthy effect of the seventies. I still attended demonstrations and marches, but I no longer felt the passion I had before; my political commitment was fading. It was an increasingly widespread feeling among those who came from those battles; I perceived my own tiredness and disenchantment.

More and more often I went to Bologna, where I also stayed for long periods. The squat in via Clavature, which was sinking more and more into decadence, reminded me of the Buendia house in some passages of *One Hundred Years of Solitude*. The Faggy Collective was concentrated on the Municipality giving the Cassero to the gays, which made their members a little more serious. In the spring they were granted a stand at the National Festival of Communist Women which took place in Montagnola Park. Inside the stand I exhibited my drawings, one of which was censored because, with a collage technique, I had stuck the close-up of a blow job on it, front and center. The exhibition of my paintings was repeated in June in the days leading up to the formal naming of the Cassero, and the initiative called me "the gay painter Porporino," as the short article under my photo stated in the article of *Europeo* titled "Living as a Homo, What's It to You?" The article was about the dispute between the municipal council of Bologna, which had given the Cassero di Porta Saragozza to the gay community, and the curia, which claimed that place as sacred to the Madonna. Porta Saragozza is one of the ancient gates of the city, of particular importance because it leads to the sanctuary of the Madonna di San Luca, protector of Bologna. A dispute that was still possible at the time, both because the left was able to play the left, and because the Vatican diktats were not recognized with as much power as they are granted today. Today, after so many years, that request would be impossible, given the enormous interference of the Church in Italian political life. What changed?

One spring morning Luciano Parisi and Anastasia Romanov picked me up to go to the transsexual demonstration in front of parliament. We demonstrated for the passing of a law that would allow sex changes and recognition as transsexual persons. On April 14 of that year, Law 164 was approved, which allows sex change through surgery, the second law of this type in Europe after Germany, and the first and above all the only one in Italy; after that, in fact, our parliament has not approved any others, not even for lesbians and gays. I had never seen so many trans people{f} all together and above all I had never seen them demonstrate. We were there out of solidarity, out of curiosity, and to meet some trans friends{f} who had come from Milan and Turin to demonstrate. All very blonde, elegant, and super feminine—real Venuses in fur. A very different event, at least in form, from what I was used to. A trans woman with a sign hanging around her neck was chained to a lamppost in the square and I remember that in the end she couldn't find the key to the padlock. We later learned that her friends, I don't know whether for fun or envy, had thrown away the key. Paradoxically, the police took care of freeing her with a pair of giant bolt cutters.

Although I had been hanging around with trans women for some time, I was unaware of their complex problems, especially those related to sex change, identity, and prostitution. I understood and in part shared their marginalization and total social exclusion, but I did not yet know the real human side. Over time I would immerse myself more and more in that experience and only by being inside it would I have the clarity of the path. Although Valerie was a trans woman, her acquaintances in that environment were not regular. Above all, it was her great friendship with Merdaiola, the Neapolitan transvestite who came to live with me, which allowed me to enter what at the time was still a world apart.

That morning in Piazza Montecitorio there were about a hundred transsexuals, some radical sympathizers and some politicians, among whom I recognized Pennella, Mimmo Pinto, and Adele Faccio, the one you'll find by your side always and everywhere. Among the most aggressive that day I remember Roberta, who would later become my best friend, Pina Bonanno, Paola Astuni, Gianna Parenti, Luciana (Frascatana), Franciolini, Roberta (Bucio). There was also a crowded press conference at the Hotel Nazionale which I attended out of curiosity. I only remember that the smoke from the cigarettes was so thick that it prevented a clear view of those present. At the table of the lecturers Bonanno reigned upright and proud, while in the hall Gianna, with a showy black hat and a lit pipe, continued to mutter and stir things up. From that moment I began to attend the MIT assemblies, which were held on a regular basis in the Radical headquarters in via di Torre Argentina. These assemblies almost always ended in shocking brawls between the most beautiful, the oldest, the most Roman, the most trans, the most transvestite, the most real, the most fake. Each time you had to submit to that hubbub, with no conclusions or sensible arguments other than the eternal quarrel about who should beat the streets and who shouldn't, who worked where and who controlled one area or another, who were the respectable ones and who weren't. Let's say that the most sensible item on the agenda was the defense against the constant harassment of the police. All this until all attention was absorbed by the "Brazilian sos." In fact, there was a rumor that the Brazilians would descend by the thousands, like the Huns pressing beyond the Alps, from Paris, and from Spain, ready to invade the Bel Paese. Strangely, the alarm was raised by two South Americans, a Colombian, and an Argentine, who described all the ugliness and aberrations of the Cariocas.

More than the Brazilians, the greatest risk was the local police who continued with roundups, warnings, fines, and beatings. At the MIT assemblies one of the most debated issues was the notorious Article 1 which pressed a knee on the neck of almost all those present, depriving them of their license, passport, and many other things, including dignity. I remember that dimension as the "suffocating trans captivity," when embarking on the path of self-fulfillment was like taking a leap in the dark because one faced all kinds of oppression, violence, repression, and marginalization. When I was appointed secretary of MIT Lazio—and it was already 1985 by then—I am not exaggerating in saying that our main activity was to telephone lawyers to help all those who had been stopped or arrested the previous night. We were also trying to carry out the necessary procedures to have Article 1 canceled from the records of those who had been convicted of it; let's say that in that period the change began with police headquarters which stopped assigning it and the lawyers who got rich to have it canceled. The detainees were there every evening and at least twice a month the famous paddy wagon passed by for the general roundup. They usually took us to the Third District in Santa Maria Maggiore, locked us up in the courtyard because we didn't all fit in the cells, and three at a time we were accompanied to the filing office, photographed from the front and in profile, dripping with ink for fingerprints, and at eight in the morning, when the city resumed its rhythm, we were released with the previous evening's clothes and makeup, sometimes with no money to take a taxi. Despite the tragedy, self-irony has always distinguished us: in the courtyard of the police station it was like being on the set of Fellini, with the policemen making fun of us from the windows of the five floors above and all those crazy women in the arena screaming, swearing, and responding in kind to the insults. It should be emphasized that in that luxurious parterre many of the soubrettes present had lovers among those on the windowsills. As they say, "the charm of the uniform." But the fascination of the uniform was on both sides given the considerable interest that trans women and transvestites aroused among the zealous guardians of public order.

Gay Occupations

Teresa and Lucy at that time had occupied a sort of shack that we called a "casetta": a mixture of a brothel, a commune, a gay center . . . let's just say a liberated and liberating zone. Casetta was located in the lower area of Pigneto, inserted in a hamlet of hovels occupied by criminals, drug addicts, prostitutes, dogs, and cats. It was like being on the set of the film *Ugly, Dirty and Bad* or a film by Pasolini who set some of his scenes right in that area. It was accessed by a rickety gate submerged in brambles that opened onto a courtyard. Around that, a series of structures that were half-houses, half-barracks were arranged among ancient ruins and acacia trees that offered shade in the summer and pleasant scents in the evening. In one corner Teresa had also managed to create a small vegetable garden where she had planted parsley, basil, rosemary, and tomatoes.

As in all occupied houses, the electricity connection was illegal, as well as the water, which was drawn from the common fountain located in the courtyard, a meeting point for the local fauna which, with the arrival of the transvestites, was truly complete. There was Barabba, a rough and nasty gangster who was continually arrested and sent to Regina Coeli; Rosa, his partner with eight dependent children who spent her time reading photo novels or the papers to us transvestites. Then there was a couple of addicts with two small children struggling with the thousand problems that come with addiction. In order not to miss anything, there was also Samantona, a Roman Junoesque villager who walked the streets at Porta Maggiore at night. To complete the geography, the small house attached to ours was subsequently occupied by other comrades who worked at Pinzimonio.

A special corridor for walking and cruising had been created between my house in San Lorenzo and the one in Pigneto. The two neighborhoods, close and communicating, united by an identical popular tradition, represented for us a protective refuge, quiet enough to allow us some longed-for visibility. Various groups of the more or less extreme left had their political headquarters there, together with those old cheap wine shops of which Rome was full. The famous Wines and Oils that have now disappeared still persisted, where people ate and drank with very little money, or those little shops where you could do your shopping by charging it to a bill that would be paid in better times. The most expensive goods such as makeup, fishnet stockings, creams, and perfumes we stole from downtown shops. Teresa was a real expert in this. At home, for a change (ha ha), there were always guests, at the dinner table and in bed. At lunchtime, at tea time, at dinner, and after dinner, masses of crazed fehgs flocked and got crazier and crazier. During the day we indulged in deep and imaginative self-awareness, at impromptu performances or assemblies during which, in addition to talking about politics, we took care of the personnel. In fact, while we were waxing, applying beauty masks, tweezing, sewing clothes, and arranging wigs, we discussed the future gay world, we dreamed of fuchsia and polka dot worlds. Often the other inhabitants of the village took part in the cheerful symposiums and, curious, lost themselves in our delirium.

In the evening we dressed up and went out in the center, in Trastevere or Campo de' Fiori. The Pantheon was already too posh for our tastes; the club environment had invaded the square, and also the first reissued baby fascists. After several ups and downs along the "corridor" (as we used to define the path that winds between the Pantheon and Trastevere through Piazza Farnese, Campo de' Fiori, and Piazza Navona) we strolled over to drink or chat at the Pinzimonio and then hitchhiked home. In reality, hitchhiking was the pretext for picking up guys and therefore having sex, which worked very well to the point of confirming itself as the most enjoyable activity of the period. The best places for hitchhiking were piazza Venezia, piazza Vittorio, and Porta Maggiore, being very careful to avoid San Giovanni and the Colosseum (areas which from a certain hour onward became dangerous from fascist ambushes that, unfortunately, we had to count more than once). Despite these fascist attacks, we still managed to run the city and take possession of the night. Hitchhiking was a great way to meet guys and deepen relationships. The corner of Porta Maggiore was the best because the guys from Prenestino and Casilino passed through them, the cream of Roman hormonal charm! We didn't pick guys up only while hitchhiking but everywhere, even on the bus. Like that time on line 14 when, in the company of Teresa, we entered into hormonal harmony with a group of tantalizing guys from Pigneto who invited us to pick flowers in a meadow in Torpignattara, where we were later joined by groups of young people from the neighborhood. We found ourselves surrounded by dozens of guys who, with their breeches down, wanted to broaden their horizons. I see that experience as distant; looking back on it today it's an impossible, risky, unreal thing: thirty guys who collectively let themselves go, even if in a so-called active way, to a homosexual relationship, which is unthinkable today. Perhaps it was the thrust of the libertarian wave that allowed the materialization of experiences that today can be defined as fantastic or surreal!

The widespread feeling was that everyone was happy with it, that everyone wanted to discover new things, that sexuality was breaking the rules, opening up to pleasure, chasing/following desire. Nineteen sixty-eight had opened the breach, 1977 had blown up the barriers, questioned everything, and what ensued was a sparkling mixture, initially restricted to areas of movement and then expanding to larger parts of the population, without these having the blue sticker attesting to a precise political path. In other words, the seventies were extending their lifestyle to everyone; maybe it was a fad, but it was definitely a good fad! I don't know if sexuality, the way of having sex in a spontaneous and uncontrolled way was a prerogative of our environments, but from what I observed, it didn't seem like it.

Beaches

Another mythical place was the Hole, the nudist beach of Castelporziano, at the ninth kilometer of the coastal road to Torvaianica. It was named for a passage, made by faggolas in previous eras, in the fencing network that delimited a beautiful and uncontaminated area of Mediterranean scrub a few kilometers from Rome. A white beach among the clean sea, sand dunes, and evergreen bushes where, restless and tireless, hundreds of hunting faguettes roamed. Behind the beach, in the scrub beyond the dunes, the first and most daring pioneeresses had created a masterpiece of rural architecture known as "the cathedral," because it resembled the nave of a church. It was a huge depression between the dunes of about two hundred square meters covered by a thick vegetation of evergreens that created walls and a huge vault, hidden and shady, which was accessed by narrow tunnels dug into the sand and hidden by brambles. From the outside you couldn't see anything or imagine what was happening inside, so when you entered you were suddenly catapulted into an incredible dimension. What from the outside looked like a quiet wild spot, inside was a lively anthill with a continuous coming and going of fehgs of every age and extraction. Someone stopped to point or scrutinize, others perched on cliffs or tree trunks, some masturbated, others secluded themselves in special niches built between the sand or the bushes where they indulged in real and succulent orgies. The beach became crowded in the afternoon and had its highlight on the weekend. Strictly nudist, it was frequented not only by gays but also by quiet people who loved nudism, including some zealous soldiers from the nearby Pratica di Mare barracks who, for pleasure, came to taste the delights of the place. The sea, the sun, and nudism created magical atmospheres, freed the minds and above all the bodies which, naked, showed all their splendor. We were naked, everyone was naked, and while naked we connected, without major problems, and this was enough to create other dimensions, liberated and liberating.

A little further away there was another beach, even more beautiful: the Hundred Steps, named that because of the long, steep stairway that led to it. It was near Gaeta, halfway between Rome and Naples, therefore frequented mainly by Romans and Neapolitans. We went there during the weekends with a tent, and sometimes we even stayed to camp for the whole week. It's a beach that is difficult to access and therefore is a true paradise for nudists, naturists, and poets. Often similar dimensions to gay campsites were recreated, with tents that served as ateliers, tea rooms, or brothels. On Friday afternoon, like the bats of Benares, a coming and going of women and young ladies began from the road to the beach along the steps, carrying circus tents, colored drapes, food supplies, evening dresses, jewels, amber, resins, and incense. At sunset, the beach looked like an enchanted place, a large camp that was part Indian, part gypsy. As darkness fell, groups of Neapolitan guys began to descend in search of adventures, and the camp was transformed into a temple dedicated to Dionysus. There was room for everyone, for those who loved group relationships with self-proclaimed straight people and for those who preferred gay ones, or a more romantic relationship, for those who wanted to take a quiet midsummer night trip . . . Around large bonfires we ate, drank, played, and danced. Magical full moon nights, summer solstices, shooting stars with many wishes expressed and fulfilled, and all our ravings dedicated to the sea. The trips with Marco Sanna, Cocca, Teresa, and all of Narciso are alive one by one in my happy gay memory. Like when a sudden and violent summer storm hit us and our four-man tent had to accommodate ten, a lively company of Neapolitan guys who found escape and a welcoming refuge inside that harem, in a pleasant and audacious huddle under a storm of lightning, thunder, and arrows of all kinds.

That coming and going was not located on the ramps of the Hundred Steps or among the dunes of the Hole, but between the cities, the collectives, and all the karst paths of that exciting nascent gay scene. Throwing coal into the roaring locomotive were the collectives of Rome, Bologna,

Turin, and Pisa, but also the Pistoia enclave and that of Torre Annunziata. General attention was dedicated to the first homosexual pride festival which would take place in Bologna on the occasion of the delivery of the Cassero to the gay community. We had left en masse for the capital of Emilia a few days earlier. The whole royal family stayed in Valerie's house. I don't remember sleeping, as day and night had no precise boundaries; those days were great celebrations for all of us. We went from show rehearsals at Anastasia's place to parades in Piazza Maggiore, from political passion to the madness of the party. That famous kiss that Ilaria gave to Mayor Zangheri caused a stir. The scene was immortalized by photographers while the agreement was being signed in the Municipality and then reported in all the newspapers.

That fabulous summer of 1982 went on until the magical appointment of *gay camping* in Vieste, a beautiful campsite between the sea and the olive trees of the Gargano.

I was traveling with the wind at my back. I felt right, carefree{f}, in perfect shape, with a thousand projects and many beautiful intentions. In Vieste I felt a trail of sparkling stars around me that shined along the way, making me feel effervescent. We rented a bungalow with Albertina, la Merdaiola, Teresa, Agata, and my brother. The bungalow immediately became one of the main crossroads of the campsite: dinners, aperitifs, parties, and shows were organized on our veranda, with some surprises due to the irrepressible exuberance of the vacationers. There was in fact a quarrel in very heated tones between Merdaiola and Albertina, which degenerated into a brawl, causing the very continuation of the campsite to be in dispute. That was the busiest campsite; about two thousand site passes were issued. There were many German, French, and Dutch fags. At the Babylon party I was elected Miss Babylon for an exceptional Babylonian queen costume that my brother had improvised for me on the spot. I must confess that the jury was biased because the most beautiful costume of the evening was that of Romana from the Great Faggotty Collective of Taranto, who emerged from the pine forest with a lyrical-electronic piece by Klaus Nomi in the background, on a bed of reeds carried on the shoulders of ten fabulous naked slaves that she kept on a leash with red ribbons.

In addition to the evening in Babylon, I remember the phantasmagorical procession of the Madonnas with an attached pagan celebration where each group represented a gay version of the Madonna. At our bungalow there was the Madonna of the Scabies, protector of sick fehgs who were ailing and in poor shape. Next to it was Porka Madonna, protector of transvestites played by a super sexy and glittering Luna di Bologna. I also remember the Italy-Germany soccer match that the queers resumed two months after the historic one in Madrid in which Italy had won the World Cup. There were also cheerleaders cheering. It's impossible to mention everything because the show was continuous; our days, our nights, our personal, and our political, everything became a show.

Another unscheduled event was the invitation by the owner of the campsite to sip champagne in his home, following his exhilarating falling in love with me. To tell the truth, I didn't care much, actually not at all, because I had so much else to think about, but my roommates, careful and calculating, insisted that I accept in order to have the bungalow where we were staying for free. A deal that I didn't know how to close and when I came out of there, half-drunk, there was the magic touch of the fairies, something truly amazing that marked my life: Luca.

In the square in front of the campsite I had met Marco Sanna, Andrea Pini, Poppea, and others who were chatting happily with a group of local guys. What a magical full moon night! I remember feeling a little cold, so I told those present that I would go get a sweater in the bungalow, but someone behind me placed a warm pink sweater on my shoulders: "Wear this," he said. I turned around and was shocked. It was the prince of fairy tales who smiled at me; his eyes entered me like the sea, deeply, flooding my whole universe. It was a moment! From those eyes shot the arrow that pierced the moon, the summer, my heart, and my whole life, making me dissolve into the most shocking love of my life. Luca invited me to sleep with him in a bungalow with a friend of his and Barbara, a beautiful trans woman from Milan. From that moment my life was never the same. The camp ended and with it the summer. I was no longer able to rest until Luca, after a few months, ran away from home and came to live with me in Rome.

The Cassero

But let's go back a few months, to the historic victory of the capture of the Cassero, which represents one of the most exciting pages of the Italian gay experience and beyond. The procession, as colorful and politically cheerful as any we had ever seen, set off from Piazza del Nettuno at around four in the afternoon. There were about six hundred of us{f}: rowdy, joyful, few but determined. One of the first times that queers paraded proudly, proud to be gay, transvestite, transsexual. We paraded for *pride* but above all for a great victory. We were wearing the colors of war but ours was not a violent and bloody war, but rather a party, the one we had always been denied. That beautiful page was attributable, politically and symbolically, to the famous "laughter that would have buried them." That day in Bologna our pride paraded, far from all the holes in which it is stuck today. The problem of how to participate in *pride* did not belong to us, with all the mega bullshit of today's controversies on alleged sideshows, bare breasts, and all those vulgarities that, according to the political right, characterize our celebration. There wasn't even the great dilemma, all Italian, of location of the *prides*, simply because the movement was one and marched together without splits if not for purely aesthetic reasons. There wasn't even a precise knowledge of that experience; after all we were tracing the path gradually, nothing was taken for granted, and everything had to be built from scratch. The only certainty was our conscience that was rebelling against 2,000 years of oppression, taking back what we had always been denied.

Let's try to think before that date in Italy or before June 28, 1969, all over the world. And let's try to think of all the action that led the Municipality of Bologna to grant a place, not just any place but a gate of the city dedicated to the Madonna. Do you think it would be possible today? The left that governed the city and the region was still very strong, enough to win negotiation with the Church and collect the victory. A big political and symbolic gesture, after which the downward game began that would lead the LGBT movement to beg for rags of rights that still haven't arrived. That fabulous queer procession, after crossing the center of Bologna, arrived at Porta Saragozza around 7 P.M., giving rise to a huge circle around the Cassero, even blocking traffic on the avenues for a few minutes. Pugnales, Beppe, and Prussi cut the ribbon while Merdaiola and Wonder unrolled the banner from the battlements of the tower. We were all happy and satisfied{f}; it was a great victory, a tangible sign of construction and emancipation.

After a while we sat down to rest at a table in a bar in the square. Of that moment I report my testimony given in 2002 for the Cassero's twentieth birthday:

For June 29, 1982, the royal family had made an appointment in full force, empresses, tsarinas, queens, princesses, and grand duchesses. As usual, we camped in the residence of Giuseppina of the Two Sicilies in via Clavature: a hall of about twenty meters, occupied by the occupants of an occupied house. The previous year, her aunt Anastasia Romanov, supported by her mother the Empress Ilaria, had publicly kissed the communist Zangheri, and for this she was accused of opening up to the Bolsheviks and thus preparing the end of the empire for what we had to do! We discussed this and above all other things in the occupied residence, for two days and two nights without ever closing an eye, and not only that. We supported ourselves with substances and substitutes; we had to decide what to do after seizing the Winter Palace! And the next day, after the queens confused with the courtesans had placed the banners on the crenelated towers and were sitting around, exhausted but happy, observing the new Porta Saragozza from afar, an old lady, astonished and amazed, in a strong Bolognese accent whispered: "Scembra che sciano arrivati gli uomini-donna socmel!" (Damn, it appears that the she-men have arrived!)

~ 4 ~

Transition, An Epic Passage (1983…)

Life's beauty unsettles me
And leaving it is an open wound
So many things left to do, but it's over.
—Marco Sanna

Then Night Came!

That was a memorable summer, full of stars and sparkles, but dark clouds threatening a storm loomed large on the horizon. One of the most popular weekly publications of that time had printed an article titled, "The Gay Plague." In particular, that article had struck me because of the usage of one of my pictures, front and center on top of a blurb that read, "The gay plague hasn't appeared in Italy yet, but there is a widespread fear that people who may have contracted the illness from American homosexual tourists will be sooner or later identified in our country as well."

Back then, when newspapers talked about homosexuality, they would also publish pictures of the most notorious members of the gay movement, usually taken at public gatherings or protests. Pictures of me, Valerie, Ilaria, Anastasia, René, and Teresa appeared in *Espresso*, *Europeo*, *Photo*, alongside a number of other local and national daily publications. Up until then, those pictures had generally accompanied stories about coming out in Italy alongside sensationalistic headings like, "Now even homosexuals are demanding their rights," all of it peppered with a healthy dose of sarcasm, moralism, and prudishness.

From that moment on, those same pictures started being used for different articles, and acquired different meanings. They became, for all intents and purposes, unofficial portraits of wanted lepers or infectors. To make matters worse, none of us had any legal recourse, because those pictures had been taken at public events. The same picture of me in a black undershirt with yellow stripes and big purple sunglasses shot at a protest in Campidoglio was first used to talk about the popularization of the gay phenomenon, then in an article on Warsaw titled, "Hard times for the marginalized in Warsaw," and lastly for a piece on the latest research developments on the gay plague. Those publications started generating a number of problems for me because my family, who was still residing in my hometown, was constantly under scrutiny given the incessant attention that curious townspeople devoted to those pictures and news. Personally, I had taken into account the possibility that, by taking part in public events, my visibility would greatly increase. That article on the gay plague was the first one, the proverbial bolt from the blue. Slowly but surely, things started to change, and more articles followed, and more still until they successfully turned us into the "lepers," or the "infectors" according to other publications, and then night came!

Reminiscing about happy memories is always nice; I could spend hours, days talking about them, and reliving them, because it does the soul good: my soul, and that of the LGBTQIA+ movement, as well. Reminiscing about the times that followed, however, means to reopen old, deep wounds. Gray times made of fear, confusion, and pain. Like quicksand, the more we tried to move on the more we'd get swallowed, every action seemingly making things worse, both on an individual and a collective level. Those news articles would confuse, terrorize, and above all destabilize us. Those among us who were the most visible got attacked and ridiculed. I still remember the porter in a building I lived in for some time, who would brazenly spray the handrail with alcohol every time I came down the stairs and leaned against it. I also remember groups of fascists who patrolled Monte Caprino or Stadio Flaminio at night—where trans sex workers could regularly be found—yelling over the megaphone to anyone who'd pass by that lepers were all over that area. Oscar, a trans woman who was also a dear friend of mine, was attacked and kicked out of a bar after patrons recognized her from a picture that had been taken and published without her knowledge. All of it felt unreal at first, some sort of a colossal lie, because there was no demonstrable truth to those accusations. People were talking about an illness, about a gay plague, but there was still no tangible sign that could help us understand what they were actually referring to. The signs of this illness, which we'd later learn to recognize as they started to appear on friends and acquaintances, didn't exist yet. Not only physical but cultural, social, psychological, and, why not, political signs: like all signs, they describe a reality, they represent it, or actually, they construct it.

The Gay Plague

The first AIDS victim I knew in person was a gay Roman artist who had moved to New York whom I would occasionally bump into at various nighttime parties when we used to be in Rome. The news was particularly upsetting to me because that entire campaign that had started a year earlier now felt real, close to me, rooted in reality. It was 1983. Immediately after that, almost in a domino effect, the head count of people admitted to hospitals who would then succumb to the illness began. In Rome as in other cities, among different groups and communities, day after day this list grew longer. AIDS faced us with a new reality that made us think about everything twice—our lifestyles, our habits, our routines.

So many questions, so much doubt, so much uncertainty, so many of us asking ourselves what to do, how to confront the illness, how to think about death. More and more, these became solitary reflections, considering that the collective experience that had characterized the preceding years was starting to fall apart little by little. Thinking about death isn't easy. It isn't now and it wasn't back then; a physical and political death, the disappearance of friends and, with that, the disappearance of an entire experience. Even though everybody tried to exorcize it, to find distractions, our attention would always end up there; the illness had become the focus of our discussions, the center of our attention and our debates, and we began to internalize it until it made us sick.

A psychological illness—even before a physical one—a political plague that in time we renamed the "reflux."

Self-consciousness gave way to self-help, self-defense to mutual care, liberation to cure. All our meetings in Narciso were suddenly about the AIDS crisis—no more time for political reunions, debates on sexuality or liberation. It almost felt as though talking about liberation was sacrilegious or inappropriate, a lack of respect and sensitivity. It was no longer appropriate to talk about sexuality since our sexuality had become the main culprit. All debate got shut down because of the illness, pushed back indefinitely and then, little by little, completely forgotten.

We didn't know how to go on, or even if we were supposed to. Everybody was so focused on this issue and on all the different, absurd ramifications involved in it, that we were unable to connect any other threads as everything kept falling apart in front of us. We were faced with illness, desperation, and death. During a natural calamity, you'll either grab the most basic necessities as you run for cover, or you'll help the victims, ignoring everything else, and this tension finally made us lose our purpose. We were no longer able to talk, reflect upon, and grow in our liberation because there was so much more to do and, frankly, we just didn't have the heart for it.

When AIDS arrived, we turned to each other trying to understand. This black wave hit us unannounced, with incredible violence, a catastrophe for our community, tearing friends, accomplices, and lovers away from us, leaving us unable to understand. We had to somehow intellectualize an event that was affecting us very deeply—our feelings, our sexuality, and our entire way of being. Many, too many vultures now had a justification to attack us and who we were. According to them, this was a divine punishment against all sinners. Donat Cattin, the health minister at the time, took it upon himself to send all Italians a letter announcing not to worry, that AIDS was affecting only the people who were out there asking for it, that it would only hit the so-called at-risk categories, like homosexuals, prostitutes, and drug addicts. This letter was a gateway to a new witch hunt; religious authorities eager to discredit us further joined in, denouncing the deprivation that had started in the '60s or even before then, maybe, all the way back to the French Revolution. These attacks, in return, forced us to retreat and hide. We had to hide everything—our symptoms, our fear, even the fact that we belonged to those at-risk categories. When that devastating illness attacked us, we didn't know what to do. Who would take care of the ill? Who were left to fend for themselves? Families, friends, even medical personnel and nurses were not adequately trained. Not knowing what to do was incredibly scary for us. Dario, a friend and lover of mine, was rejected from all hospitals in Lazio, and was finally admitted to a hospital in Latina at death's door in inhuman conditions. They locked him up in an isolated area, where nurses would walk around in some kind of a diving bell; even the priest asked to give him his last rites from behind a closed door. His sister, utterly distraught at that point, had to move the body into the casket by herself because all funeral homes, in spite of the exorbitant amounts of money asked to organize our funerals, were afraid to touch us or even set up any plans. As I recall it now, this reads like science fiction. Yet, this was the raw reality of the '80s. Each one of us would think about what we had done, how we had done it, and with whom, and the simple thought itself would annihilate us. If contagion, as we thought back then, happened by way of all direct unprotected contact, including kissing, then all of us, no matter how fabulous the experience in question, were automatically at risk. So it was better not to think—since it didn't help much with anything—and just keep doing our thing, because there was no cure other than to continue living until it was our turn.

Fear, suspicion, and isolation had replaced the exuberance and joy that we had known up until then. That yearning subject, cause and effect of all of our battles, began to melt like snow in the sun; the body that we had placed at the center of the universe all of a sudden failed us, betrayed us, and everything had to be revised as a result. Our happiness, like Ithaca for Ulysses, got further and further away under the rage of the storm. The very first informational brochures, created by different gay collectives, listed risks, symptoms, and different behaviors. Among the high risk factors I recognized all, literally all the behaviors that I, like many others, had enacted up until that moment: unprotected intercourse, deep kissing, drug use that would weaken the immune system, the exchange of drug paraphernalia. I mentally revisited all my liaisons, years of wild and joyous sex; but, in spite of my fears, the guilt that doctors, moralists, bigots, and vultures tried to pin on us did not stick to me. It was like returning in front of the priest to receive the Holy Communion but, instead of fifty Hail Marys and three days of fasting, my act of penance was abstinence for life and fifty doses of penicillin instead.

Some advised getting tested every month, others every two months, others every six. Getting tested also entailed preparing oneself emotionally, both during and after. Oftentimes, people would get tested but never pick up their labs out of fear of the results. Those who did went by themselves because, if the test result was positive, you would have to hide it from everyone. It was impossible to socialize this illness until it was in the later stages and assistance from friends became indispensable. In Rome, Narciso started offering public services by the Manifesto location in San Lorenzo, where you could receive consultation and assistance; tests were available every Thursday at the Epidemiological Observatory in Nomentano. At the beginning, we all{f} went to the San Gallicano hospital in Trastevere where they had a gay doctor in charge of the STD ward. He was very capable and very open, and we had nicknamed him "Doctor{f} Pampanini." It was a hub where all the Roman faguettes would hang out, even before the AIDS epidemic, a sort of communal living room where you would bump into friends and acquaintances, engage in conversation to kill time, and you would hear if so-and-so had gotten pregnant, or if those red spots were syphilis, smallpox, or just smeared lipstick from the night before. Usually, when friends and acquaintances came out of the doctor's office, you could guess their test results right away from their facial expression and general disposition. Many stopped showing up altogether around those times, always for the same exact reason. Some literally disappeared, leaving no trace behind. This illness was a solitary one, lived out in an absence of feeling or trust in others, and without the gay scene around you, that had suddenly become problematic, especially in terms of visibility. You would run away from others but also from yourself. For years, every morning after washing my face, or in the evening before going to bed, I would examine my neck, my armpits, my groin in front of the mirror to check my lymphatic glands. Any swelling there could be a symptom of the disease. I remember the fear I would experience every single time I touched one that felt even just slightly enlarged. In my mind I could no longer attribute it to simple inflammation, or to a cold, but I immediately imagined all those collateral afflictions and infections that accompany the dehumanizing progress of the disease.

The only glands that were actually swelling up at that point were my breast ones, because of the hormones I was on, which I would take methodically. They kept growing, and I kept changing. After a few months I had already upgraded to a B cup, which I wore with pride. It was then that Luca gifted me a bra that, every evening, he'd get to take off of me.

Blows to the Heart

And the count began, the obituaries: Marco, Sandro, Bruno, Antonio, Valerio, Ursula, Olga, Stefano, Marco, Ciccio, Roberta, Fabio, Alberto, Franco. One by one, sometimes distant and sometimes closer, our friends passed away. Big voids, lumps in the throat, melancholy, impotence, total absence of reactive stimuli. Shocking news arrived from New York, San Francisco, London, Paris: thousands and thousands of deaths that cleaved the largest LGBT communities in the world. Mapplethorpe, Foucault, Freddie Mercury, Sylvester, Derek Jarman, Rudolf Nureyev, Keith Haring: all the fabulous gay patchwork was falling apart.

I quote a passage from Marco Sanna's diary, profound and poignant, written during his illness, which best of all conveys the situation:

> I think of Dominique, I can't help it, it's a heartbreaking memory, it hurts like this herpes in my mouth, it burns and it's a sweet spring evening, the colors of this abandoned place are almost poetic, the colors of Rome, yellow, ochre, white, a tree covered in white flowers, an apricot tree, far away from the noise of traffic when I get home, once again I come to terms with my illness, with its manifestations, with its progress. It's really difficult, the wind thins out the tree's flowers and carries around the

white petals and I have a yeast infection and it seems very difficult to eradicate, the idea of chronicity destroys me, every time there is a new manifestation it brings up the phrase "Nothing will ever be the same again."

The gloomy atmosphere and sad feeling of helplessness took over as the good days became an ever more fading memory. Slowly our fabulous gay journey was forgotten, and in its place, a new way of being, of thinking, and of thinking about oneself took hold. No longer friends, accomplices, and lovers but strangers, unknown and dangerous. Mistrust began to characterize our relationships; less and less did our hand rest on the other to know and welcome him. Lips were no longer a meeting place and conjunction but a source of endless talk about what we would have liked to do and were no longer able to do. Our genitals were no longer part of our bodies, but an unrelated extension aimed at orgasm; detachment, separation that would gradually involve body and conscience, conscience and action, needs and politics, orgasm and passion, ass and cock, and so on up to that solitary and schizophrenic body of which today we are passive owners, a body of which we do not have more consciousness and not even perception.

Slowly our culture, that of the times, introjected the need for social control over bodies and, without realizing it, we entered the society of prevention where the body is medicalized, monitored, virtualized; a society based on fear, in which the removal of fear itself creates other, new enemies which from time to time are different of all kinds: of sex, race, gender. Slowly, everything we had tasted and experienced vanished, withered, and the void remained. That sexual revolution discovered in *Paradise Now* at Studio Uno Underground, enjoyed until then, went underground. The greatest effort remains to convey the meaning and soul of that revolution because it remains unknown to most. Passages are missing, the links between that dimension and the current experience, between the modern and the postmodern. Perhaps when we recover those connections we'll also be able to be indignant about everything that is happening today. Maybe we'll be able to say enough to that homophobic culture that offends our dignity. For me, who lived through that phase, today it's difficult to understand the immobilism of gays, lesbians, and trans people in light of the violent attacks of our old enemies. They took back what they lost and we are losing what we took back.

Luckily love distracted me, consoled me, and intoxicated me, managing to make me estranged from that reality. I began to wake up from the languid dream of love when the time came for Luca to leave for the military: two years in the navy. The mere thought of detaching myself from him annihilated me; I could no longer conceive of my life without him. As an alternative to two years in the navy, he chose the civil service, which he carried out at ARCI, exactly in that office where Arcigay was being born. The manager and creator of that office was Marco Bisceglie, a mature ex-priest from Melfi in Lucania, calm and jovial, excommunicated by the Vatican for his positions in favor of divorce, abortion, and for siding with the workers on strike, but especially for his coming out as gay. His fervent collaborator in that office was Nichi Vendola, who, while very young, took his first steps in politics. I had shared a path of life and struggle with both of them, so there were no major problems in accepting Luca's civil service.

In March of that same year, another tragic piece of news arrived which left everyone amazed and astonished: Mario Mieli had taken his own life. The news circulated, ran on all channels, increasing our sense of bewilderment.

It seemed that Pandora's box of negativity had been uncovered and misfortunes were arriving in a rhythmic and growing way. When I learned of Mario Mieli's suicide, I had the distinct and clear sensation that an era had come to an end. The one that opened up was uncertain and, given the signs, difficult and tiring. That was the watershed, the dividing line between a before and an after, *entre le début et l'histoire*. I still can't understand if there is an awareness of this passage, if what I'm talking about might seem like reality or fantasy.

In Italy, grappling with a thousand problems, with a reality that is now hostile to us queers, we haven't had the opportunity to develop our own thoughts, a culture that wasn't the boring one of the disco, a reflection on our experience, a reconstruction of our history. It's also true that up until now we{f} have been too far inside it to be able to detach it from ourselves and see it objectively and clearly. I have the feeling that awareness of those complex passages is lacking rather than knowledge. Everyone knows of Mario Mieli's suicide but few have reflected on its political and cultural significance, on the influence that gesture has had on our community. Everyone knows about AIDS and its effects on health, but few know its implications on culture, politics, history, the political significance of an epidemic, plague, or rather of the gay plague, as it was defined at the beginning. History, sociology, anthropology, politics, law, and sweat, so much sweat from the effort of building a world that looked more like us. Who is it up to say who we are if not us; what is our story? When, how, and why, and if not now, when?

Putting the pieces together is not easy; it's sometimes painful, and other times pleasant, but it is essential to build our future.

On October 17, 1983, two years after my last exam, I managed to graduate; I defended a thesis in modern history on peasant reality in Italy during the First World War. I got a score of 95 percent. Love cradled me, sweetened me, and intoxicated me. I was saved by it during a time when everything had turned around and the darkness seemed like it would never abandon us.

Mi rapì e mi salvò l'amore che move il sole e le altre stelle.
—Dante Alighieri, *Paradiso* XXXIII v. 145

Author Acknowledgments

I thank Silvia Fracaro for her valuable collaboration in revising the book.

Thanks to Mario Di Martino, Stefania Voli, and Antonella Ciccarelli, for the fabulous accompaniment.

Thanks to all the people and characters who have given and continue to give substance to the book, to our experience, and above all to our history.

Appendixes

Associations and Collectives

Arcigay: born from the original version at the beginning of the '80s in Palermo. Among its founders is Marco Bisceglie, ex-priest/workman who was excommunicated by the Church because he publicly came out as gay and sided with the FIAT workers in their fight. The association would later take on a national aspect with a reformist connotation and would find its headquarters in the LGBTQIA+ Cassero headquarters of Bologna.

CASL (Comitato autonomo San Lorenzo): collective in via dei Volsci, active in Rome in the late '70s.

Circolo Mario Mieli: the club was born in 1983 from the merger of preexisting Roman organizations FUORI! and Collettivo Narciso.

Collettivo Frocialista (Faggy Collective): born in 1977 in Bologna from the antagonist movement, its initial headquarters were in via Castiglione at the headquarters of the Bolognese Socialist Party. In 1978 it became the "Circle of homosexual culture of June 20th," and in 1982, after the assignment of the headquarters in Porta Saragozza, it became the LGBTQIA+ Cassero.

Collettivo di via dei Volsci: Roman collective of Workers' Rights based in the San Lorenzo district of Rome.

COM (Collettivi Omosessuali Milanesi; Milanese Homosexual Collective): based in the occupied houses of via Morigi in

Milan. They stage provocative shows including *La Traviata Norma*. Mario Mieli served on the board.

COP (Collettivi Omosessuali Padani; Paduan Homosexual Collective): founded in 1976 in Parma. From it the Pumitrozzole was born, the first gay theater group in the underground scene of the '70s, from which the TV star Platinette emerges.

Facciamo Breccia (2005–2011): libertarian and antifascist LGBTQIA+ movement against the Vatican regarding sexual and gender issues, resistant to any conservatism and religious orthodoxy.

FUORI! (Out!; Italian Revolutionary Homosexual Unitary Front): formed in Torino in 1971, the first big gay Italian association, later affiliated with the Radical Party.

Indiani Metropolitani: the most libertarian and creative area of the movement of 1977.

Lambda: gay, revolutionary collective in Turin, born in the political workers' area of the FIAT factory; from it the homonymous newspaper directed by Felix Cossolo, which later turned into the monthly publication *Babilonia*, was born.

Lotta Continua: formed in 1969 as a formation of the extraparliamentary left with a revolutionary communist orientation, it dissolved in 1976.

MIT (Italian Transexual Movement; later Transexual Identity Movement): officially born in 1981. It contributes with its battles for the approval of Law 164. It is currently based in Bologna in via Polese 22.

ML: Marxist-Leninist groups with various names, very active in these years.

Narciso (Homosexual Revolutionary Collective): born in 1979 within the antagonist movement. It combines the homosexual experience with broader cultural and political instances, typical of the radical left. Its headquarters is at the San Lorenzo anarchist club (Anomalia) in via dei Campani 70. It later became "Circolo Mario Mieli."

Open Mind: opposition movement and LGBT association of Catania; organized the first Pride in Sicily and the famous event "Always fags and fascists never."

Psicoanalisi Contro: Freudian group founded by Sandro Gindro that theorized a free and natural homosexuality. Self-placed in the revolutionary left, it guaranteed and offered support at political prices.

PSIUP (Socialist Party of Proletarian Unity): also known as Manifesto PSIUP, founded by Rossana Rossanda, Luigi Pintor, and Lucio Magri.

Vampire Gotiche Folli: Gay, Roman collective of the '70s of which any trace has been lost.

Clubs and Hangouts

Alibi: gay disco in Testaccio, Rome.

Aula VI di Lettere: at the University of Rome La Sapienza. The classroom was occupied and liberated from 1977 through 1980.

Bistrot: theater/cabaret/trattoria in via de' Coronari in Rome, run by Dominò, who performed there cross-dressed.

Cage aux Folles: gay disco near the Piazza di Spagna (ca. 1982–1986).

Cento Scalini: nude beach close to Gaeta (Lt).

Christiania: "Free City of Christiania" is a partially self-governed quarter of the city of Copenhagen, founded in 1971 by a hippie commune; on January 1, 2006, the city lost its special status of an alternative community.

Circo Massimo: historic gay hook-up site in Rome.

Comune di Isola Capo Rizzuto: campsite run by companions of the extraparliamentary left.

Convento Occupato: ancient, deconsecrated convent in via del Colosseo in Rome, occupied for many years by the Stella Rosa group that transformed it into an important meeting place.

Easy Going: meeting place of the emerging gay disco scene close to piazza Barberini (ca. 1983–1985).

Gay House: also called Ompos, in Testaccio, Rome.

Governo Vecchio: building occupied by the feminist movement in the center of Rome on the street of the same name; within it were active counseling, legal service, and self-help and self-awareness groups. Nonaccessible to men.

Il Buco (the Hole): nude beach at Castelporziano (Rome) that had become a gay hotspot.

Il mago di Oz (the Wizard of Oz): alternative meeting place in Trastevere run by gays, functioning as a restaurant, bookstore, and theater.

Lurido: nighttime bakery in via Borgonuovo in Bologna, a meeting place for all the creatures of the night.

Monte Caprino: the most famous gay hook-up place in Rome, more or less from the '70s until the end of the millennium.

Ompos: historic meeting place and gay archive founded by Massimo Consoli, its headquarters in Testaccio in the structure of the former slaughterhouse.

Piazza del Cinquecento: in front of Termini station, historic meeting and cruising place for gays, transsexuals, hustlers. Very crowded during the day and especially at night, also with famous people. Today it is completely transformed.

Pinzimonio: alternative restaurant in via Borgo Pio adjacent to the Vatican, frequented by gays and fellow members of the extraparliamentary left.

Quartiere Latino (the Latin Quarter): the area of Paris frequented by artists, intellectuals, activists; it surrounds the Sorbonne University where the May '68 revolt broke out.

Saint James: famous gay disco bar in the via Veneto area, gay meeting place frequented by the international jet set (born in the Dolce Vita period).

Studio Uno Underground: fabulous youth meeting place in a small Southern town.

Suburra: restaurant and alternative meeting place for the extraparliamentary left in Rione Monti.

Super Star: night disco bar and meeting place in Scanderbeg alley, Trevi Fountain area, considered a place of infamy, frequented by transvestites{f}, transsexuals, gays, and alternative types (ca. 1979–1989).

Radio Stations

Radio Alice: founded in Bologna in 1975 by students of the libertarian area and of the DAMS (Fine Arts at University of Bologna) collectives. Historical headquarters in via del Pratello 41. It broadcast from 1976 to 1977, and closed down with the accusation of having directed the clashes in the aftermath of the killing of Francesco Lorusso.

Radio Città Futura: founded in Rome in 1975, defined as "the free voice of the capital," it was born in the political area of the left (PDUP, Avanguardia Operaia and the publisher Giulio Savelli).

Radio Onda Rossa: founded in Rome in 1977 by Autonomia Operaia militants. Historical headquarters in via dei Volsci; is one of the main free radio stations of the '77 movement, still active today.

Magazines and Newspapers

Ciao 2001: one of the most important music magazines of the seventies. It was born in 1968, voice of the Italian public counterculture until the early nineties, with sporadic publications between 1999 and 2000.

The Fag Page: weekly insert on Thursdays in *Lotta Continua*, published throughout the year 1980.

Lambda: magazine founded in 1977 by the Lambda collective of Turin, it was the first gay counterinformation sheet in Italy; in 1981 it became *Babilonia*, the most popular gay newspaper.

Lotta Continua: political newspaper of the homonymous group, main information organ of the extraparliamentary left with national circulation, published from 1969 to 1982.

Il Male: political satire newspaper, published from 1977 to 1982.

Metropolis: fortnightly formed in 1977 as an organ of political analysis of Autonomia Operaia, published until 1979.

Il Pane e le Rose: periodical launched in 1973 as a supplement to the *Quaderni piacentini*, published until 1976; themes: condition of youth, sexual freedom, music, very attentive to the nascent feminist movement.

Re Nudo: the longest-running and most widespread underground magazine in the seventies, published from 1970 to 1980.

Rosso: born in 1973 as a bimonthly of the Gramsci Group, a point of reference for the Autonomia Operaia area, published until 1979.

Vanguardia operaia: national newspaper formed in 1974 from the organization of the same name, published until 1976.

La Voce del Popolo: newspaper of Marxist-Leninist groups.

Zut A/Traverso: underground magazine founded in Bologna in 1976 by the collectives headed by Radio Alice, published discontinuously until 1981.

People

Adele Faccio: feminist, famous activist, and militant of the Radical Party.

Alfredo Cohen: famous gay political actor; one of the founders of FUORI!; his show *Mezza femmena e sa 'Camilla* is unforgettable. All traces of him have been lost. He died in Tunis on December 3, 2014.

Anastasia Romanov (Ciro Cascina): famous actor of the movement. Her show *The Madonna of Pompeii* is unforgettable. She lives on Mount Vesuvius.

Andrea Pini: writer, journalist, activist; wrote *Homocides: Homosexuals Killed in Italy* (Rome: Stampa Alternativa, 2002), and *When We Were Fagots: Homosexuals in Italy of the Past* (Turin: Il Saggiatore, 2011).

Angela Davis: philosopher, fabulous activist, and activist of the Black Panthers. Tried and arrested for subversion. She teaches at UCLA.

Angela Putino (Naples 1946–2007): feminist, philosopher, writer.

Angelo Pezzana: founder of FUORI! and organizer of the first gay protest in Sanremo.

Antonia Iaia (known as Antonella): trans actress and performer, she worked with the Falso Movimento theater company.

Antonio Frainer (Trento 1959–Bologna 1994): gay activist and member of the KGBB.

Beppe Ramina: activist, intellectual, journalist of the gay scene, and one of the founders of the Bolognese Faggy Collective.

Bruno di Donato: activist of the first gay movement and founder of FUORI! He died in the night between April 5 and 6, 1991.

Dario Bellezza (Rome 1944–1996): homosexual poet and writer.

Enzo Cucco: activist of the first gay movement and founder of FUORI! Active today in the Certain Rights association.

Erio Masina: actor and theater director; his show *Bella All in Black without Make-Up* is famous.

Felix Cossolo: activist of the gay movement in the seventies, founder of the gay newspaper *Lambda* and of the *Babilonia* magazine. Organizer of the first gay camps.

Francesco Gnerre: writer, intellectual, activist, author of *The Denied Hero: Homosexuality and Literature in the Italian Twentieth Century* (Milan: Baldini & Castoldi, 2000).

Helena Velena: transgender activist; author of *From Cybersex to Transgender* (Rome: Castelvecchi, 1995).

Ilaria (Vincenzo Moretti): born in Sassari; fervent gay activist; died in a car accident in 1985.

Ivan Teobaldelli: activist of the gay movement in the seventies and eighties; collaborator on the magazine *Babilonia*.

Joe Dallesandro: actor/sex symbol of the Factory; interpreter of *Trash* and *Flesh*.

Judith Malina: actress, director, anarchist-activist; companion of Julian Beck with whom she founded the Living Theater.

Julia Murray: Sylvia Rivera's partner.

Julian Beck (New York 1925–1985): intellectual, American anarchist-activist; he founded the Living Theater, and moved to Europe and later to Italy where he performed together with his partner in the squares with his irreverent and provocative shows. He died in New York on September 14, 1985.

Lina Pallotta: intellectual, photographer, reporter; her book covers for the three books by Porpora Marcasciano are: *Tra le rose e le viole* (Rome: Manifestolibri, 2002), *Favolose Narranti* (Rome: Manifestolibri, 2008), and *AntoloGaia* (Milan: Il dito e la luna, 2007), as well as various reports on the LGBTQIA+ scene.

Lindsay Kemp: famous mime, director, performer; his show *Flowers* is extraordinary.

Lola Pugnales (Samuel Pinto): considered the essential founder of the Cassero.

Luciano Parisi: activist of the gay movement at the end of the seventies. Animator of famous clubs and Roman evenings.

Lud (Ludovico C.): bohemian artist; lives in the Castelli Romani.

Marcella di Folco (Rome 1943–Bologna 2010): historic passionate leader of the Italian trans movement; first transsexual to hold the position of city councilor in Bologna; founder of important MIT services in Bologna.

Marco Melchiorri: gay activist, one of the founders of the Narciso Collective. Died in 1995.

Marco Sanna: intellectual and passionate activist of the gay scene. He founded the Narciso Collective with Porpora Marcasciano, Enzio Ienna, Sergio Pellegrini, Enrico Giordani, Marco Melchiorri. He wrote several articles in *Manifesto* and *Lotta Continua*. Author of poems and creative protests. He died on November 11, 1990.

Marco Mieli (1952–1983): activist, intellectual, actor, performer, provocateur; today we would say "queer." He wrote *Elements of Homosexual Criticism*, the most important text of Italian gay culture.

Massimo Consoli (Rome 1945–2007): a leading figure in the Italian gay world. Writer and essayist; organized the most important archive of gay culture.

Medusa (Claudio C.): gay activist among the founders of the Cassero.

Merdaiola (Antonello P.): Neapolitan transvestite, gay, activist, performer. He died in Bologna in 2006.

Mimmo Pinto: parliamentarian of Proletarian Democracy.

Monique Wittig (1935–2003): intellectual, feminist writer.

Nicoletta Poidimani: philosopher, activist, and writer; author of *Beyond the Monocultures of Gender* (Milan: Mimesis, 2006) and *We Will Survive* (Milan: Mimesis, 2007).

Nocciolina (Gavina V.): born in Alghero, companion of journeys and adventures, she took her own life in July 1979.

Ottavio Mai (Rome 1946–Turin 1992): director and homosexual activist. In 1986 he founded, with Giovanni Minerba, who still directs it, the LGBTQIA+ Turin Film Festival—From Sodom to Hollywood.

Paolo Poli: brilliant theater actor.

Penny Arcade: actress and performer of the New York scene and Andy Warhol's Factory; actress in *Women in Revolt*.

Pier Paolo Pasolini (Bologna 1922–Rome 1975): one of the most important intellectuals of the twentieth century, writer, director, provocateur.

Prussy (Valerio Cacciari): very high gay activist, essential member of the Cassero KGBB theater group. Died in 1994.

René (Renato F.): gay activist.

Sergio Pellegrini: Roman gay activist, one of the founders of the Narciso Collective.

Stefano Casagrande (Rome 1960–Bologna 2000): known as Casarina; activist, president of the Cassero, artist, creator of Miss Alternative and of the KGBB.

Sylvia Rivera (New York 1951–2002): historic world leader; she threw the bottle at the policemen, triggering the Stonewall revolt. She was a guest of MIT in 2000 for Transiti and World Pride Rome 2000.

Teresa (Marilina A.): trans activist, lives in Rome.

Ugenio (Anna M.): the only lesbian activist of the Narciso Collective. She died in 1990.

Valerie Taccarelli: passionate trans activist, irreverent animator of the first Italian gay scene.

Vanni Piccolo: gay activist, intellectual.

Vladimir Luxuria: activist, actress, singer, writer, provocateur, one of the most famous characters in the LGBTQIA+ world.

Zanza (Enzo I.): gay activist, unsurpassed and creative provocateur. He died in 2003.

Juke Box

Alfredo Cohen, "Valery" (1979), dedicated to Valerie Taccarelli and covered by Milva, who renamed it "Alexanderplatz."

Area, famous Italian rock group.

Banco Mutuo Soccorso, famous Italian rock group.

Candeggina Gang, legendary punk band led by Jo Squillo.

Claudio Lolli, "Michel" (1972), "Gli zingari felici" (happy gypsies, 1976).

Cream, famous English rock group.

David Bowie, *Ziggy Stardust* (1972), *Aladdin Sane* (1973).

The Doors, *The Doors* (1967).

Eugenio Finardi, famous Italian singer-songwriter.

Gabriella Ferri, singer, artist, performer, and representative of popular Rome; committed suicide in 2005.

Genesis, famous English rock band.

The Grateful Dead, famous psychedelic rock group from the West Coast; with Jefferson Airplane, passes through American counterculture.

Jefferson Airplane, *Surrealistic Pillow* (1967).

Lou Reed, "Take a Walk on the Wild Side" (1972), "Vicious" (1973).

Mia Martini, "Minuetto" (1973).

Napoli Centrale, famous Italian rock group headed by Pino Daniele.

Paolo Pietrangeli, "Contessa" (1966).

Patti Smith, the priestess of rock.

Patty Pravo, "Pazza idea" (1973), "Ragazzo triste" (1966), "Oggi qui domani là" (1967), "La bambola" (1968).

Pink Floyd, *Ummagumma* (1969), *Atom Heart Mother* (1970), *Meddle* (1971).

The Police, "Message in a Bottle" (1979).

Premiata Forneria Marconi, famous Italian rock group.

Renato Zero, famous singer, more or less gay.

The Rolling Stones, *Sympathy for the Devil* (1968).

Sex Pistols, *Anarchy in the UK* (1976).

Transsexuals and Transvestites

Aracne (Claudia Capriati): performer, trans woman, MIT activist throughout the Bologna alternative scene from 1994 to 2007, the year of her death.

Cocis: transvestite from Bologna famous for her protests in the courtroom that tried her for transvestism.

Frascatana (Luciana C., Rome 1945–1998): trans pioneer and founder of MIT.

Gianna Parenti (Florence 1945–2009): trans pioneer, artist, and actress, founder of MIT.

Giraffe: famous en travesti character of classical and popular Bologna.

Nadia Ventura: among the trans Bolognese pioneers, a famous character of alternative and popular Bologna. She died in 2012.

Paola Astuni (Modena 1941–1989): trans pioneer from Bologna and founder of MIT.

Pina Bonanno: trans pioneer and founder of MIT; author of the famous protest at the Idroscalo in Milan in August 1979.

Roberta Bucio (Rome 1956–Bologna 2001): trans activist.

Roberta Ferranti: trans pioneer, philosopher of life with an excellent mind, founder of MIT. She lives in the Castelli Romani.

Roberta Franciolini (Rome 1943–2012): trans pioneer, ardent activist, and founder of MIT.

Romina Cecconi (known as La Romanina): historical character of the trans world. She was sent to internal confinement for two years because she was considered socially and morally dangerous.

Ursula (Rome 1948–1992): pioneer of the trans movement and founder of MIT; animator of the capital's nightlife scene.

Shows, Books, and Theatrical Performances

The Art of Loving, Erich Fromm (Milan: Mondadori, 1963).

The Ballad of the Shepherds, text and research by Pino Simonelli.

Bury My Heart at Wounded Knee, Dee Brown (Milan: Mondadori, 1972).

. . . *But My Love Does Not Die: Strategies of the Counterculture and the Underground in Italy*, edited by Gianni Emilio Simonetti, Ricardo Sgarbi, Guido Vivi et alia. (Rome: Arcana, 1971).

Do It! Scenarios of the Revolution, Jerry Rubin (New York: Simon & Schuster, 1970). Italian translation *Fallo! Scenarios of Revolution* (Milan: Mimesis, 2008), text of the American counterculture.

Elementi di critica omosessuale, Mario Mieli (Einaudi, Torino, 1977) (Mieli's university thesis in philosophy, it represents the manifesto of the homosexual movement).

Fuga, Timothy Leary (Rome: Arcana, 1996).

La Gatta Cenerentola, show by Roberto De Simone.

Half a Woman and Zia Camilla, text and performance by Alfredo Cohen (1980).

Homosexual: Oppression, and Liberation, Dennis Altman (Rome: Aracna Editrice, 1974).

Jennifer's Five Roses, the famous play by Annibale Ruccello.

Living Theater, a living theater company founded by Julian Beck and Judith Malina.

The Master and Margarita, Mikhail Bulgakov (Turin: Einaudi, 1967).

One Hundred Years of Solitude, Gabriel Garcia Marquez (Milan: Feltrinelli, 1968).

Other Libertines, Pier Vittorio Tondelli (Milan: Feltrinelli, 1979).

Paradise Now, text and performance by Julian Beck.

The Rocky Horror Picture Show, musical film; performance by Tim Curry.

Seven Meditations on Political Sado-Masochism, show and political text by Julian Beck and Judith Malina.

The Teachings of Don Juan, Carlos Castaneda (Rome: Astrolabio-Ubaldini, 1970).

To Have or to Be?, Erich Fromm (Milan: Mondadori, 1976).

Timelines

Timeline of Key Events

1968: youth revolts explode all over the world; famous for conflicts and occupations like May in Paris.

1969: (June 28) Stonewall riots in New York.

(August) Woodstock festival on the Isle of Wight.

1972: first coming out in Sanremo with the activist protest, including Mario Mieli, Angelo Pezzana, Alfredo Cohen, Enzo Cucco, and Enzo Francone who, with others, constituted the first core group of FUORI!

1973: (September 11) coup d'état in Chile. Pinochet deposes socialist Allende and makes the country collapse into a savage dictatorship.

1974: (May 12–13) divorce is legalized.

(May 28) massacre by neofascists in Brescia; eight dead.

(August 4) massacre by neofascists on the Italicus train; twelve dead.

1975: (November 2) Pasolini is killed.

1976: (summer) *Re Nudo* festival at Parco Lambro in Milan and pop festival in Ravenna.

(December 8) violent confrontations at the Scala Theater in Milan.

1977: (February) occupation of almost all Italian universities.

(February 17) Luciano Lama (CGIL secretary) ousted at the University of Rome.

(March 11) Francesco Lorusso killed by police in Bologna.

(May 12) Giorgiana Masi of Lotta Continua killed by police in Rome.

(September 23–25) movement against repression convention in Bologna; more than 100,000 people participate.

(September 30) Walter Rossi of Lotta Continua is killed by fascists in the Balduina neighborhood in Rome.

(October 18) suicide (homicide?) of Andreas Baader and two other Raf members at the Stammheim prison in Germany.

Mario Mieli publishes *Elements of Homosexual Criticism*, the most important text of gay/queer culture in Italy and Europe.

1978: (March 16) kidnapping of Aldo Moro by the Red Brigades; his corpse is found on May 9.

1979: (April 7) after a ruling by judge Pietro Calogero in Padua—called the Calogero Theorem—a massive repression of revolutionary groups begins.

(May) the Narciso Collective is born in Rome; in 1983 it eventually becomes the Circolo Mario Mieli.

(July) Festival dei Poeti on the Castelporziano beach in Ostia; Allen Ginsburg, Gregory Corso, Lawrence Ferlinghetti, and Peter Orlovsky participate.

(August) first gay campsite at the Comune di Isola Capo Rizzuto.

(November) first conference of the gay revolution movement at the Convento Occupato on via del Colosseo in Rome.

(November 24) first demonstration of gay visibility in Pisa organized by Collettivo Orfeo.

1980: (June 27–29) Homosexual gay pride days in Bologna.

(June 27) massacre in Ustica by persons still unknown; eighty-one dead.

(August 2) fascist massacre at the Bologna train station; eighty-two dead.

(August) second gay campsite at the Comune di Isola Capo Rizzuto.

(November 23) an earthquake in Irpinia kills about 3,500 people.

1981: (June 28) demonstration and conference of the gay movement in Bologna and other cities.

(August) third gay campsite at Ortona (CH).

1982: (April 14) passing of law 164 allowing sex changes.

(May) first rehearsal of Pride in Rome; a procession of about one hundred people parade around Piazza del Campidoglio at the Pantheon.

(June 28) Pride and takeover of the Cassero in Bologna.

(August) fourth gay campsite at Vieste.

1983: AIDS, known as the gay plague, begins to spread in Italy.

(March 12) Mario Mieli commits suicide

(August) fifth gay campsite at Porto Sant'Elpidio (AP).

Porpora Marcasciano's Timeline

September 15, 1957: born in San Bartolomeo, a small town in the province of Benevento, where she remains until her scientific high school diploma in 1976.

1976–1977: enrolls in the first year of the Faculty of Sociology in Naples.

1977: moves to Rome.

1979: establishes the Narciso Collective.

1981: performs civil service at the Rome headquarters of Italia Nostra.

1982: becomes a member of MIT.

1983: graduates in the Department of Sociology with a thesis in modern history.

1985–1990: secretary of MIT Lazio.

1991: moves to Bologna.

1994–2010: vice president of MIT.

2005: founds the Sylvia Rivera Trans National Coordination.

2006: helps found and organize Facciamo Breccia.

2010: National MIT president.

Key Words

Articolo 1: given to people considered socially dangerous, it provided for the withdrawal of drivers' license, passport, and other documents, special surveillance, and in some cases even internal confinement.

Articolo 28: exemption from military service for homosexuality.

Baffe: slightly effeminate and very or too masculinized faggots.

Coming out: to come out, declare oneself homosexual.

Criptochecca: closeted homosexual.

Down: waning phase of LSD understood also as a heavy and depressing condition.

Educastrazione: term and concept introduced by Mario Mieli in his *Elements of Homosexual Criticism*.

Femminiello: typical Neapolitan figure that includes homosexual, transvestite, transsexual, transgender, and everything that is not male.

L'Internazionale: hymn of the October revolution and of all the leftist movements of the world, it also represents an area of thought.

LSD or LSD 25: hallucinogenic drug linked to the personal search for oneself in the counterculture of the sixties and seventies. The *Acid Test* ritual is famous among West Coast hippies, which consisted of taking it collectively during musical happenings.

Magic bus: means of transportation of hippies traveling to India. They left from Istanbul and, via Ankara, Tehran, and Kabul, arrived in Delhi. First because of the Iranian revolution and later the war in Afghanistan, they stopped working.

Ordine veterosessuale: term and concept introduced by Nicoletta Poidimani in the book *Beyond the Monocultures of Gender* (Milan: Edizioni Mimesis, 2006).

Queer: it can be understood as a theory, as a practice, or both, aimed at undermining education and giving a nonstraight meaning to life and the universe.

Straight mind: term and concept taken up by Monique Wittig, recast to unique Western thought.

Terzo Distretto: police district located in Piazza dell'Esquilino where all the trans victims of roundups were taken.

Trip: journey with LSD and all hallucinogenic substances; the word and the associated concept refer to the physical and cultural journey of a generation, also understood as beautiful, astounding, strange . . . hallucinating.

Porpora's Publications

Tra le rose e le viole: La storia e le storie di transessuali e travestiti
(Castel San Pietro Romano: Manifestolibri, 2002)

AntoloGaia, sesso genere e cultura degli anni '70 (Milan: Il Dito e la
Luna, 2007)

*AntoloGaia. Vivere sognando e non sognare di vivere: i miei anni
Settanta* (Rome: Alegre, 2015)

Favolose narranti. Storie di transessuali (Castel San Pietro Romano:
Manifestolibri, 2008)

Elementi di critica trans (Castel San Pietro Romano: Manifestolibri,
2010)

She has published essays in various anthologies, including: *Porneia.
Voci e sguardi sulle prostituzioni* (Padua: Il Poligrafo, 2003); *Altri
femminismi. Corpi cultura lavoro* (Castel San Pietro Romano:
Manifestolibri, 2006); *Gay. La guida italiana in 150 voci* (Milan:
Mondadori, 2006); *Transessualità e scienza sociali* (Naples:
Liguori, 2008); *T* Sguardo sui confini dell'identità di genere*
(Bergamo: Libri Aparte, 2009); *Vite clandestine. Frammenti
racconti e altro sulla prostituzione e la tratta di esseri umani*
(Naples: Gesco Edizioni, 2010); *Queer in Italia. Differenze in
movimento* (Pisa: Edizioni ETS, 2011); *In un corpo differente*
(Bologna: Comma 22, 2011); *Otokongo* (Empoli: Ibiscos Edizioni,
2012); *I clienti del sesso. I maschi e la prostituzione* (Naples: Intra
Moenia, 2013); and *Infiniti amori* (Rome: Ediesse, 2013).

Notes on Contributors

PORPORA MARCASCIANO is the president of MIT (Trans Identity Movement) and a city council member serving as head of the Commission of Equality and Equal Opportunities in Bologna, Italy, where she has lived since 1990. She received a degree in modern history from the University of Rome "La Sapienza" and has been an activist in political, social, feminist, gay, and trans movements since the 1970s. Her publications include *Dawn of the Bad Transwomen: Stories, Gazes, and Experiences of My Transgender Generation*; *Fabulous Narrators: Transexual Stories*; and two editions of *AntoloGaia*. She is the subject of the 2021 biographical documentary film *Porpora* (directed by Roberto Cannavò), and also stars in the documentary *The Fabulous Ones* (directed by Roberta Torre).

FRANCESCO PASCUZZI received a PhD in Italian from Rutgers University where he currently teaches English writing as an assistant teaching professor. In 2015, he edited *Dreamscapes in Italian Cinema*, an anthology that examines the oneiric realm in Italian film history and has since published book chapters and essays on filmic representations of motherhood, mourning, and identity. In 2020, he coedited *The Spaces and Places of Horror*, an anthology that explores the complex horizon of landscapes in horror film culture to better understand the use that the genre makes of settings, locations, spaces, and places, be they physical, imagined, or altogether imaginary. He is currently researching a project on heterotopias and horror film culture. Francesco's main field of research encompasses comparative and transnational studies between Italian and foreign cinema, and his current interests include modern and contemporary horror film, Hallyu and contemporary Korean cinema, Italian auteur film of the new millennium, and contemporary queer cinema.

SANDRA WATERS received her PhD from Rutgers University with a dissertation on the figure of the narrator in the Italian historical novel. Her research interests include gender, trauma, and film theory; the historical novel; the collective author; and horror. Her recent publications include articles and chapters on Luther Blissett and Wu Ming, Dario Argento's Three Mothers trilogy, Maria Rosa Cutrufelli's *The Woman Brigand*, Paolo Sorrentino, and surveillance in contemporary American horror film. She coedited *Spaces and Places of Horror* with Francesco Pascuzzi, and coedits the Other Voices of Italy series for Rutgers University Press. She is the managing editor of *Italian Quarterly*.

SARA GALLI holds MAs in modern philology and Italian language education for foreigners from the University of Genoa. She is currently a PhD candidate in Italian studies at the University of Toronto, where she researches Dante's didactic project and the influence that Augustine of Hippo had on him. She is a cofounder of the Women's and Gender Studies collective in the American Association of Italian Studies.

MOHAMMAD JAMALI is a doctoral student in Italian studies at the University of Toronto, where he has been working on Mario Pratesi's archives. He is a cofounder of the Women's and Gender Studies collective in the American Association of Italian Studies.

Printed and bound by CPI Group (UK) Ltd, Croydon, CR0 4YY

09/06/2025

14685731-0001